AF600305

JAPANESE SOCIETY AND THE POLITICS OF THE NORTH KOREAN THREAT

JAPAN AND GLOBAL SOCIETY

How has Japan shaped, and been shaped by, globalization – politically, economically, socially, and culturally? How has its identity, and how have its objectives, changed? *Japan and Global Society* explores Japan's past, present, and future interactions with the Asia Pacific and the world from a wide variety of disciplinary and interdisciplinary perspectives and through diverse paradigmatic lenses. Titles in this series are intended to showcase international scholarship on Japan and its regional neighbours that will appeal to scholars in disciplines both in the humanities and the social sciences.

Japan and Global Society is supported by generous grants from the Shibusawa Eiichi Memorial Foundation and the University of Missouri–St Louis.

Editorial Advisory Board

For a list of books published in the series, see page 183.

Japanese Society and the Politics of the North Korean Threat

SEUNG HYOK LEE

UNIVERSITY OF TORONTO PRESS
Toronto Buffalo London

Toronto Buffalo London
www.utppublishing.com

ISBN 978-1-4426-3034-5

Library and Archives Canada Cataloguing in Publication

Lee, Seung Hyok, author
Japanese society and the politics of the North Korean threat / Seung Hyok Lee.

(Japan and global society)
Includes bibliographical references and index.
ISBN 978-1-4426-3034-5 (bound)

1. Japan – Foreign relations – Korea (North). 2. Korea (North) – Foreign relations – Japan. 3. National security – Japan. 4. Economic sanctions – Korea (North). 5. Ballistic missiles – Korea (North) – Testing. 6. Kidnapping victims – Korea (North) – Public opinion. 7. Kidnapping – Japan – Public opinion. 8. Public opinion – Japan. I. Title. II. Series: Japan and global society

DS849.K7L43 2016 327.5205193 C2015-906943-2

University of Toronto Press acknowledges the financial assistance to its publishing program of the Canada Council for the Arts and the Ontario Arts Council, an agency of the Government of Ontario.

Canada Council for the Arts
Conseil des Arts du Canada

Funded by the Government of Canada
Financé par le gouvernement du Canada

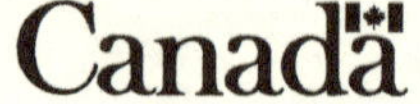

Contents

Foreword vii

Acknowledgments ix

1 Introduction 3
The Case Study and Its Significance 4
Public Opinion and Public Discourse in the Japanese Context 7
Setting the Scope and Dimensions of the Case 12
Western Studies from the 1990s and 2000s on Japanese Foreign Policy 14
Overview of the Book 21

2 Relations after the First Missile Launch 24
Japan's Security Identity and the Postwar Consensus 24
Relations with North Korea before 1998 27
Relations between 1998 and 2000: Issues and Responses 30
Conclusion 37

3 Relations prior to Koizumi's Visit to Pyongyang 39
New North Korea–linked Incidents 39
Societal Reaction 40
Koizumi's Emergence and Responses to North Korea, 2001–02 43
Koizumi's rise and structural changes in political decision-making 45
Adjustments to national security policy 48
Koizumi's early approach to North Korea 52
Conclusion 54

4 Japanese–North Korean Relations, 2002–04 56
The Koizumi–Kim Summit of 2002 56
The Post-summit Societal Discourse on North Korea 61
Discourse immediately following the summit 61
The political fallout from the abductions issue 64
Additional implications: A "sense of victimhood" 69
Heightening societal criticism of social elites 72
Media reaction 74
The Government's Response to the Changing Societal Discourse 79
Readjustment of the policy towards the abductions 79
Links to other security policies 82
The passage of emergency legislation 85
Conclusion 87

5 Japanese–North Korean Relations, 2004–06: Debates about Unilateral Sanctions 89
Koizumi's Second Visit to Pyongyang and the "Return" of the Abductees' Families 90
The Origin of the Unilateral Sanctions Legislation 93
The early proposals 93
Sanctions legislation in 2004 96
The Final Dissolution of the Pyongyang Declaration Framework 100
The last straw: The Yokota Megumi DNA incident 100
Koizumi's shift towards unilateral sanctions 102
The North Korean Nuclear Issue Takes International Centre Stage 103
North Korea Policy, 2004–06, before the Second Missile Launch 108
Denouement: The Second Taepodong Launch and the Imposition of Unilateral Economic Sanctions 110

6 Conclusion 115
The Origin and the Nature of the Sanctions 115
The Future of Japanese–North Korean Relations 119
Implications for the Debate on Revising the Constitution 124

Notes 129

Bibliography 161

Index 177

Foreword

University of Toronto Press, in cooperation with the University of Missouri–St Louis and the Shibusawa Eiichi Memorial Foundation of Tokyo, has launched an ambitious new series, "Japan and Global Society." The volumes in the series explore how Japan has defined its identities and objectives in the larger region of Asia and the Pacific and, at the same time, how the global community has been shaped by Japan and its interactions with other countries.

The dual focus on Japan and on global society reflects the series editors' and publishers' commitment to globalizing national studies. Scholars and readers have become increasingly aware that it makes little sense to treat a country in isolation. All countries are interdependent and shaped by cross-national forces so that mono-national studies, those that examine a country's past and present in isolation, are never satisfactory. Such awareness has grown during the past few decades when global, transnational phenomena and forces have gained prominence. In the age of globalization, no country retains complete autonomy or freedom of action. Yet nations continue to act in pursuit of their respective national interests, which frequently results in international tensions. Financial, social, and educational policies continue to be defined domestically, with national communities as units. But transnational economic, environmental, and cultural forces always infringe upon national entities, transforming them in subtle and sometimes even violent ways. Global society, consisting of billions of individuals and their organizations, evolves and shapes national communities even as the latter contribute to defining the overall human community.

Japan provides a particularly pertinent instance of such interaction, but this series is not limited to studies of that country alone. Indeed, the books published in the series will show that there is little unique about Japan, whose history has been shaped by interactions with China, Korea, the United States, and many other countries. For this reason, forthcoming volumes will deal with countries in the Asia-Pacific region and compare their respective developments and shared destinies. At the same time, some studies in the series will transcend national frameworks and discuss more transnational themes, such as humanitarianism, migration, and diseases, documenting how these phenomena affect Japan and other countries and how, at the same time, they contribute to the making of a more interdependent global society.

Lastly, we hope these studies will help to promote an understanding of non-national entities, such as regions, religions, and civilizations. Modern history continues to be examined in terms of nations as the key units of analysis, and yet these other entities have their own vibrant histories, which do not necessarily coincide with nation-centred narratives. To look at Japan, or for that matter any other country, and to examine its past and present in these alternative frameworks will enrich our understanding of modern world history and of the contemporary global civilization.

Akira Iriye

Acknowledgments

In the course of this project, I have been privileged to receive support from a long list of mentors. I first became interested in Japanese foreign policy towards North Korea – particularly with regard to the abductions issue – while pursuing my first graduate degree in Japan. During this period I wrote my first English-language working paper on the topic, as the case had not yet been covered in depth by English-speaking academics. I recently reread the paper with some embarrassment after many years (I am glad to have made progress since then!), but I am happy to say that I maintain my main argument, which is presented in the pages that follow. I certainly did not expect that this initial interest would bear subsequent fruit, first in the form of a doctoral dissertation and eventually as a book.

In writing this book, I am most indebted to Professor David A. Welch of the University of Waterloo, the Balsillie School of International Affairs, and the Centre for International Governance Innovation. I doubt that I will ever be able to repay fully everything I owe him. He has been my supervisor, mentor, boss, and true friend. He has influenced me in almost every aspect of my life over the past ten years, and his objective and keen observation and logic have encouraged me to push my ideas in directions I had not thought possible before. I also thank my former supervisor at Waseda University, Professor Yamamoto Takehiko. Now that I look back, I see that my years at Waseda University helped me to be an understanding friend of Japan, but also an honest critic when the need arises.

My very special gratitude also goes to Professor Tadokoro Masayuki at Keio University. I cannot adequately express my appreciation of the support he has given me over the past six years, in both public and private settings, as well as in his capacity as a dissertation committee member. My work certainly would have been less nuanced without his deep local knowledge and generous feedback. Professor Soeya Yoshihide at Keio University graciously offered assistance in arranging some of my interviews for this project, and I will never forget his kindness. I am indebted to the Shibusawa Eiichi Memorial Foundation – in particular, the president, Mr Shibusawa Masahide, and the research director, Dr Kimura Masato – for hosting me for my research and teaching stay at Keio University in 2008–09, which turned out to be a highly comfortable and productive experience, and to Professor Joseph Wong at the University of Toronto for hosting me as a visiting scholar at the Asian Institute at the Munk School of Global Affairs in 2013–14 so that I could focus on this book.

I would also like to express my sincere appreciation to my other former doctoral dissertation committee members and readers – Professor Michael Donnelly and Professor John Kirton of the University of Toronto, and Professor Kawasaki Tsuyoshi of Simon Fraser University – for their thorough and encouraging comments. During my return trips to South Korea, Professor Park Cheol Hee of Seoul National University and Professor Suh Seung-won of Korea University shared their insights on various topics related to Japan, and I am very grateful for their generosity. I would also like to thank all my interviewees for their time and for agreeing to provide valuable feedback.

Numerous Keio friends – especially Shiratori Junichirō, Gōroku Tsuyoshi, and Hayashi Seiichi – made my short stay at their university a pleasant and enjoyable learning experience for widening my views about crucial Japanese perspectives. I am most grateful to Aladdin Diakun at the Balsillie School of International Affairs and Amy Goertz for their dedicated English proofreading, to Barry Norris for his thorough and professional copy editing, to the two anonymous reviewers, and to Daniel Quinlan and Wayne Herrington at the University of Toronto Press for all their invaluable feedback and assistance in the publication process; this book certainly would not have come to light without their help. My sincere appreciation also goes to Jaemin Kim and friends at the Newman Centre at the University of Toronto for their spiritual support and encouragement during this endeavour. But my highest gratitude, of course, goes to my beloved family: Sangkyu Lee, Chongnam Suh, Kyuhey Lee August, and Gamja.

JAPANESE SOCIETY AND THE POLITICS OF THE NORTH KOREAN THREAT

Chapter One

Introduction

The Democratic People's Republic of Korea (North Korea) twice conducted ballistic missile tests close to Japan in 1998 and 2006. Although Japan responded in 1998 with non-coercive condemnations to demonstrate its disapproval, in 2006 it imposed unilateral economic sanctions on North Korea, marking the first instance since the Second World War that it applied substantial coercion to punish a neighbouring state. In this book, I examine why Japanese policy towards the North shifted between 1998 and 2006 for a seemingly identical type of provocation, and I highlight the underlying domestic processes through which changes in the Japanese public discourse on national security and North Korea influenced the policy shift.

I argue that the unilateral sanctions imposed in 2006 were not a calculated strategic response to punish the missile launch (or the North Korean nuclear programs) per se, but instead were a direct consequence of a deeper shift in societal discourse in Japan that took place in the years between the first and second missile tests. During that eight-year period, other highly publicized provocations and shocks from the North, especially the sensational revelation in 2002 of past North Korean abductions of Japanese citizens (*rachi jiken/rachi mondai*), caused the Japanese public to become increasingly conscious of their country's security weaknesses, and encouraged a re-evaluation of Japan's historical relations with its neighbour. The resulting shift in societal security discourse interacted with concurrent structural changes in the Japanese government and mass media – which made them both highly susceptible to discursive currents among citizens – and led to a hardened domestic environment in which the idea of pressuring the North became a feasible option when the opportunity arose in 2006.

As of 2014 the Japan–North Korea bilateral relationship was moving forward again, as the two sides finally resumed negotiations to resolve the abductions issue. Although we do not know how the ongoing negotiations will unfold, it is timely to look back on the origin of this issue and see how it became the most serious obstacle in the bilateral relationship. The purpose of this book is thus to illustrate the context in which the abductions issue influenced and was closely linked to Japanese assertiveness towards North Korea on all foreign policy fronts over the past decade, and also to demonstrate how the issue helped Abe Shinzō[1] to achieve his first prime ministership in 2006.

The Case Study and Its Significance

On 31 August 1998 North Korea launched a multistage Taepodong-1 ballistic missile eastward. The missile flew over northern Japan, and a portion of it then fell into the Pacific Ocean.[2] Although US intelligence sources eventually confirmed that it was a failed satellite test launch,[3] the fact that North Korea's intention was not to strike Japanese cities directly did not ameliorate the shock it caused in Japan. After all, this was the first instance in the post–Second World War period that a ballistic missile from a neighbouring state had flown through its airspace, without any official prior notification of the launch's schedule or of the North's exact intentions. The incident and its subsequent impact in Japan rightly deserved the term "the Taepodong shock."

The Japanese government reacted to the North Korean provocation by launching verbal condemnations, especially at the United Nations, where it pushed for an official statement of protest by the UN Secretariat but eventually had to settle for a less assertive press statement. Japan also placed a temporary hold on food aid whose delivery to the North had been scheduled before the launch, and froze the payment of its financial contribution to the Korean Peninsula Energy Development Organization (KEDO), an international agreement reached in 1995 to supply North Korea with a light water reactor as part of the attempt to persuade the North to give up its nuclear program, which had come to light in 1994.[4] (See Chapter 2 for the reaction of KEDO and Japan's role in this international institution after the Taepodong-1 launch in 1998.) The freeze on food and financial aid was not a unilateral Japanese decision, however, but closely coordinated moves with other member states of KEDO, such as the United States and South Korea. The hold on Japan's portion of the KEDO contribution was lifted in October 1998, and food aid resumed in December 1999.[5]

Considering that a potentially catastrophic missile belonging to a not-so-friendly neighbour had violated its airspace, Japan's reaction as a sovereign state was highly limited and controlled. It did not take any directly coercive countermeasures to punish North Korea's provocation, even when faced with a military threat to its national security, and it refrained from implementing any substantive, punitive measures to dissuade North Korea from taking future actions of the same nature. Furthermore, the actions that Japan did implement were not in any sense unilateral decisions led by Japanese initiative.

Then, on 5 July 2006, after an eight-year gap, North Korea conducted a series of short- and medium-range missile exercises, during which it launched a multistage ballistic missile, the Taepodong-2, from its eastern seaboard, with the debris falling into international waters a few hundred kilometres away, between the western part of Hokkaidō and the Maritime Province of Russia.[6] This time, unlike in 1998, the missile neither penetrated Japanese airspace nor flew over Japan towards the Pacific Ocean. Although the maritime security of other regional neighbours, such as Russia and China, was equally affected, the same day the Japanese government implemented a series of twelve unilateral sanctions against North Korea, including banning its ferry *Mangyongbong-92* from entering Japanese harbours and North Korean nationals from entering Japan.[7] In the following months, Japan would stop the bilateral flow of capital and trade, extend the measures of 5 July to other North Korean vessels, and reiterate its ban on North Korean citizens entering Japan.[8]

In drastic contrast to its settling in 1998 for a UN Secretariat press statement, in 2006 the Japanese government also took the leading role in drafting a UN Security Council resolution condemning North Korea, and actively persuaded other member states to join its unilateral sanctions.[9] The Security Council resolution that eventually passed did not require UN member states to join the Japanese sanctions or impose their own against North Korea, as Japan had hoped. Still, the policy reaction Japan demonstrated in 2006 was strikingly different from its stance in 1998: for the first time in the postwar era, Japan had unilaterally imposed sanctions against a regional state or taken the most active part in drafting and submitting a UN resolution specifically targeting a neighbour. It is true that Japan had participated in other multilateral sanctions and boycotts during the Cold War as a member of the

Western bloc and an ally of the United States. For example, as a member of COCOM (the Coordinating Committee of Multilateral Export Controls), Japan had regulated its exports of strategic equipment to the Soviet bloc states.[10] It had also boycotted the 1980 Moscow Olympics to protest the Soviet invasion of Afghanistan, joined the European export sanctions against Iran the same year,[11] and cancelled loans and aid to China after the Tiananmen Square Incident in 1989.[12] However, these were not in any sense direct coercive measures designed and exercised to force those states to alter their policies towards Japan, nor were they punitive retaliations for actions threatening Japanese security.

Why, then, did the Japanese reaction to the two similar North Korean provocations eight years apart differ so substantially, and why did the unilateral sanctions of 2006 materialize in their particular form? I argue that the reasons can be understood only by tracing the domestic process in Japan between 1998 and 2006. The main emphasis here is Japan's public/societal sphere and the observable trend of its widely supported security discourse towards North Korea. The overall "societal discursive shift" towards the North among the public, in conjunction with its interaction with mass media and politics, is the most important key to understanding the puzzle.

I use the term "public/societal" to encompass the notion of the domestic, non-governmental interest groups in Japan linked to North Korean issues or national security, and to broadly embrace ordinary Japanese citizens at the mass level of all occupational, educational, and regional backgrounds. By "discourse" I mean a contextual and narrated-in-detail form of public opinion, formed by societal debates and discussions (often through mass media) concerning a foreign policy issue. Public opinion, as expressed in opinion polls, is citizens' responses to predetermined and framed questionnaires. Societal discourse, on the other hand, points to the background ideational current or narratives that lead citizens to answer opinion polls in a particular way. It is a source from which one can understand contextually the nuanced background (or ideational origin) of how and why citizens in the societal sphere react in a certain fashion on a particular issue. Discourse, therefore, embeds the meaning of the social-communicative process through which the public forms mainstream preferences and values concerning a political issue, while the expressed result of discourse constitutes public opinion. Furthermore, the "expressed" portion, by itself, does not constitute "the whole story"; it is, rather, a simplified and partial indicator of the societal discussions through which discourse is derived.

Public Opinion and Public Discourse in the Japanese Context

Although this book relies comparatively heavily on public discourse, rather than on public opinion, it is also important to emphasize that, in the Japanese context, there is no clear demarcation between *yoron* or *seron* (public opinion) and "public discourse," as there is no equivalent vocabulary for the latter in Japanese.[13] Compared to the more detailed and operational definitions in use in North America,[14] the term *yoron* is used much more broadly in Japan.

Japanese society and politics broadly understand public opinion as a "viewpoint of society that is perceived and recognized by its members to be strong and influential in a particular issue area." And for the viewpoint to be recognized as such, it is essential that the idea exude an impression of being – or has the clear potential to be – conceded to by the majority of the public in a visible manner.[15] Japanese newspapers also provide equally general definitions of their own. The largest circulation daily, *Yomiuri Shimbun*, takes public opinion as "an inclination of ordinary citizens on a certain issue."[16] The second-largest, *Asahi Shimbun*,[17] maintains that it is "an opinion or an attitude (bearing/demeanor) of everyone (i.e., every citizen) toward a problem that concerns everyone."[18] Two additional terms that are widely interchangeable with public opinion in the Japanese context are *iken no kazamuki* and *kūki*,[19] which have connotations of societal inclination towards a particular viewpoint and a strong – albeit indirect, unofficial, and subtle – pressure on individuals to conform to the mainstream ideational current.

The Japanese understanding of public opinion, therefore, is closest to a particular North American view of the term as signifying a reflection of the beliefs and values of the majority of citizens. That Japanese do not distinguish clearly between the societal-value-forming process (discourse) and expressed-value inclinations is an indication that they understand the concept not merely in terms of numbers, but also as the very representation of social communication. Since the Japanese definition largely overlaps my use of the term "discourse" in this book, I examine both public opinion and societal discourse concerning North Korea in subsequent chapters, sometimes interchangeably. However, I emphasize discourse as the key to understanding the observed policy change that took place in Japan between 1998 and 2006.

Public opinion and its background societal discourse are powerful influences on Japanese politics, and both the public and the government accept Japanese mass media as their prominent reflective medium. All sectors of political actors and societal elites rank the mass media as the most powerful and influential agent in Japanese politics.[20] Public opinion has a tremendous influence on Japanese politics because it constitutes the most powerful source of legitimacy in policy-making. Even when the actual policy-making process involves coordinative negotiations among the cabinet, the ruling party, and the bureaucracy, the agents in power are nevertheless constantly pressured to monitor the reactions of citizens and the degree of their support.[21] Whenever the government launches a new initiative, it is thus obliged to consider whether it will be seen as legitimate in the eyes of the public,[22] and for this reason "the policy orientations of the political leadership will never stray far from the basic values of the citizenry."[23]

Government officials and policy-makers thus constantly monitor the expressions and interpretations of the people's mandate: "Voices from all strata of the public, comments and editorials of journalists, letters from ... ordinary readers and ... viewers, columns with coverage on how ordinary citizens are reacting to a certain issue, and opinion polls" – all introduced and transmitted through newspapers, magazines, and television.[24] Newspapers are especially important, as "everyone around the Japanese government seems to read three papers a day and to take from them his or her own notions of what problems facing the nation deserve attention and what might be done about them."[25] The viewpoint that they recognize as the mainstream current in society on a given topic constitutes unignorable public opinion in their minds.[26]

Looking into the content of mass media, therefore, is a direct means of tapping into the nature of public opinion and the background societal discourse on any widely discussed and engaged political matter in Japan. This is especially the case when an issue is shocking enough to affect citizens' nationalism and to stir their emotional involvement. International incidents with direct implications for Japanese identity, national pride, and security understandably rank among the top such examples. Thus, when a particular political or foreign policy issue is widely discussed and engaged by the public – that is, *publicized* – any analysis of Japanese governmental policy on that issue that does not incorporate the role of public opinion and the background discourse is incomplete.

What needs to be emphasized here is that the nature of the relationship among the media-public-government triangle differs according to the degree of publicization of a given news topic. Therefore, it is crucial to understand these nuanced differences before moving on to the subsequent chapters, to prevent any misunderstanding as to the influence of the media and the public on Japanese foreign policy.

Japan, like any advanced democracy, consists of citizens who have interests in various political and social issues, and anyone and any group can present their opinion publicly. It is also natural, however, that not everyone is concerned with the same issue to the same magnitude, and not all political issues are perceived by the public to be equally dramatic or significant. This is especially true with respect to foreign policy: the scope of societal interest in an issue and the degree of its publicity can differ vastly, depending on the country to which the policy is directed and the policy's domestic implications.[27] Therefore, when a particular issue is not sufficiently publicized, or when the nature of the issue makes it difficult for ordinary citizens to "personalize" it – to relate it to their own lives, interests, and their national identity and pride – the societal discursive current surrounding the issue could be nebulous, in the sense that it might be difficult to locate the majority opinion.

Political issues generally do not enjoy wide societal attention when they fall into the type of everyday politics that have little consequence for the economic and security well-being of ordinary citizens; the same can be said for international topics that involve routine intergovernmental contacts and negotiations. When the degree of societal engagement is relatively soft and thus without any clear, dominant public attitude, Japanese mass media can be highly versatile in their style of presentation. In such cases, mass media outlets are relatively free to reflect diverse voices from the interested public and to provide their own interpretations of the issue's societal implications with a sense of neutrality and pluralism. The media can even facilitate awareness and provide a public stage where diverse voices can engage in domestic discussions of their viewpoints as part of the process of forming a new societal discourse. In turn, this helps the media eventually to focus on the mainstream societal interpretation once the overall "atmosphere"[28] is pinpointed later on.

On the other hand, certain political topics invite much wider societal engagement from the start. These are the ones involving strong emotional or moral dimensions; topics such as international issues that provoke citizens' nationalism (by the action of an external force) or touch upon traditional societal taboos are bound to be at the centre of public attention.[29] When the nature of the topic is such that there is a strong societal emotional participation from the beginning and the voluntary formation of a clear, mainstream, public discursive undercurrent, the media often end up amplifying this ongoing trend. In such a scenario the media generally are compelled (by correctly "reading" the societal atmosphere) to report on the majority opinions of the public, and thus to provide a more concrete, discursive "focal point" by their own act of news coverage.

In effect, in their treatment of such topics, the mass media perform a social bonding function. Some journalism specialists lament that this particular characteristic of the Japanese media sometimes results in an overly nation-centric selection and presentation of topics and interpretations that appeal only to the Japanese.[30] Nonetheless, the media's bonding effect certainly has facilitated wide political participation by promoting psychological involvement and political knowledge for everyone, including "opinion leaders" and those of lower socioeconomic status.[31]

Ōtake Hideo argues that the Japanese media have a strong tendency to fawn over readers and viewers, and are especially prone to be swayed by direct criticism from the public.[32] Accordingly, when faced with a strong societal atmosphere on a given subject, one of the characteristics of the Japanese media is their strong predisposition for *yokonarabi taishitsu* (following the crowd/not standing out).[33] When all media consequently adopt a similar tone of interpretation concerning a particular topic, it is thus not as a result of deliberate collusion but of jumping on the bandwagon. As we shall see later, in certain instances where the majority public atmosphere is overly dominant, a phenomenon resembling what Elisabeth Noelle-Neumann has called a "spiral of silence" can become noticeable.[34]

I do not claim that *all* aspects of Japanese foreign policy are a simple function of public opinion – there are numerous examples of issues where societal influence does not play a crucial role. What I do argue, rather, is that certain foreign policy issues result in a wide discursive engagement by the citizenry, and that these highly publicized cases are the ones in which public opinion must be regarded as a highly influential factor for gauging likely government policy reactions.

Which kinds of media sources should one use in this analysis? A number of recent works on the topic have emphasized the importance of Japanese newspaper editorials, analyses and columns, with which I concur, especially concerning editorials. For example, in his study on the origin of cabinet-led diplomacy facilitated by Prime Minister

Koizumi Junichirō, Shinoda Tomohito covers "the most traceable opinions expressed in the editorials of Japan's five major newspapers: *Asahi, Mainichi, Nihon Keizai, Sankei,* and *Yomiuri*" as the most expressive of public opinion.[35] He argues that since the Japanese press is considered in Japan to be the most reliable source of information and also enjoys a significant influence on policy as a result, jointly using major newspaper editorials and public polls can be a highly effective approach to accessing the empirical unfolding of the interaction between domestic actors.[36] Another contribution, by Linus Hagström and Jon Williamsson, which assesses Japanese foreign security policy changes, also treats editorials and *kaisetsu* (analyses) from *Yomiuri Shimbun* and *Asahi Shimbun* as a "shortcut to gauging normative change" in Japanese society.[37] In addition, not only are these two the largest circulating newspapers in Japan, but the former takes a moderately conservative stance while the latter is more liberal and progressive,[38] which enables the researcher to examine the general discursive tone of Japanese society in a more balanced fashion.

When one looks at how editorials are written each day by the major Japanese dailies, the rationale for adopting them as the chief representation of public sentiment becomes even clearer. Every day, editorial boards decide on the theme and the argument for the day, and the decision must always, in principle, be unanimous. An editorial is considered to be the official product of "integrating everyone's voices in the company," and is never regarded as the personal opinion of an individual writer.[39] Also, when the theme of an editorial relates to a publicized topic in which citizens' emotions are highly charged, the tone is carefully framed to present the newspaper's stance in a controlled and balanced manner, so as not to sound too distant from the dominant, public interpretation and discursive atmosphere. This is because editorial boards are aware that taking a greatly different stance could provoke a strong adverse reaction from the public and would be counterproductive for the position that the editor or newspaper actually stands for in the long run.[40] Therefore, dailies invest a great deal of effort in their choice of themes and tones in order to carefully convey opinions that reflect their political and ideological leaning, while staying within the confines of what they perceive to be ongoing societal discursive trends. Relatedly, politicians, bureaucrats, and opinion leaders in various societal strata pay close attention to the editorials of major newspapers as among the most definite grounds for gauging their policies' legitimacy.[41]

Public opinion polls and *yoron chōsa* (surveys) are another media source popularly regarded as directly reflecting the societal inclination. Japan as a whole, not just the government, depends heavily on opinion polls as the lens through which to observe society in "real time." Polls have been respected as a symbol of Japanese democracy throughout the postwar period, and have served as a "mock referendum," substituting for actual direct voting by citizens on socio-political themes of public interest.[42] As mentioned earlier, it is impossible to understand fully the discursive context in which the majority of respondents answer poll questions by relying only on the resulting figures. It is therefore crucial to supplement data from polls with editorials to develop more detailed insight into societal discursive trends and linked public opinions.

The final media source I employ in this book is articles in Japanese monthly journals. Although not as scholastic as the typical academic literature, they are nevertheless highly reflective of ongoing societal trends, and offer much more nuanced and in-depth analyses of background societal discourses on the topics raised in newspaper articles and editorials of the day. For balance and comprehensiveness, I use pieces from the following five major monthly journals (the order reflects their overall political inclination from conservative to progressive/liberal): *Seiron, Bungeishunjū, Chūōkōron, Ronza,* and *Sekai.*

Setting the Scope and Dimensions of the Case

In addition to the missile tests and the disclosure of the abductions of Japanese citizens, other North Korean security threats with direct implications for Japanese sovereignty also materialized between 1998 and 2006; I incorporate these, too, into the analysis to reveal their linkage to the societal discursive shift.

One of the most publicized developments during this period was the renewal of North Korea's nuclear program, suspicions about which were confirmed by North Korea's official declaration of its possession of a nuclear weapon in 2005 and its first atomic test in October 2006. Not surprisingly, academic and policy circles that embrace the traditional definition of state security regard the nuclear topic to be of the greatest significance, yet I exclude the issue from analysis in the main chapters of this book for two reasons.

First, the suspected North Korean nuclear program, at least during the period between 1998 and 2006, was not a direct, concrete, visible threat to Japanese territorial or maritime sovereignty, unlike the two missile launches. It also did not involve Japanese citizens, as in the case of the abductions issue. Although suspicions about the program were confirmed in 2006 after North Korea's first atomic test, it is hard to argue that Japan was "victimized" in the same manner as in the other cases, since the test was conducted deep within North Korea and did not violate Japan's sovereignty in any strict sense. For this reason, I suggest that the different nature of the nuclear threat requires a separate inquiry from threats that had a direct impact on the Japanese societal sphere.

Second, the manner in which the nuclear issue was handled also differed. Although the missile launches in 1998 and 2006 were perceived to be a security hazard to the region, states in the region had diverging estimates of the degree of threat they posed, and the launches did not easily facilitate the establishment of an international intervention mechanism – indeed, they were interpreted as mainly the concern of Japan and the United States.[43] In contrast, the nuclear issue was handled by a firmly established and long-term multilateral institution, the International Atomic Energy Agency (of which North Korea had also been a member), and by the Six Party Talks devoted solely to the resolution of the issue among all related parties, including both Japan and North Korea.[44] As a result, although Japan adjusted and coordinated its policy concerning the atomic issue with that of other members of the Six Party Talks – namely, China, Russia, South Korea, and the United States – its policy in the missile cases was less locked into international institutional constraints. The main negotiating parties in the missile cases in any event were North Korea and the United States, and Japanese policy-makers perceived that Japan was not in a position to deal directly with North Korea in the international setting.[45] Accordingly, Japan took part in the bilateral negotiations between the United States and North Korea only indirectly, through policy coordination with the United States. Thus, although Japanese policy-makers were acutely aware that the missiles' potential danger to Japan was arguably even more serious than that posed by North Korea's nuclear program, the missile issue never achieved the same degree of consistent international engagement as did the nuclear issue with the Six Party Talks because, as mentioned earlier, other states in the region had different estimates about the threat the North Korean missiles posed.[46] Since Japanese policy on the missile issue was not directly incorporated into a concrete international institution, the launches were linked more easily with other already-materialized North Korean threats perceived by Japanese society. These conditions made the missile issue a more domestically politicized topic, allowing it to become part of a "North Korea issue package" in societal discourse.

Of course, I do not assert that the nuclear and missile issues are mutually exclusive or that the domestic debates surrounding each issue were totally unrelated to each other. However, even when there was some convergence, differences in the policy environment in which the Japanese government dealt with the issues – and also the domestic discursive environment in which the public interpreted their nature – must not be overlooked; thus they should be approached as two separate inquiries.

The much-publicized deadlock of the SPT certainly deepened negative images of North Korea in Japan during the period. Although the nuclear issue undeniably provided further justification for regarding North Korea as the main threat to Japanese security, suspicions about its nuclear program by themselves were not the origin of the negative image of the North, at least from the societal perspective. Rather, the nuclear suspicions reinforced for the Japanese public the direction of the societal debate on Japanese security that had been generated by other, already-materialized provocations from North Korea with direct implications for Japanese sovereignty.

It should also be remembered that, in 1994, during the first nuclear crisis on the Korean Peninsula, Japan cooperated with the United States and South Korea to persuade the North to freeze its existing nuclear program. The security threat it posed to Japan at that time was equally as significant as the subsequent threat in the next decade. In the absence of an actualized and visible threat to its home islands, however, Japan's subsequent relations with North Korea did not become dramatically more hostile. Even more significant, when North Korea officially declared its possession of nuclear weapons in 2005, Japan did not proceed immediately to impose sanctions, even though legal obstacles had been removed and some voices in the government and the media were calling for tougher measures.[47]

In light of the swift Japanese policy reaction after the second ballistic missile launch in 2006, these examples further support my view that the nuclear issue, by itself, cannot account fully for Japan's societal discourse and its eventual policy shift towards North Korea.

Western Studies from the 1990s and 2000s on Japanese Foreign Policy

A variety of academic literature on Japanese foreign policy was published from the late 1990s to the mid-2000s, while the events that are analysed in this book were taking place. Most of the literature published in the West,[48] however, dealt mainly with the "big question" of whether Japan's general foreign policy trajectory was experiencing a fundamental strategic transformation away from its traditional post–Second World War national principles – that is, those based on the Yoshida Doctrine and the Peace Constitution.[49] In other words, most literature on Japan's foreign policy posture focused on explaining its overall trajectory in the midst of the system-level international changes affecting Japan in the post–Cold War era, rather than specifically delving into the details of its relations with North Korea. Indeed, works devoted solely to Japan–North Korean relations were rare, especially those that focused on the abductions issue and on relations between the first and second missile launches in 1998 and 2006. Although this academic trend began to change in the late 2000s, Japan's relationship with North Korea was treated largely as a small part of the broader context of its complicated and strained relations with its East Asian neighbours in the post–Cold War period.

It should be noted that Japanese academia has, naturally, also produced a significant amount of empirical work on Japan's relations with its neighbours. These Japanese sources provide contextually rich and detailed empirical interpretations – particularly concerning societal discourse and the subtle domestic processes behind discursive shifts – that have often been overlooked in Western research. For this reason, I use such sources extensively throughout the main parts of this book, but since most of the Japanese literature is non-theoretical and inaccessible to Western readers not trained in the language, I review here only those works that have been published in the West.

Most Western literature published during the 1990s and 2000s can be categorized in two main ways. One is based on the works' *predictions* – that is, on the writer's position on whether a fundamental change in Japan's overall post–Second World War security strategy was likely to occur or had already taken place. The other category is based on the *theoretical assumptions* the writers apply in their analyses.

Of works in the first category, one group argued that Japan had indeed undergone a clear shift, or that it was on the verge of discarding its long-held postwar principles and doctrines based on the Yoshida Doctrine and the Peace Constitution. Scholars in this group – for example, Kenneth B. Pyle and Richard J. Samuels – analysed changes in Japan's strategic choices in the midst of ongoing shifts in the global order after the Cold War, and provided grand explanations of the nature and the significance of such changes.[50] Pyle argued that Japan's future foreign policy would be very different from the grand strategy that Yoshida Shigeru had pioneered, and that Japan would maintain its traditional postwar role as a "merchant nation" for only a limited time.[51] Samuels claimed that, although there were still ongoing debates about the validity of the traditional doctrines that had contributed to Japanese prosperity and stability, it was nevertheless apparent that these doctrines had been "challenged, perhaps fatally."[52] Pyle and Samuels also agreed that external factors had played an important role in the shift; transformations in international power dynamics after the Cold War, such as the rising influence of China, the threat from North Korea, the possibility of "abandonment" by the United States, and Japan's relative economic decline, had all had a tremendous impact on how Japan perceived itself, the region, and new threats.[53]

Michael J. Green concurred that significant alterations in international and regional relations were at the core of Japan's increasing sensitivity to the revision of its domestic institutions of national security.[54] He also placed particular emphasis on the economic side of the analysis – namely, Japan's frail material edge in international markets vis-à-vis China in a world dominated by balance-of-power politics. As Japan was pressed to assess its national economic resources in order to "get more 'bang' for the shrinking diplomatic 'buck,'" it would be compelled to be more serious about its foreign and security policies.[55] Christopher W. Hughes similarly took the position that Japan was likely to become a more assertive and "normal" military power as a result of international environmental changes.[56] Hughes emphasized that Japan would aim to transform itself while concurrently strengthening its existing alliance with the United States. This calculation was purely strategic: since Japan could not trust or rely on an East Asian or United Nations–centred multilateral security framework, which could involve China or North Korea, it would have little choice but to maintain the existing alliance, although it would also desire to become a more active player within it.[57]

Another group of scholars in the first category, however, took the opposite view, emphasizing the continuity of the postwar security principles in governing Japanese foreign policy-making and their resilience in the face of pressures stemming from the system-level changes in the post–Cold War environment. The best known of this group are Peter J. Katzenstein and Thomas U. Berger. They emphasized the consistency of the pacifist dimensions of Japanese foreign policy, and they highlighted the "stickiness" of postwar Japanese domestic identities and norms despite the tectonic shifts in international power relations that had occurred after the end of the Cold War.[58] Japanese ideas about national security and Japan's position in the world had been produced by societal ideational factors that, in turn, were produced by Japan's distinct historical experiences; from Katzenstein and Berger's perspective, it was understandable that Japan had not fully discarded its postwar security institutions. Therefore, Katzenstein and Berger's work in the 1990s emphasized Japan's antimilitaristic identity as the reason for the consistency of its foreign policy orientation and the resilience of its postwar security institutions.

Like the scholars who emphasized fundamental changes in Japan's posture, however, the scholars emphasizing continuity still faced empirical evidence of certain security policy changes, as well as increasing domestic questions about the validity of the postwar security principles. As a result, these scholars have acknowledged the changes in their more recent publications without fundamentally revising their earlier arguments.[59] For example, Andrew L. Oros acknowledged that, since the end of the Cold War, various external factors had facilitated domestic debates on national security. But although Japan was undeniably responding to new threats, Oros – as well as Berger – asserted that newly proposed measures to deal with them did not necessarily constitute a fundamental shift in its security principles.[60] Such policy adjustments were said to be evolving along a "predictable path" guided by the same "central tenets" that had characterized the Cold War period, and thus the "constrained nature of recent 'new' security policies" illustrated that Japan was still "far from enacting a major shift."[61] According to Berger, the origin and nature of this "duality" – of changing policies but consistent overarching security principles – came down to Japan's characteristics as a "liberal adaptive" state.[62] Berger claimed that Japan was pushed to adapt more "realist tools of foreign policy" to realize its "wishes to move the world in a more liberal direction," while maintaining its traditional liberal principles.[63]

The second category of Western literature on Japanese foreign policy is based on the theoretical assumptions the writers apply in their analyses – indeed, the scholars mentioned in the first category apply two different theoretical frameworks. Their explanations as to whether Japan was fundamentally changing were based, after all, on their distinct "worldviews," which prompted each author to emphasize the importance of particular aspects of Japan's situation and behaviour, with different implications for interpreting and predicting state foreign policy. It is not a stretch to suggest that the scholars in the first category who emphasized change were applying the tenets of "realist" or "neo-realist" international relations theories, while those who emphasized continuity can be understood as belonging to the "constructivist" camp.

The two strands of realism in international relations theory understand state behaviour to be rational and strategy driven.[64] From this perspective, it is not difficult to see that the scholars who argued that changes in Japan signalled a fundamental transformation in the country's orientation developed their explanations based on assumptions about the primacy of rationality and security considerations in determining state behaviour in the international system. By prioritizing Japan's well-proven trait of adeptly calculating its interests in the changing external environment, the scholars writing in the realist tradition were compelled to perceive Japan's foreign policy as the product of the state's rationality.

Scholars such as Samuels, Pyle, and Mochizuki showed a strong tendency to focus on structural shifts in the international system. North Korea was frequently mentioned in their work, but predominantly as an *additional and secondary* justification for Japan's re-evaluation of its postwar "grand strategy"; the true motive behind Japan's behaviour, according to these scholars, had more to do with "big power relations" between China and the United States. Moreover, these scholars predicted the future trajectory of Japan's foreign policy and security posture as a product of rational and strategic thinking by political elites.

The two main assumptions of these realism-based analyses – the primacy of system-level big power politics, and rational policy-making by governmental elites to maximize Japan's national interest and prestige in response to turbulent international power shifts – led these scholars to predict that Japan's traditional postwar security principles, as symbolized by the Yoshida Doctrine and the Peace Constitution, were on the verge of being discarded or at least fundamentally revised. The authors concluded, therefore, that, although Japan would maintain the Peace Constitution for the time being, it would soon replace the ideas of "economy first" and "no external military power projection" embedded in the Yoshida Doctrine and the Constitution as a result of the country's heightened sense of vulnerability in the face of changes in the global order. From this perspective, North Korea, rather than being the primary cause, served as a more up-close-and-personal source of additional legitimacy to push for this new grand strategy, since the true goal was much more substantial in scope.

The second category also includes scholars such as Katzenstein and Berger, who are widely regarded in the discipline as "constructivists." In contrast to the realists, these writers reintroduced the importance of cultural and societal elements in empirical analyses by emphasizing the primacy of ideational and normative influences on Japanese foreign policy. From a constructivist perspective, politics in general and foreign policy in particular are shaped by cultural characteristics. Cultural characteristics are domestically institutionalized through reiterated political interaction and projected outward in domestic actors' collective national security identity. The form of national interest a state defines for itself is, therefore, a consequence of the state's distinct domestic understanding of what it stands for in the international system.[65]

During the 1990s the constructivist scholars successfully emphasized that a consistent internal "antimilitarist" and "pacifist" identity framed Japanese postwar strategy. Although they did not face a significant challenge to their overall conclusions, policy shifts since the late 1990s – especially during the early 2000s – eventually forced them to update their original claims somewhat. The constructivist works published in the 2000s started to employ a subtle change in their arguments, asserting that the observable policy changes in Japanese foreign policy were predictable minor adjustments or adaptations to the changing international environment. This nuanced change of interpretation is characteristic of constructivism, which is well equipped to explain continuity of a certain identity but limited in comprehending the nature of ongoing changes. Thus, rather than being evidence for the weakening of the constructivist authors' original assertions, the changes in Japanese policy were, in fact, understood as the newest iteration of Japan's own skilful manoeuvring to strengthen its postwar "liberal" and "antimilitaristic" identity by implementing peripheral adjustments.

For example, Berger and Oros created and promoted definitions of "normalcy" and "continuity" that were distinctly different from those of mainstream Japan researchers. Berger's claim that Japan is an "adaptive state" was based on his belief that, since the 1990s, Japanese elites and the Japanese public had reached a political consensus on their country's future direction and purpose in the world, based on their continuously liberal view of international politics. He asserted that, despite certain policy modifications, Japan was still heavily guided by a liberal belief that "progress in international affairs is both possible and necessary and that Japan can contribute to a progressive shift in international relations."[66] In the case of Oros, the most distinct part of his theme was defining the term "normal." Rather than abstractly arguing whether Japan was, or was trying to be, a "normal state," he argued that the question scholars should be asking instead was "what is considered normal by Japan, and by Japanese?"[67] and he posited that we must understand that domestic contestations over various security issues had always constituted what defined "normal" in Japanese society.[68] In other words, Oros claimed that this very process of socially defining the meaning of the central tenets and making practice-level changes within that framework – embedded as it was in contentious politics – was what Japanese had always defined as "normal."[69]

As we have seen, the two categories of literature on Japanese foreign policy published during the 1990s and 2000s significantly expanded our knowledge of the overall Japanese post–Cold War security trajectory. However, the very strength of these paradigmatic interpretations also caused detailed, small-case analyses of Japanese–North Korean bilateral relations during this crucial period to be sidelined. It is not that the scholars did not acknowledge the importance of the "North Korea factor," but that it constituted only a part of the larger – and more popular – themes of this body of literature, such as constitutional revision, Japan's possible nuclearization, its rivalry with China, the alliance with the United States, and the future international role of the Self-Defense Forces. Moreover, analyses of the interaction between the Japanese public and the government and the actual role of the former in setting both limitations and opportunities for decision-makers were not given central attention. Scholars did acknowledge that the democratic elements of Japan's political system imposed heavy burdens on foreign policy-making,[70] and that politicians and bureaucrats, despite their considerable power in designing foreign policy strategies, also prioritize in response to the public voice at key moments.[71] However, although the writers admitted to the multiplicity of actors involved, subsequent empirical portions of their works were, nevertheless, still heavily tilted towards highlighting government-level decisions and the vocal preferences of key political figures.

There are a few notable exceptions. For example, Hughes published an article in 2006 highlighting the domestic political processes through which Japanese sanctions were designed and implemented in response to North Korea's nuclear and missile programs. By tracing how organized political groups interacted, Hughes demonstrated that domestic debates and negotiations among coalitions had been more influential than international pressures in the formation of Japanese sanction policies.[72] Another example is a 2006 article on Japan's North Korea policy by Hyung Gu Lynn, which highlighted how the media, particularly television programs, generated a narrow and biased public perception of North Korea following the summit meeting between Koizumi and Kim Jong Il in September 2002.[73]

One can point to a welcome trend, however, in more recent years. Since 2009 there have been additional publications solely dedicated to bilateral relations, the abductions issue, and Japan's security policy towards North Korea. Such work – by, for example, Heigo Sato, Brad Williams and Erik Mobrand, Anthony DiFilippo, Atsuhito Isozaki, and Samuels – has further facilitated the accumulation of our empirical knowledge on the topic, as these publications are also examples of more case-specific findings.[74] This book is thus a further contribution to the case-specific body of literature, especially concerning the link between the Japanese government's policy shift in response to the North Korean missile threat and the abductions on the one hand, and the change in Japanese societal discourse on the other.

Overview of the Book

Chapters 2 to 5 constitute the main empirical body of the book. Each chapter, except Chapter 5, traces three factors – namely: (1) incidents involving North Korean breaches of Japan's territorial, maritime, and human sovereignty in a given period; (2) Japanese societal reaction and the public's interpretation of these incidents, and the consequential unfolding of societal discourse on security as seen through the Japanese media; and (3) the nature and the behaviour of government decision-makers, and their increasing susceptibility to the public discourse.

In Chapter 2 I start by exploring Japan's overall national security principles during the post–Second World War and post–Cold War periods, as well as its traditional diplomatic stance towards North Korea prior to 1998. I then trace bilateral relations from right after the Taepodong-1 missile launch in 1998 up to 2000. I highlight the reasons Japan took only modest measures to protest the missile provocation and the appearance of so-called *fushinsen* (mystery/spy ships) near the Japanese coast during this period, and explore the highly nuanced and multifaceted view towards North Korea that the mainstream Japanese public still embraced in the late 1990s.

Chapter 3 covers 2001 and 2002, up to the point just prior to the first historic bilateral summit meeting in Pyongyang between Prime Minister Koizumi and Kim Jong Il in September 2002. During this brief period, another appearance of *fushinsen*, which resulted in Japan's first postwar maritime live-fire engagement, and the bizarre entry (and swift deportation) of Kim Jong Il's son, Kim Jong Nam, made the Japanese public anxious about North Korea as the most unpredictable and proximate concern to national security. I also analyse the significance of Koizumi's emergence, as public opinion and the subsequent restructuring of the decision-making mechanism that empowered the cabinet would have a direct impact on subsequent policies of the Japanese government towards North Korea.

Chapter 4 covers the period from the time of the Koizumi–Kim summit meeting in Pyongyang in September 2002 to the end of 2003. Here I focus on the Pyongyang Declaration signed by the two heads of government, which laid the foundation for future bilateral diplomatic normalization and the comprehensive resolution of all recent security instabilities caused by North Korea. I demonstrate that one "achievement" of the Japanese side during the summit – the open admission by the North that it had abducted Japanese citizens – ended up causing unprecedented shock and anger in the minds of the Japanese public, despite the balanced nature of the Declaration. Although forcing the North to make the admission was originally designed to push bilateral normalization ahead, the disclosure of the abductions issue soon became the most prominent obstacle for normalization after the summit. This unintended consequence made it impossible to implement the originally agreed-upon framework, as skyrocketing negative societal discourse towards North Korea dominated the vast majority of public emotions, and the mass media, in turn, jumped on the bandwagon in a manner consistent with the trend. The chapter demonstrates how, in the aftermath of the summit, this domestic mechanism started to substantially limit and frame the governmental policies towards the North from this stage on.

In Chapter 5 I trace how the idea to pressure the North through unilateral sanctions developed and unfolded in the domestic Japanese context, originally as a consequence of the disclosure of the abductions issue. In the rest of the chapter, I illustrate how the proposal then became formal legislation as a result of pressure from the societal sphere by the end of 2004, and how and why sanction were finally implemented in 2006, even though they had in fact been originally planned as potential coercive measures to force North Korea to comply with Japanese demands concerning the abductions.

In Chapter 6 I conclude that the imposition of unilateral sanctions in 2006 was neither part of a consistent, long-term, grand strategy on the part of the Japanese government in the post–Cold War environment nor an instant reaction by the government to punish North Korea's missile launches. Instead, it was more of an unintended "joint enterprise" brought about by the collective inputs of three factors: accumulating, highly provocative, and publicized international incidents offered by the North; domestic societal discursive shifts; and the Japanese government's embrace of the public "atmosphere" that had developed between 1998 and 2006.

Koizumi – and the governments of other prime ministers who preceded him – originally preferred normalizing bilateral relations as a way to resolve North Korean threats peacefully, despite rising negative societal discourse against the North. Indeed, Koizumi was not openly supportive of sanctions even up to 2004. Therefore, the changing trajectory of the Japanese government's planned approach to North Korea from the one envisioned in the Pyongyang Declaration of 2002 to the eventual imposition of unilateral sanctions in 2006 is one of the most vivid illustrations of how Japanese postwar foreign policy was led into a particular direction by societal influence.

Chapter Two

Relations after the First Missile Launch

Before moving on to an examination of Japanese–North Korean bilateral relations after the Taepodong-1 missile launch in 1998, it will be helpful to set the stage by covering Japanese security principles and identity during the post–Second World War period and their connection to Japan's policy towards North Korea prior to 1998.

Japan's Security Identity and the Postwar Consensus

Scholarly interpretations of the origin and nature of Japan's security identity after the Second World War differ on what that identity has meant for domestic politics and society. They generally agree, however, that, in the aftermath of the war, the majority of the Japanese public strongly supported a new Japan that distanced itself from the past, from great power ambitions, and from the use of military force, especially towards its neighbours. Scepticism about the use of armed force was a fundamental attitude of many Japanese and influenced Japan's subsequent decisions on defence policy; this scepticism also expressed the "postwar consensus," which was built on remorse over the nation's wartime aggression in Asia.[1]

During the postwar period, Japanese regarded military power as ineffective in ensuring their country's security. Instead, Japan promoted economic development by aligning itself with the United States based on the Yoshida Doctrine, which held despite subsequent changes in both internal and external conditions during the Cold War.[2] At the same time, there was a widely held view that the postwar Constitution, and particularly Article 9, the "Peace" clause, had been imposed on Japan by the United States. Iokibe Makoto argues, however, that, even as the so-called MacArthur draft of the Consitution was being developed, Japanese government officials, including Prime Minister Yoshida Shigeru, were directly involved in a constitutional draft of their own that reflected the same antimilitaristic principles prevalent in public attitudes, and that their ideas were subsequently incorporated into the final version.[3] Indeed, on 27 May 1946, in one of the first postwar opinion surveys on the constitutional issue, *Mainichi Shimbun* asked the public whether it saw the need for a clause repudiating Japan's sovereign right to conduct war, and 70 per cent responded yes. Thus, the Peace Constitution was generally supported by the majority of citizens as the ideological backbone on which Japan should reconstruct a new state.[4]

Of course, contrary to claims of the "Japanese origin" of the new Constitution, one still might argue whether, or to what extent, Japan's rejection of militarism and hegemonic power ambitions was derived purely from remorse over past actions towards its neighbours and the international community. Some scholars have pointed out that this ready embrace of pacificism after their defeat in war, rather than stemming from a moral conviction, merely reflected Japanese "sense of relief and liberation" from a war to which they never considered themselves fully devoted in terms of ideas or causes: a memory many Japanese simply tried to make sense of as "a misfortune that befell them" due to powers beyond their control.[5] In this view, the notion of peace as a defining value of Japan's postwar era originated more from "a determination never to be horribly victimized by war" themselves than from remorse towards outsiders.[6]

Other scholars likewise doubt the sincerity of the Japanese government's postwar, antimilitaristic policies and conciliatory gestures towards Japan's neighbours. These scholars point out that, rather than automatically embodying pacifist ideals, right-leaning conservatives, left-wing socialists, and communists continued to engage in heated debates about the direction of Japan's foreign and security policies. From this perspective, the meaning of Japan's numerous apologies to its neighbours is interpreted as the product of political cost-benefit calculations and mere compromises among politicians and bureaucrats for the sake of domestic politics.[7] Miyashita Akitoshi also argues that the postwar norms of antimilitarism and pacifism were not necessarily products of internal, normative convictions – that although the public and Japanese politics did indeed wholeheartedly embrace them, this was due, not to remorse, but to a realization that doing so would best serve Japan's material interests in a new, postwar world structure.[8]

At the same time the existence of heated debates among politicians and politically active citizens should not lead one to conclude simply that they were the only ones leading actual security policy formulation, or that there was no broader consensus about antimilitarism and the rejection of great power ambitions. As Iokibe argued in an interview with this author, "despite intragovernmental debate and animosity, socialists and mainstream conservatives, especially in the newly formed Liberal Democratic Party, could still agree that Japan must discard its traditional *Fukoku Kyōhei* (rich nation, strong army) doctrine and instead find a realistic means to pursue the *Fukoku* (rich nation) portion in line with widespread societal demand for a peaceful development strategy."[9] Although there was open disagreement about the implementation of individual policies, in debates about national security, it is important to note that Japanese reached consensus on the fundamental issue of preventing the resurgence of prewar militarism and fascism. The absolute majority of the public agreed that the principle of democratic control of Japan's security policies must be central, and the political elites agreed to the institutionalization of democratic principles in security and foreign policy areas.[10]

Renouncing Japan's previous conduct because it had resulted in tragedy for Japanese themselves – or for their neighbours, depending on one's interpretive priority – constituted the most significant element of the departure from the past. The renunciation was embedded in new security principles that oriented the country towards limiting its military power projection and conducting non-coercive and pacifist diplomacy through the institutionalization of democratic control. Of course, as numerous scholars have noted, individual policies have not always seemed to be in line with this mainstream public perception. However, any divergence between certain issue-specific policies and broad public sentiment during the postwar period was the result of "tactical," rather than "strategic," decisions on the part of the Japanese government, since Japanese political elites shared the orientation of Japanese society.[11]

Throughout the Cold War, this consensus enabled Japan to prioritize its economy and maintain its national security without burdening itself with the dangers of international entanglements or excessive military buildup. The success of this security strategy through the postwar period led to increasing confidence among Japanese that they had made the right choice and that they could live without fear of a plausible, direct external threat. Except for the outbreak of the Korean War in

1950, neither the Japanese public nor the political elite thought it credible to expect an attack from abroad, and opinion surveys during the 1960s and the early 1970s strongly confirmed this majority perception.[12]

The prevalence of the postwar, antimilitarist identity and the institutionalization of mainstream society's consensus around balancing idealism and reality in security policies surely were not welcomed by everyone. Some right-leaning politicians and academics considered the identity and security design to be too naive.[13] Even moderate conservative elites with a more *realpolitik* understanding of the international system argued that the public, through education, should be enlightened as to the more assertive military capability necessary for Japan to achieve a truly functional deterrence.[14] Throughout the Cold War period, however, such proposals never won a wide following, either in society or in politics as a part of the mainstream discourse.

Relations with North Korea before 1998

As a natural extension of its postwar identity, it is not surprising that Japan's relations with its neighbours were sensitive to possible charges of resurgent neocolonialism, or that Japan strove to avoid direct political and economic confrontations as well as military conflicts.[15] Japanese foreign policy in Asia, therefore, was geared more towards confidence building and reconciliation, mainly using the formula of diplomatic normalization and economic cooperation through the provision of official development assistance as a means of paying war reparations.[16] With respect to Japan's basic stance towards the Korean Peninsula in general, and North Korea in particular, its principle foreign policy goal was largely confined to the careful support of regional stability and the status quo.[17]

In postwar diplomatic interactions with the two Koreas, Japanese was reluctant to openly express their concerns about the peninsula's security issues, since any Japanese initiative beyond supporting inter-Korean dialogue could be perceived by Koreans as a sign of interference.[18] Such caution was not confined to government foreign policy. The public was equally passive concerning Japan's role in any potential contingency on the peninsula, even if it would have a direct consequence for Japanese security. For example, as late as 1997, a year prior to the Taepodong-1 missile launch, 39 per cent of Americans who were asked about contingencies in Korea responded that they expected a military response from Japan, as an ally, should the United States get involved, while only 2 per cent of Japanese respondents favoured their country's participation.[19]

In line with societal perceptions, Japan's foreign policy doctrine towards South Korea was to maintain cordial bilateral relations while sidestepping any direct military cooperation in the United States–South Korea–Japan triangular alliance. Likewise, its doctrine towards North Korea was to maintain non-political contacts on a case-by-case basis in order to circumvent unnecessary disputes[20] – indeed, such contacts were well maintained throughout the Cold War. After signing private sector agreements on trade in 1972 and fishing in 1977, other moderate steps were taken in economic and cultural spheres,[21] and bilateral trade was stable at around US$500 million per year even into the 1990s.[22] Again reflecting the general societal trend, Japanese media throughout the 1960s, 1970s, and 1980s emphasized the need to maintain *heiwa to yūkō* (peace and friendship) between Japan and the North, despite North Korean terrorist activities against South Korea that occasionally destabilized regional security.[23]

With the end of the Cold War, the Japanese government reached out to improve official bilateral relations with the North, in a way updating its previously cautious stance. This was an interesting development, since many Japan experts interpret the years immediately following the end of the Cold War as having been the starting point of Japan's "rightist" foreign policy orientation, especially after Japan's diplomatic embarrassment in the First Gulf War of 1990–91. These Japanese initiatives started with Prime Minister Takeshita Noboru's statement in the Diet on 30 March 1989 in which he expressed *ikan* (deep remorse) to the people of the peninsula and his willingness to improve official relations with North Korea.[24] That same day the first Diet delegation, made up of representatitives of the Liberal Democratic Party (LDP) and the Japan Socialist Party (JSP) headed for Pyongyang.[25] In September 1990 another LDP-JSP delegation – this time led by Kanemaru Shin, the "godfather of the LDP" – visited North Korea. Kanemaru agreed with Premier Kim Il Sung that negotiations on diplomatic normalization should start, and that Japan would acknowledge its responsibility for damages incurred by North Koreans during *both* the pre– and post–Second World War periods. Although the agreement to make such an acknowledgment caused an uproar in the Japanese government, negotiations nevertheless started, and continued until February 1992.[26] This "Kanemaru mission" was then followed by two more delegations: a 1995 mission led by the influential Katō Kōichi of the LDP and made up of LDP, JSP, and Sakigake Party members of the Diet, which presented the North with 500,000 tons of rice to "move a step closer to diplomatic normalization," followed by a 1997 mission led by the even more influential Mori Yoshirō of the LDP.[27] For our purposes, the 1997 delegation is especially significant, as it illustrates the extent to which the Japanese government was willing to compromise with the North in order to better bilateral relations after the Cold War.

During the period immediately following the end of the Cold War, ambitious LDP leaders perceived diplomatic normalization with North Korea to be a political winner that could help ensure their names would be engraved in Japanese history.[28] Contrary to the risk-averse stance of Japan towards North Korean affairs during the Cold War, LDP leaders, and even those of the opposition parties (socialists and communists who had been emotionally pro-North all along), started to see a better political relationship with the North as a risk worth taking, even if it involved problematic and appeasing agreements. They viewed it as a highly symbolic and politically beneficial achievement for themselves and for Japan as a whole if they were able to secure amicable relations with the last neighbouring state with which Japan did not have official diplomatic ties. This goal would remain unchanged until Koizumi Junichirō's visit to Pyongyang in 2002.

The Japanese public, however, was still generally neutral with respect to governmental interaction with the North, neither openly supporting nor opposing the changing bilateral dynamics, although the societal atmosphere was largely in favour of "peace and friendship" in principle. It is important to note, therefore, that, in contrast to the public's heightened attention to North Korea and the perceived threats emanating from the North that would be seen in the early 2000s, there was not yet open opposition to the normalization of relations in the early post–Cold War period. Japanese society was also somewhat lenient on domestic issues involving pro–North Korean communities in Japan. For example, huge amounts of funds had been flowing into the LDP and JSP from the pachinko industry, which is largely owned by ethnic Koreans in Japan, many of whom have attachments to North Korea, and Chōsen-Sōren (in Korean, Jochongryun), a pro–North Korea organization made up of Korean ethnic communities residing in Japan and considered the de facto representative of the North Korean regime in Japan, was able to send a wide range of financial support to Pyongyang.[29] In a climate of public apathy, therefore, politicians and pro–North Korean organizations could interact freely with North Korea without facing public scrutiny, and friendly links with the North were not necessarily career-killers for politicians, as would become the case a decade later.

Relations between 1998 and 2000: Issues and Responses

Then, two incidents between 1998 and 2000 served to galvanize the Japanese public's perceptions of North Korea. The first was the launch of a Taepodong-1 ballistic missile across Japan in August 1998; the second was the appearance of so-called *fushinsen* (mystery/spy ships) off the Japanese coast near the Noto Peninsula in March 1999.

Around noon on 31 August 1998, North Korea launched a new, two-stage ballistic missile, later confirmed as the Taepodong-1, eastbound in the direction of Japanese airspace. A portion of its warhead landed in the Pacific Ocean, marking the first time a missile had flown over the Japanese isles.[30] During the missile's flight, seven commercial aircraft were flying near its trajectory.[31] At the time of the incident, it could not be confirmed whether the missile's trajectory was in or above the atmosphere – if the former, it would have been a violation of international law on sovereign airspace – and it was also presumed that the purpose of the launch was an exercise, not an attack on Japan.[32] A multistage ballistic missile from a neighbouring country flying over the homeland without prior warning for the first time in postwar history spread an unprecedented shock throughout Japan. The next day Chief Cabinet Secretary Nonaka Hiromu issued an official statement of protest, saying that the missile gravely undermined the peace and security of Japan and Northeast Asia.[33]

The second incident occurred on 25 March 1999, when two unidentified vessels appeared off the Noto Peninsula on the northwest coast of Japan, heading north. Although they were disguised as Japanese fishing boats, they were equipped with numerous antennas and were extremely fast. They were presumed to be North Korean, but the Japanese government could obtain no such proof at the time. However, then-Prime Minister Obuchi Keizō ordered the Maritime Self-Defense Force (MSDF) and the Japan Coast Guard (JCG) to the area. During the chase that followed, the MSDF and JCG ships in fact considered shooting the rudders off the mysterious intruders, but they eventually limited themselves to firing warning shots, the first time since the Second World War that Japanese naval vessels had taken such action.[34] In choosing that option the officers aboard were reluctant to take responsibility for the consequences of an "excessive misadventure" in the event of *kashitsu-chishi* (accidental death or injury) among the personnel aboard the *fushinsen*.[35] The Japanese government confirmed that the two boats had entered a North Korean harbour after their successful escape, and again issued a statement of protest, although it did not demand that the boats or their crews be handed over.[36]

After the Taepodong-1 launch North Korea understandably became a serious security concern to Japanese. Although policy-makers had already known that Japan was vulnerable to an attack of that kind, the provocative missile launch publicly confirmed that fact and amplified the Japanese public's threat perception of North Korea.[37] The *fushinsen* incident, barely a year later, provided an additional source of anxiety to Japanese who now believed their country lacked even the basic means of enforcing its maritime sovereignty. The controlled reactions of the MSDF and JCG and the relatively mild verbal protest of the Japanese government to a clear breach of Japan's sovereignty served only to worsen Japanese perceptions of North Korea and of their own country's handling of the situation.[38] From then on there were more frequent criticisms in certain major media outlets of the government's "almost theological adherence" to the "*heiwa-boke* (peace naivety)" of the postwar period, which had prevented Japan from taking realistic and effective countermeasures against a clear and present violation of its sovereignty.[39]

The repercussions of the two incidents, therefore, went further than simple Japanese agitation with respect to North Korea. Security-conscious sectors of the media reflected on the structural failure of Japan's postwar regional diplomacy, which had been conducted without an adequate backing of "power" to secure the counry's rights, as demonstrated by North Korea's taking advantage of these Japanese practices.[40] The exposure of the national contingency plans' limitations provided ample opportunity for the Japanese public to pay more attention to the regional environment from a more realistic viewpoint, and led to a questioning of the persuasiveness of "pacifism as the only means to prevent entanglement in international conflict," a postwar dogma long espoused by progressive factions in society.[41] Confirming this subtle reconfiguration of security perceptions in the late 1990s, former prime minister Asō Tarō, in an interview in 2006, commented that: "*the prevailing winds of Japanese public opinion* apparently changed direction with North Korea's test launch of its Taepodong missile" (emphasis added).[42]

The Japanese public's anxiety about North Korean actions and the response of the Japanese government was widely reflected in security debates. However, contrary to some interpretations that this new development marked the beginning of Japan's "shift to the right" in the security realm, it was not necessarily the prelude to Japan's discarding its postwar security principles. Despite the genuine shock caused by North Korea's actions and their impact on Japanese perceptions of the North, the security discourse that unfolded between 1998 and 2000 remained well within the framework of the postwar security identity.[43] Nonetheless, compared to the security discourse prior to the missile launch, the period of 1998 and 1999 can be interpreted as a transition of sorts, but mainly visible in the way Japanese society expressed its concern and anxiety more openly about the demonstrated limitations of Japan's response. Contrary to the expectations of many observers, the transition certainly did not involve a wholesale transformation of the societal view of North Korea as an enemy or the public's rejection of Japan's traditional postwar security principles – indeed, in the domestic elections that followed in 2000, security was not a critical issue for all constituents.[44] Rather, the true significance of this period is that it marked the preliminary stage of Japanese societal anxiety about North Korea and the basis of the security discourse that followed additional North Korean provocations in later years.

The eye-opening experience of the North Korean shocks thus caused the general public to be more conscious about national security, but this consciousness remained largely abstract once the actual incidents had passed. Despite the heightened concerns and anxiety, Japanese society was not yet sufficiently mobilized to influence government policy on alternative security preferences, and decision-makers could formulate policy relatively independent of societal pressure. Instead the societal and media discourse of the late 1990s was confined mainly to debates about the adequacy of measures the government was taking despite the new security consciousness.

Concerning countermeasures against possible future missile threats, the debate in Japan centred on the feasibility of two government proposals: joining the US Theater Missile Defense (TMD) system, and starting its own spy satellite program. It should be noted, however, that both proposals were defensive countermeasures that did not have direct consequences for North Korea. Although the heightened threat perception helped both proposals obtain a green light, the mainstream media on the moderate left and right debated their merits in light of the postwar security identity. For example, *Yomiuri Shimbun* supported both the TMD and the satellite program, claiming that any sovereign nation would seriously consider an air defence system against a possible attack from abroad.[45] However, as an example of how the postwar security identity still largely set the boundaries of acceptable discourse, it is interesting to observe that *Yomiuri Shimbun* emphasized repeatedly that it did not regard the programs as in conflict with Japan's *senshu-bōei* (exclusively defence-oriented) security principles of the postwar period.[46] *Asahi Shimbun*, on the other hand, while not taking an opposing stance in the midst of societal anxiety, shifted focus to the potential negative consequences of the programs – such as the inefficiency of allocating a huge budget to untested projects, or the risk of initiating a new arms race in East Asia – and proposed that Japan place heavier emphasis on alleviating the general threat level in the region.[47] A similar pattern of debate is visible concerning the *fushinsen*. Although both streams of the security debate recognized the seriousness of the situation, *Asahi Shimbun* took a more cautious stance on the MSDF's involvement and the firing of warning shots, which, if not regulated properly, could undermine the doctrine of *senshu-bōei*.[48] *Yomiuri Shimbun*, on the other hand, focused on the failure to seize the vessels, arguing that overly stringent standard operating procedures for the use of MSDF weapons were at fault.[49]

The North Korean provocations also heightened the sense among Japanese parliamentarians of the existence of the external threat and their consciousness of and frustration about Japan's feeble response, as evident in Diet debates in autumn 1998 and spring 1999.[50] The incidents, however, did not lead to the government's restructuring its North Korea policies in the direction of confrontation. Although it implemented certain defensive policy measures to better manage similar threats in the future, the government chose to maintain the strategy of diplomatic normalization through dialogue. Concerning the ballistic missile threat, Japan limited itself to coordinating its policies with those of the United States and South Korea, rather than undertake direct negotiations with the North, as the government felt it lacked diplomatic leverage to conduct bilateral talks on this particular issue.[51]

In addition to weak societal influence on security policies during the late 1990s, the composition of the ruling LDP and the security decision-makers also contributed to the limited nature of the Japanese policy response. Compared to the strong leadership and populist tendency of the Koizumi administration in the next decade, which was more open to societal input and political risk taking in foreign policy, the LDP in 1998 and 1999, led by Prime Minister Obuchi, was still in a relatively weak position within the ruling coalition with the Liberal Party and in a difficult process of political recovery after the resignation of Prime Minister Hashimoto Ryūtarō.[52] As maintenance of the coalition and political stability took priority, policy-making was characterized by an aversion to drastic risk taking, as any reshuffling of traditional security policy practices might also invite unintended political consequences. Some media argued, however, that the ruling party's focus on maintaining harmony within the coalition and the Diet compromised its ability to prepare for future security contingencies.[53]

In the end the Japanese government undertook four policy responses to the North Korean ballistic missile incident. The first response was multilateral in nature: after expressing "*kiwamete tsuyoi ikan no i* (a strong sense of regret or dissatisfaction)" to the North Korean ambassador to the United Nations,[54] Japan demanded that the UN Security Council pass a resolution condemning the launch. The resolution did not materialize, however; instead, the UN issued a Security Council President's press statement – a merely symbolic gesture.[55] Confining itself to limited vocal criticism, Japan did not press for further measures at the UN.[56]

The second response was also multilateral in nature. Just before the Taepodong-1 launch, the member states of the Korean Peninsula Energy Development Organization (KEDO)[57] were in the process of allocating each member's financial contributions for the construction of a planned light water reactor in North Korea. After the launch, the executive board members of KEDO – the United States, South Korea, Japan, and the European Union – agreed on 3 September 1998 to postpone this decision.[58] Although it could be interpreted as a type of sanction, this measure was fundamentally different from the sanctions Japan imposed in 2006 in three respects. First, contrary to the later sanctions, when Japan acted unilaterally, the 1998 KEDO decision was fully multilateral. Second, in contrast to the 2006 sanctions – most of which were still in effect as of September 2014 – the suspension of financial contributions through KEDO was a symbolic measure lifted on 21 October 1998, after just a few weeks, and Japan agreed to provide its share through a multilateral agreement with the other member states.[59] Finally, the 1998 decision was not intended to inflict damage directly on the North, as the member states of KEDO, especially South Korea and the United States, did not want to break up the framework of the organization, which had been negotiated with difficulty.[60] In the case of the 2006 sanctions, however, flows of money, people, and goods from Japan to North Korea were summarily prohibited.

The third and fourth security policy responses involved the abovementioned Japanese participation in the US TMD initiative and the launching of Japan's own spy satellite program. As with societal and media consideration of the issue, domestic politics went through extensive internal debates on Japanese participation, but the government eventually confirmed its intention to take part in joint research of TMD with the United States in December 1998. Because TMD was purely defensive and did not infringe on a previous Diet resolution concerning the "peaceful use of space," the system was interpreted as compatible with the basic principles of postwar Japanese national security. Legislation authorizing four new Japanese spy satellites to be launched by 2002 soon followed.[61] Finally, besides TMD, Japan also agreed to further cooperation with the United States to develop Ballistic Missile Defense (BMD), another pillar of the missile defence system.[62] The relatively swift implementation of these proposals and the lack of strong opposition from either the public or other political parties testify to the effect of the North Korean shock.

Concerning the *fushinsen*, Japan made no direct demand that North Korea investigate the incident or prevent such an event from happening in the future; instead, the changes that followed as a result of the incident were all internal to Japan. The Japan Defense Agency (JDA) requested the budget to establish three platoon-sized special teams in the MSDF to enable the boarding of such vessels.[63] Then, in March 2000, the JCG and JDA jointly published a new manual for responding to maritime incursions, stating that although the JCG would be responsible for interception, the MSDF could be dispatched in a supporting role with the consent of the prime minister.[64]

In short, the Japanese government responded to the missile and *fushinsen* shocks with moderate policy shifts in its defensive capabilities, but did not undertake a significant reformulation of its postwar security principles. Although others have already well analysed this aspect of the Japanese reaction, another aspect of the Japanese government's North Korea policy during the same period, which actually better characterizes its basic stance towards North Korea, has been comparatively overlooked.

After the mission to Pyongyang in September 1990 led by the LDP's Kanemaru Shin, the LDP had fostered a channel of dialogue with the North throughout the 1990s, a "default engagement position" the party maintained even after the events of 1998.[65] As a result, even as both the government and the public were struggling to make sense of their increased awareness of North Korean threats in a confusing atmosphere, the government, surprisingly, initiated a concurrent diplomatic move. Another multiparty delegation of Diet members, this time led by former Socialist prime minister Murayama Tomiichi, was sent to Pyongyang to mitigate tensions, a visit that symbolized the complicated and multifaceted nature of the Japanese government's and public's views on North Korea. It almost gives the observer the impression that the Japanese were simply too eager to normalize diplomatic relations with the North despite the recent provocations. In short, although the Japanese opened their eyes to the actual threat from North Korea and partially updated their defensive capabilities, the shock was not yet fundamentally earthshaking or long-lasting enough to force the government and the public to discard their traditional postwar approaches towards the North.

The Murayama delegation arrived in Pyongyang on 4 December 1999, about eight months after the *fushinsen* incident. The prime objective of the visit was to pave the road towards diplomatic normalization, and both sides promptly agreed to restart negotiations.[66] Aside from reopening the official channel of dialogue, however, what deserves special attention, as it reflects the Japanese stance towards the North during this period, is the mutually agreed-upon official agenda for the talks. Although the Japanese initially commented on the ballistic missile issue, the North Koreans declined to discuss it, arguing that any state had the right to possess such missiles. And neither side even mentioned the *fushinsen*.[67] As a result the Japanese delegation, concerned that annoying the North Koreans by raising those issues could break up the negotiations altogether, let slip the opportunity to directly address their two most serious security concerns in the subsequent normalization talks. Also, when the Japanese cautiously asked for North Korean cooperation in investigating the *still-unconfirmed suspicion* that Japanese citizens had been abducted by the North,[68] the North Koreans flatly denied any connection, asserting that the very use of the term "abduction" was an expression of aggression towards North Korea.[69] The North Koreans "offered" to conduct an internal investigation of the "missing persons" through the International Red Cross from a humanitarian standpoint,[70] but this issue likewise failed to become an official intergovernmental agenda item in the subsequent diplomatic normalization talks.

Following the Murayama delegation's recommendations to both the Japanese and North Korean governments, diplomatic normalization meetings were held on 8 April 2000 and again on 25 August, these being, respectively, the ninth and tenth times such negotiations had taken place since the Kanemaru mission of 1990. Prior to the April meeting, probably as an initial trust-building measure, the Japanese government sent 100,000 tons of rice to North Korea at the request of the World Food Program.[71]

In the April negotiations, the Japanese representatives assured their North Korean counterparts that Japan would sincerely respect the "Murayama statement of wartime remorse and apology to Asia" made on 15 August 1995 (not to be confused with the same person's statement in Pyongyang as the head of the delegation in 1999) and apply it to its dealings with North Korea, even though the ballistic missile, *fushinsen*, and abductions issues had not been included in the mutually agreed-upon official agenda for normalization. Concerning the ballistic missile issue, the North Koreans demanded that the Japanese delegation refer to it as a "satellite," rather than as a missile.[72] When Japan nevertheless requested that North Korea abandon the future development, production, deployment, and test-launching of such missiles, even if not as an official condition of the negotiations, the North simply responded that the topic was to be discussed only bilaterally with the United States. The April and August 2000 negotiations, therefore, in effect "did nothing but register Japan's concerns."[73] Despite the Japanese government's agreement to provide an additional 500,000 tons of rice in October 2000 in response to another request from the World Food Program[74] – an unprecedented scale for Japanese grain aid – the eleventh negotiation, which took place on 13 November 2000, also failed to make much headway.[75]

Conclusion

North Korea's Taepodong-1 missile launch on 31 August 1998 and the incursion of *fushinsen* on 25 March 1999 marked the first instances in the post–Cold War period in which Japanese citizens could visualize direct security threats to their homeland. After these incidents, even ordinary Japanese were forced to contemplate potential contingencies and the inadequacy of the post–Second World War security principles in a new context. North Korea began to be embedded in the Japanese psyche as a destabilizing factor. As one survey from this period demonstrates, the security-related topic the public was most interested in was the situation on the Korean Peninsula. The same survey found that many

Japanese felt the regional dynamic to be even more dangerous after the end of the Cold War than during it, with 31 per cent worried that there was now an actual possibility of Japan's entanglement in a war, the highest that such concerns had placed in opinion polling since 1969.[76]

Although the Japanese public experienced an acute new sense of the threat from North Korea and became more susceptible to the need for more "realistic" security policies, the period between 1998 and 2000 did not mark a fundamental shift away from the traditional Japanese perception of the North, as exemplified by the media debates that followed the missile launch and *fushinsen* incidents. The media, following the societal atmosphere, approached the North Korean threat from various perspectives and presented diverse opinions on the desirable Japanese response. Absent a publicly preferred, widely shared, or organized policy orientation towards North Korea, it is natural that there was no strongly visible policy proposal from either the public or the media during this period. In this regard, while the period can be understood as transitional in certain respects – with the public trying to make sense of the North Korean shocks and embracing a more realistic security awareness – the extent of this transition should not be overstated.

Policy-makers in the government also largely shared the societal atmosphere of the period. Similar to the reaction among the public to the North Korean shocks, the government's several defensive security measures – joining the TMD, spy satellites, and new guidelines for the MSDF to handle maritime incursions – were still within the scope of Japan's traditional postwar security principles. Equally important, however, if not more so, was the emphasis the government placed on maintaining a policy of engagement with North Korea. The behaviour of the LDP-led government clearly gives one the impression that it preferred negotiations on diplomatic normalization as the desirable path to enhancing Japan's security from North Korean threats, even in the aftermath of the Taepodong-1 launch.

In retrospect the most significant characteristic of the period between 1998 and 2000 is that, although there was no transformation of Japanese security policy towards North Korea, the effects of the missile launch and *fushinsen* incidents began to accumulate in the Japanese societal psyche. Along with additional issues that came to the fore over the next decade, these eventually would provide the public discursive stage on which postwar security discourse in general, and Japanese default policy towards North Korea in particular, would be debated in the early 2000s.

Chapter Three

Relations prior to Koizumi's Visit to Pyongyang

A further worsening of North Korea's image in Japan occurred in 2001 and early 2002 as a result of two new incidents. As in the 1990s, however, this period did not produce any concrete Japanese foreign policy directly targeted against North Korea, although the impact of accumulating provocations on the minds of the Japanese public led to some domestic policy changes concerning the national "emergency."

The most important factor during this period, which would have lasting consequences for subsequent Japanese policy towards North Korea, was the rise of Koizumi Junichirō as prime minister and the strengthening of the society-policy linkage as a result of his "populism." Although this populist tendency was not always clean-cut and visible in his early policies towards North Korea, the domestic changes he facilitated in the midst of ever-accumulating North Korean threats were, nevertheless, significant. As we shall see in Chapter 4, the realignment of the structure of domestic influence eventually would play a crucial role in the process that enabled public anxiety to pressure the Japanese government to harden its policy towards the North.

New North Korea–linked Incidents

As if to maintain the momentum of the earlier shocks, two new incidents occurred early in the new century that kept the Japanese public's attention on North Korea and further reinforced the legitimacy of regarding this neighbour with added suspicion.

The first incident was the bizarre arrest and swift deportation of Kim Jong Il's eldest son, Kim Jong Nam, and his family from Japan on 4 May 2001. The incident began on 2 May, less than a week after Koizumi became prime minister following the short-lived and unpopular term of Mori Yoshirō, when Japanese immigration authorities detained four foreigners for entering Japan with forged Dominican Republic passports. The officials identified the male head of the group to be Kim Jong Nam, an identity the man neither confirmed nor denied.[1] He admitted that the group had used counterfeit passports, and officials presumed that they had entered Japan to visit Tokyo Disneyland and the Akihabara electronics district in central Tokyo.[2] The police advised the new prime minister to detain and prosecute them for violating Japanese passport laws, but the government quickly decided instead to deport the group. Although government officials had been certain from the early phase of the investigation that the man was indeed Kim Jong Nam, they announced on the day of the deportation – which was broadcast nationally on live television – that they could confirm neither his true identity nor his link with North Korea.[3]

Then, on 23 December 2001, barely two years after the incident in 1999 when, for the first time in Japan's postwar history, the Japan Coast Guard (JCG) fired live warning shots at a North Korean mystery/spy ship, there was another *fushinsen* incursion. This time, in Japan's first naval engagement since the end of the Second World War, the JCG vessels fired on the intruder with deadly force.[4] The two *fushinsen* incursions thus coincidentally gave postwar Japan the experience of using actual military means within its maritime sovereignty.

The *fushinsen* appeared on the night of 21 December on the high seas near the Amami Ōshima island chain of Kagoshima Prefecture in southern Japan. A JCG patrol ordered the ship to stop, and fired warning shots as in 1999, but it continued its escape, only stopping on the night of the 22nd near the Chinese Exclusive Economic Zone.[5] On the 23rd, JCG vessels and the mystery vessel exchanged fire, at the end of which the *fushinsen* sank and one JCG member was wounded.[6] Eventually, the JCG recovered two bodies from the scene, as well as lifejackets with the Korean *Hangul* alphabet written on them. Since the shape of the vessel was similar to that of the ones in 1999, the government concluded it to be of North Korean origin.[7]

Societal Reaction

Prior to the second *fushinsen* incident in 2001, the Japanese societal attitude towards North Korea was still more or less an extension of its perception from the 1990s. In other words, even as the Japanese threat perception towards the North gradually increased, as more news related to North Korea was broadcast to ordinary Japanese and its hard-to-comprehend activities were publicly divulged, there was also a concurrent societal trend that maintained that it would be unwise to provoke North Korea unnecessarily.

In this context it is understandable that the public reaction to the Kim Jong Nam incident was not overly critical of the government's decision, despite the public's bewilderment and annoyance at his strange entry into Japan and the equally strange manner in which he was deported, and the bizarre episode certainly joined the list of North Korea–linked incidents in the minds of the public. Immediately after the deportation, however, the tone of the media representing the societal mainstream was generally sympathetic to the new government, which had to consider the broader implications of Japanese–North Korean relations, although there was some disagreement as to whether the release of Kim Jong Il's son would win North Korea's gratitude. The typical media evaluation of the new government's deporting the group as ordinary "illegal aliens" in order to draw an early end to the crisis was that it indeed had been a difficult political decision, since publicizing the man's true identity through a full investigation would have caused further negative implications for the already-stranded diplomatic normalization process.[8] The media also pointed out, however, that some might question the government's expectation of reciprocal North Korean goodwill.[9] In retrospect, the Kim Jong Nam incident was a minor incident that did not have a long-lasting impact on Japanese perceptions of North Korea or on Japan's national security, as other incidents had, although it would resurface when societal discourse on North Korean threats gained momentum later on.

The new *fushinsen* incident, however, had a significant impact and wide-ranging consequences for Japanese security discourse during this period. The very nature of the incident – another direct violation of Japan's maritime sovereignty and the first instance of Japanese use of deadly force – was an indication of the threat from North Korea. Moreover, because actual footage of the naval engagement was repeatedly broadcast on Japanese television, the threat was a visible one, unlike the earlier *fushinsen* incident and the Taepodong-1 launch, and it encouraged the public's belief that East Asia was a dangerous place and that Japan must be more sensitive to the military threat from North Korea.[10] In a survey undertaken by *Yomiuri Shimbun* in August 1998, just before the Taepodong-1 incident, 19.6 per cent of respondents said they felt threatened by North Korea, but in an October 2001 poll, the figure jumped to 50.4 per cent (by comparison, only 13.8 per cent identified China as a threat).[11]

The combination of these incidents over the three-year span from 1998 to 2001 thus motivated the Japanese public to embrace a hardened understanding of national security. Both public and policy communities interpreted the second *fushinsen* incident as an example of an imminent, direct, and irregular military attack on Japan with more serious implications than mere maritime incursions. It was widely believed that North Korean agents on the vessels were conducting drug trafficking and other criminal activities, and that they possessed the real potential to launch terrorist attacks on Japanese infrastructure such as nuclear power plants, water supplies, or public transportation.[12]

As a result of the incident, considerable public discussion concerning maritime security and the role of the JCG took place. Wider audiences seemed to accept that the occasional use of force was acceptable as long as it occurred within Japan's territorial waters, for defence, and in inevitable circumstances, and that it would be necessary to integrate the JCG into Japan's more general national defence strategy.[13] Nonetheless the JCG was still criticized for having prolonged the sea chase for more than a day and for having incurred casualties, for which an overly careful response in the early phase of the operation was widely believed to be at fault.[14] The incident also spurred the establishment, rare in postwar Japan, of several loose organizations of security-conscious members of the public who were ready to volunteer for "homeland defence." For example, Nippon Zaidan – a network of conservative Sasakawa group foundations and think tanks – established a so-called Coastal Guard, a "volunteer auxiliary organization whose 100,000 members pledged to report suspicious activity along the coast to the JCG."[15]

It is also characteristic of this period that additional coverage of North Korean violations of aspects of Japanese security – sovereignty of its sea and airspace, and now even immigration laws – led to wider public reflection on national security principles, with more concrete attention towards North Korea than during the 1990s. North Korea's actions provided the most significant opportunity for increased public consciousness about the limitations of Japan's capability to protect itself effectively.

The most widely raised topic in security discourse was the discrepancy between the changing public threat perception and the existing legalistic hindrances that prevented the updating of domestic measures for national defence. In an editorial on Constitution Day in 2002, *Yomiuri Shimbun* asserted that the people and the government alike, as a result of the changing external security environment, finally had started to realize that "national security cannot be obtained for free like air and water." Although the editorial assessed this shift – whereby more Japanese felt compelled to find solutions to security threats that were more "commensurate with international standards and common sense" – in a positive light, it also pointed out that the Constitution and other legal institutions were not yet equipped to reflect the new discursive trend.[16] In another widely circulated magazine, the then governor of the Tokyo Metropolitan Government, Ishihara Shintarō, and future prime minister Abe Shinzō also positively interpreted their countrymen's greater willingness to embrace the long-overdue perception of a new, hard reality. Claiming that television coverage of the JCG and the *fushinsen* in naval engagement forced the Japanese people to face the reality that national security was indeed in danger, they argued that "[t]he visual imagery made it clear to the public that North Koreans are not one of those 'peace-loving people around the world' assumed by our Constitution."[17] Considering the well-known right-wing political inclination of these two politicians, one should not regard their comments as representing the majority's attitude towards North Korea and Japanese security institutions. Nevertheless, their statements do convey a contemporary portrayal of the subtle, but increasing, societal anxiety about Japan's national security. Although individual attitudes certainly differed, the overall trend among the public was a growing negative perception towards North Korea, particularly as Japan's own security posture became increasingly linked with the North in the minds of the people.

Koizumi's Emergence and Responses to North Korea, 2001–02

In spring 2001 a significant change took place in Japanese domestic politics when Koizumi Junichirō became the new prime minister. He won his position not so much because of his foreign policy stance, but through his successful public self-portrayal as a reformer of domestic politics and his charismatic personal character. In making friends with ordinary Japanese and the media, he distanced himself from traditional, factional turf wars within the Liberal Democratic Party (LDP) and countered opposition both in and out of his party by directly appealing to the people. As a direct result of his charisma and strong public support,

Koizumi was able to exercise strong leadership in the decision-making processes associated with both foreign and domestic policies, at the cost of undermining the traditional influence of the bureaucracy and the LDP. However, as his administration was fundamentally dependent on popular support for its survival, one result of Koizumi's "populist" prime ministership was the increased influence of public opinion on cabinet decision-making. This change in the domestic political structure eventually would have significant consequences for subsequent Japanese foreign policy towards North Korea once Koizumi's prime ministership passed its "honeymoon."

This is not to say that Koizumi and his cabinet were always directly swayed by public opinion in all domestic and foreign policy matters. On a number of occasions, Koizumi took unpopular policy decisions, especially in the domestic realm, as his plans for privatizing the postal service and curtailing budgets for regional highway projects illustrate. He was keenly aware, however, that his popularity did not depend necessarily on public support for particular policies, but on his abstract "reformist" label, and there were instances when he used his superb communication skills to persuade the public to understand and, he hoped, accept his policy blueprints. Nevertheless, as we shall see, Koizumi's populist political background, the essence of his power, gradually – and paradoxically – forced his policies to conform more to societal discursive shifts and made him accept that the balance of power was tilting in favour of society as his prime ministership matured.

Similar patterns are observable in Koizumi's policy towards North Korea, with differences between his earlier and later stances, as we shall see. At first the Koizumi cabinet undertook certain measures to update Japan's security. The cabinet also took part in the preliminary debate on *Yūji-hōsei/Yūji-kanren-hōan* (emergency legislation) in the Diet, as its politicians felt the accumulation of North Korean threats and the hardening of societal discourse against the North. However, since the public's primary focus during this period was still on internal reform, Koizumi initially had leeway to pursue his North Korean policy based on his personal ambitions (his secret negotiations with the North for a summit meeting, which eventually would materialize in September 2002) and the more traditional LDP default policy of engagement (to realize bilateral diplomatic normalization), all the while answering to the increasing public demand to re-evaluate Japan's security policies. In short, in the first year of his cabinet Koizumi's "populist" tendency was visible domestically, but not equally reflected in his policy towards North

Korea. Subsequently, however, his stance increasingly followed the societal trend, as he was forced to reorient his policy in the light of drastically increasing threat perceptions and the anger of the Japanese people towards the North, especially after his visit to Pyongyang (see Chapter 4).

In the broader context of the Japanese government's North Korea policy shift, Koizumi's emergence as prime minister is highly significant, since it laid the foundation for a clearer linkage between societal security discourse and foreign policy in subsequent years. It is an important key to understanding how and why North Korea's provocations and the resulting rise in the threat perception on the part of Japanese society became a direct influence on the government's foreign policy decision-making towards the North.

Koizumi's rise and structural changes in political decision-making

Koizumi became prime minister in spring 2001 by winning the LDP presidential election. His catchphrase, that he would "destroy the LDP," won the hearts and minds of ordinary Japanese, just as his straightforward and almost amateurish way of speech helped him to be popularly portrayed as "one of the people" at a time when the public was fed up with "professional" politicians and bureaucrats.[18] Although Koizumi himself expressed surprise at being categorized as a "populist," his means of achieving power by positioning himself not with other politicians but with popular sentiment clearly indicates that he knew how to use society's negative reaction against traditional politics to his advantage.[19]

In contrast to typical LDP prime ministers, Koizumi had never been a leader of an intraparty faction and, at least initially, was without any organized support from Diet members. Despite the handicap, he succeeded in gaining a clear upper hand in pre-election debates by deliberately "making others look bad" with his strong personality – hence his nickname "*henjin* (weirdo)" – and a standoffish approach to traditional, factional party politics, which eventually made him an "idol" among the public.[20] In Japanese politics an idol is not an everyday phenomenon, so, at a time when ordinary Japanese strongly felt the need for political reform, Koizumi's image as boldly embarking on a venture to destroy old and inept politics was extremely advantageous for his bid for the prime ministership.[21]

What one can easily surmise from this is that, from the very beginning, the most important base of Koizumi's political power was the public and therefore he was comparatively more sensitive to public opinion than previous prime ministers. He placed considerable emphasis on keeping that support by maintaining the image of a "good guy" – at which he generally succeeded – even when some of his actual policies would not have made him a "good guy" in retrospect.

It is not surprising, therefore, that Koizumi put into practice a new public affairs strategy not previously seen in Japanese politics to maintain his popular support. As he was acutely aware of the power of the media on society and vice versa, his strategy revolved around making friends out of both, by making himself constantly accessible to ordinary citizens via everyday television and newspaper appearances. To reach out effectively to ordinary constituents outside Nagata-chō (the Japanese equivalent of Downing Street), Koizumi drew media attention to himself on television debates and gossip shows and in the sports and entertainment magazines of minor media corporations, which previously had not been allowed into the *kisha-kurabu* (press club system). The diversification of Koizumi's coverage thus led to increasing competition among the media to obtain fresh and entertaining news material, a change that also influenced the way the mainstream media dealt with political news.[22]

Unlike other more traditionally styled and lordly LDP politicians, Koizumi gladly responded to the media's "*burasagari* (journalists clinging on, sometimes almost literally, to a popular politician full-time for a news scoop)." Since he rarely betrayed their expectations of an entertaining and refreshing comment or two, the practice of conducting extremely short daily interviews became the media norm in Japan. Other politicians eventually had to succumb to this new media tradition, as they learned from Koizumi the merit of doing well in "one-phrase politics." With his proven skill in directly briefing people about his intentions in simple language, however, Koizumi benefited more than anyone else from daily one-phrase politics on television.[23]

The emergence of Koizumi and the changes he facilitated in political communications between the prime minister and the public resulted in greater citizen interest in and understanding of politics. Yet, although this heightened popular interest resulted in a more intimate link between politicians and the public, it also increased the pressure on politicians to be more sensitive to societal trends. And although the introduction of one-phrase politics diversified the ways in which politicians could publicize their positions, it also had a rather powerful effect on politicians' behaviour and statements, as they were constantly "tested" by the media and society. Koizumi, more than anyone, passed these "tests" by successfully portraying himself as the politician who correctly understood and represented people's wants, thus helping to release their frustrations over Japanese politics and provide them with a sense of vicarious satisfaction.

So successful was Koizumi's populist strategy that some journalists and media observers actually started to worry that the people's support would turn into something more sinister. Admitting the result of an opinion survey – which reported 80 per cent support for the Koizumi cabinet – as a correct reflection of public emotion favouring "the reformist" and hopes for political change, an *Asahi Shimbun* editorial raised concerns that "people support almost anything, without careful and logical reflection, as long as it is initiated by Koizumi ... The trend is already turning into a general mood, and this unswerving support based on *kūki* [the collective emotional atmosphere] could, if not handled correctly, even turn into a type of indirect censoring mechanism denying alternative opinions."[24] Similar trends appeared in the political arena as well. As the rank-and-file members of the LDP realized the tremendous importance for their own electoral polls of having a popular party leader, they dared not antagonize Koizumi in public.[25] In fact, as Koizumi successfully gained grassroots popularity as a result of "audience drawing," more Diet members openly expressed their support for him, rather than turning to their factional leaders for cues as they had done in the past.[26] Even the biggest opposition party, the Democratic Party of Japan (DPJ), had to admit the merit of having a single charismatic and popular leader, and promptly copied the Koizumi model in subsequent election campaigns.[27]

It is not surprising that the nature of Koizumi's political power affected the way in which he conducted domestic and foreign policy. This was especially the case concerning the latter. Under the Koizumi cabinet, traditional consensus building among the cabinet, the bureaucracy (especially the Ministry of Foreign Affairs, MOFA), and the ruling party (especially the LDP's policy subcommittees) prior to deciding on foreign policy was weakened, and the cabinet[28] instead gained centralized power in the decision process, based on its political needs.[29] This procedural change, which enhanced the prime minister's power to delegate authority to his own cabinet to supervise and to make final decisions, made Japanese decision-making more closely resemble the British Westminster system of parliamentary democracy; it was, to borrow Estévez-Abe's words, "the Britannicization of Japan."[30] Some experts were rather concerned by this drastic shift, in which authority was concentrated in the cabinet without the necessary "general staff headquarters" – like the White House's National Security Council – to support the prime minister professionally with solid, long-term strategic feedback on important foreign policy decisions.[31] Nevertheless, so long as Koizumi was backed by the public majority, he was able to push for his domestic and foreign policy decisions and smooth out tedious Diet operations, even when professional experts did not necessarily support him.[32]

Thus, as in domestic politics, the concentration of foreign policy decision-making power in the cabinet eventually produced a paradoxical environment: so long as the public supported him as an individual, Koizumi was able to gain much leeway to put his own personal vision of Japan's external conduct into practice, but this also meant that his decision-making would face pressures if he realized that the societal majority clearly preferred other options. Rather than being contradictory, this was an inevitable consequence of conducting populist policymaking with close interaction with the public.

To reiterate, Koizumi's political power was not based on unswerving public support for his individual policies, but on his image as a reformer who would not be intimidated by breaking traditional political "taboos." Therefore, his conduct was heavily geared towards doing precisely that, in order to facilitate the people's release of stress and frustration.[33] In foreign policy, for example, openly expressing a "Japanese rationale" for the prime minister's visit to the controversial Yasukuni Shrine to Japan's war dead (plus the actual visits) and not succumbing to South Korean and Chinese criticisms on other historical issues, even at the risk of undermining smooth regional diplomacy, reflected Koizumi's political position, which had to represent increasing societal frustration over neighbours' "interference with domestic issues."

Koizumi was also adept at reaching out to citizens directly and persuading them to support his policies even when they were controversial. As time passed, however, his power showed increasing signs of being under pressure to place a heavier emphasis on unfolding societal trends and to adjust his policies accordingly.[34]

Adjustments to national security policy

What was the relationship between North Korea's provocations and their reception in Japan on the one hand, and the emergence of Koizumi and the resulting political shifts on the other, and what influence did this relationship have in shaping the Japanese government's policies towards North Korea and national security during this period? As mentioned earlier the role of societal discourse in the Koizumi cabinet's North Korea and security policy-making became much more apparent from late 2002 onward. Therefore, the empirical picture one gets from their interactions is not so clear-cut, at least during the previous year.

Certainly, the continuation of the types of North Korean security threats seen in the 1990s helped to maintain constant societal engagement on national security. Moreover, domestic debates increasingly reflected the public's growing acceptance of a more realistic interpretation of Japan's external environment and the need to re-evaluate its traditional postwar security policies. For this reason, although foreign policy directly targeting North Korea did not materialize, there was a further upgrading of the role of the JCG and stepped-up preparations for emergency legislation during this period.

In this regard Koizumi, as in other domestic policy areas, matched his stance with security policy linked to the public's increasing perception of threat, and he consequently went along with political developments in the Diet. These measures were also matched, however, by his initial adherence to the traditional LDP foreign policy stance of political negotiations for normalizing diplomatic relations with North Korea and his ambitious plan (although secret at this time) to meet Kim Jong Il in Pyongyang to resolve personally all North Korea–related threats. Though seemingly contradictory, under close examination these two characteristics of Koizumi's policy were not at odds at all. The security-conscious public, feeling increasingly threatened by the North, would support diplomatic normalization if it actually resolved the threats by peaceful means, and Koizumi knew it would be a great political victory as well as a sure way of winning further popularity at home.

After the second *fushinsen* incident in 2001, the government, and especially the Diet, actively sought ways to update the JCG's role and standard operating procedures with regard to maritime incursions. It is not surprising – considering the incident touched on core notions of military security by forcing naval combat upon Japan – that, immediately after the incident, the LDP proposed to further mitigate the legal limitations on weapons use imposed on the JCG, discussions that had already started after the first incursion in 1999.[35] For politicians who had wanted to know the extent to which the Japanese public would accept more defence spending and the use of force, the increase in societal threat perception caused by the *fushinsen* incident became a useful case study that helped them to conclude that Japanese voters were now more prepared to support such measures.[36]

Far more significant than the empowerment of the JCG, however, were the preparations undertaken in 2001 and early 2002 by the LDP and the Diet to pass emergency legislation clarifying the role of the state and prefectural governments in case of a national emergency, whether a foreign attack or a natural disaster. Such legislation had been proposed in the past but never enacted. In 1978, for example, Prime Minister Fukuda Takeo (father of Fukuda Yasuo, prime minister from 2007 to 2008) argued for such legislation in the Diet, but he was met with vicious protest and had to back down under criticism that he had "embarked on a return to authoritarianism."[37] Immediately after the Taepodong-1 launch and the first *fushinsen* incident, the media reported that some Diet members felt the time had come for official discussions on how to reduce the legal burden on the Self-Defense Forces (SDF), in order to facilitate an effective military response in case of an external attack,[38] but such discussions never materialized. In one stroke, however, the renewed North Korean threats overcame this reluctance on the part of the public and the Diet alike even to contemplate an emergency,[39] and emergency legislation became part of the political agenda in late 2001 and early 2002. This time even the opposition parties took part in the discussions, acknowledging that Japan was indeed under serious threat from North Korean missiles and *fushinsen*. Preliminary interparty debates in the Diet in January 2002 laid the foundation for drafting legislation to simplify governmental procedures in case the SDF were to be dispatched for a national emergency.[40] With more Diet members at least accepting the idea that the standard legal procedures in times of emergency should be re-evaluated, the government was able to announce in April the final draft of three bills dealing with a national emergency in case of an attack, actual or imminent, from abroad.[41]

In the end the emergency legislation was not actually put to a vote in the Diet at this time, but links between threats from North Korea and actual Japanese political initiatives to re-evaluate formal legal procedures with broader security implications became visible. The evidence strongly suggests that politicians' and the public's perception of accumulating North Korea issues facilitated these links in a timely manner. Generational change in the political sphere also played a role. From the early 2000s, especially in the LDP, traditional "mainstream pragmatists"[42] who had devoted political energy to economic development and a limited – or, rather, a prudent – foreign policy role for Japan by strictly adhering to the ideals of the Yoshida Doctrine were shunted aside, replaced by Young Turks who embraced a more active stance in pursuing Japan's national interest and security.[43] These younger politicians emerged in all parties and from diverse professional, academic, regional, and family backgrounds, but they shared one common trait: they all belonged to a postwar generation more open and sensitive to national security affairs and to Japan's demonstrated vulnerability.[44] Moreover, as their political rise coincided with the emergence of Koizumi and the domestic changes he brought to relations among society, politics, and the media, their electoral success, especially among "Koizumi's children," testifies to their greater sensitivity to public attitudes and discursive shifts than were the older generations of politicians. These young politicians, whose parents in most cases also belonged to the postwar generation, genuinely shared Japanese societal anxiety about "*ima soko ni aru kiki* (current and proximate threats)" from North Korean missiles and *fushinsen*. One questionnaire of forty-eight Diet members in their twenties and thirties revealed that 82 per cent considered it plausible that North Korea would either wage war directly against Japan or force Japan's participation in one involving the North at some point in the future.[45]

The preparation of the emergency legislation, despite its historical significance in the context of increasing linkages between heightening societal threat perceptions and political responsiveness, should not be interpreted too heavily as a sign of Japan's discarding its traditional postwar security principles. As in the case of the Japanese government's international and domestic responses to the Taepodong-1 launch and the first *fushinsen* incident, the accumulation of North Korean provocations indeed heightened the societal and political sense of external danger and facilitated the updating and re-evaluation of domestic contingency measures to a modest degree. However, these domestic security upgrades were carried out without consciously touching on the more fundamental values of the postwar era: *senshu-bōei* (exclusively defence-oriented security principles), democratic control of the government and the military, and the avoidance of direct international confrontation.

It is also significant that the emergency legislation was not automatically put to a vote in the Diet. In Diet subcommittees and elsewhere, politicians realized that there could still be questions concerning the bills' possible implications for "constitutionality and potential endangerment of civil liberties," as the central government and the SDF would be given more freedom to sidestep prefectural governments' and ordinary citizens' rights.[46] Diet subcommittees, made up of members from both the ruling and opposition parties, widely discussed the rights of individual citizens, basic human rights, and a clearer definition of exactly what would constitute an "emergency." As a result, the government was compelled to postpone actual deliberation of the bills indefinitely.[47]

Koizumi's early approach to North Korea

The "populist tendency" that Koizumi showed in his domestic politics was not clearly visible in his foreign policy designs in the early period of his administration. His cabinet's early position on North Korea, therefore, was more or less inherited from the stance of previous governments – namely, carefully engaging with the North without directly provoking the regime in the process.

The embrace of this default policy is most apparent in the Koizumi cabinet's immediate response to the Kim Jong Nam incident, which occurred barely a week after Koizumi came to power. When immigration officials detained Kim's group, interministerial debates ensued, with the police wanting the group to be arrested and interrogated, while MOFA, especially Minister Tanaka Makiko, preferred to let the North Koreans be "secretly deported by bypassing standard procedures" before the media were fully alerted. MOFA reasoned that arrests would only make the problem drag on indefinitely, as North Korea would never admit the group's identity under any circumstances.[48] With this conflicting advice, Koizumi decided to deport Kim's group publicly just three days after its detainment to prevent any further negative implications for bilateral relations, although he claimed that the measure was in "full accordance with standard legal procedures of democratic Japan."[49] To the very end, the government continued to obscure the true identity of the male, referring to him in media briefings as "the man who *resembles* Kim Jong Nam," and Koizumi is reported to have said that Japan had no choice but to deport him, since "Japan won't be able to withstand the various complications that will result if we take any other action."[50] By hurriedly exercising *yakkai-barai* (getting rid of the nuisance) before exposure by the fully engaged media spun the issue out of control, the government could credit itself for having prevented serious bilateral tension by letting North Korea save face – indeed, it was widely predicted that Koizumi's measure might have positive consequences for relations with the North.[51]

With the advantage of hindsight we now know about Koizumi's secretive negotiations with North Korea to realize a summit meeting with Kim Jong Il during his first year in office.[52] In this light the policy response to the Kim Jong Nam incident is not only coherent with the traditional LDP stance towards North Korea, but also possibly one of the earliest indications of Koizumi's personal intention to resolve all North Korea–related issues through his personal initiative. Although the incident occurred before the first secret negotiations took place, it is likely that Koizumi already possessed his own blueprint for the future of bilateral relations, and did not want a nuisance to complicate its implementation unnecessarily. Again, during this period, the increased perception of the threat from the North did not equate to a wholesale societal opposition to diplomatic normalization in principle, if normalization resulted in the mitigation of the threat. By correctly understanding the nuanced societal perception of the North, it is likely that Koizumi preferred that minor incidents such as Kim Jong Nam's intrusion not hinder the realization of a political solution that would be welcomed domestically. In short, it seems Koizumi regarded the secretive foreign policy target of a diplomatic breakthrough with North Korea as a win-win strategy for securing both his popularity and his political legacy in Japan's postwar history.[53]

Koizumi's early hope to realize such a historical breakthrough was also evident in his handling of the second *fushinsen* incident. Not only did his government refrain from actually punishing North Korea – although it strengthened the readiness of the JCG – but it also took its time (deliberately, some would argue) to have the hull of the sunken *fushinsen* salvaged, as its recovery inevitably would divulge the vessel's nationality and purpose. At first, the government had planned to bring the ship to the surface the day after the incident, since it was technologically feasible.[54] Yet, for one reason or another (one being that the location of the sunken ship was within the Chinese Exclusive Economic Zone), the government took until 19 June 2002, a full six months after the incident, even to *decide* to undertake the the salvage operation, and another three months passed before the ship was finally recovered and its nationality identified on 12 September, just five days before Koizumi's planned summit in Pyongyang.[55]

Although concrete proof is lacking, the timing of the recovery gives the unavoidable impression that Koizumi, perhaps along with a few insider politicians and bureaucrats involved in the secret negotiations for a summit meeting, delayed the vessel's recovery without informing the government agencies involved of the true reason for the delay. Circumstantial evidence from the way the recovery process unfolded suggests that the recovery was put on hold until those privy to the negotiations could be sure that the North Koreans would not oppose them or that the talks had progressed sufficiently for both sides not to consider turning back. One media source supports this speculation by reporting that, during the latter phase of the secret negotiations, the chief North Korean delegate indeed expressed that North Korea would not oppose the recovery and that it would exercise "*mokunin* (connivance)."[56] Considering that, during the Kim–Koizumi summit, which took place only five days after the recovery, North Korea not only "exercised connivance," but Kim actually admitted and apologized for the *fushinsen*, it would not be far-fetched to suppose that Koizumi timed the salvage to occur after he had already received sufficient guarantees on the scheduled summit and the promise of a North Korean apology.

Conclusion

During 2001 and the first half of 2002, Japanese societal perception of the threat from North Korea continued to grow as a result of additional incidents linked to the North. As in the 1990s, however, the Japanese government took no concrete foreign policy response directly targeting North Korea or punitive measures to put pressure on Kim Jong Il's regime. Nevertheless, the accumulation of North Korean provocations and their impact in the minds of both the Japanese public and politicians resulted in certain domestic policy changes with respect to the role of the JCG and to postwar Japan's traditional stance on how to deal with episodes of national "emergency." In this context, even though the draft emergency legislation did not become law, the preparation of the bills and the active debates in the Diet represented a noteworthy change in the political discourse, as the North Korea threat began to be linked to a more general discussion about Japan's national security.

The most significant political change during this period, which eventually would play an important role in the unfolding of Japanese policy towards North Korea, was the emergence of Koizumi Junichirō as prime minister and the realignment of relations between society and politics that he brought with his "populism." Although Koizumi's personality and adept "showmanship" won him wide public support, the significance of the "Koizumi factor" is in the long-lasting *structural* and *procedural* consequences he brought to Japanese domestic politics. Structurally, his success in winning the prime ministership by directly reaching out to the public strengthened societal and media influence in Japanese policy-making and made politicians increasingly susceptible to the public atmosphere. Procedurally, the structural shift in the power balance among society, the media, and the government, in turn, resulted in more cabinet-led political decisions on foreign policy (reflecting societal discourse), at the cost of weakened party and bureaucratic engagement in decision-making procedures. These two changes of Koizumi's, more than his individual popularity, had a lasting impact on subsequent policy towards North Korea, as the nature of Koizumi's political power gradually led him to reflect the shifting societal discursive trend towards North Korea in the years after his visit to Pyongyang in September 2002.

From the perspective of the argument I present in this book that societal discourse was the most important influence on the change in Japanese foreign policy towards North Korea in 2006, the significance of the above changes in 2001 and 2002 for subsequent Japanese–North Korean bilateral dynamics cannot be overstated. Since societal discourse does not simply and automatically *become* foreign policy, there must be an inevitable connecting link. The rise of Koizumi in 2001 – whether or not he was consciously aware of it – enabled the public's abstract security anxiety to be incorporated directly into the Japanese government's subsequently hardened policy posture towards North Korea. This chain was further reinforced by the concurrent emergence of a young, postwar generation of politicians who were keenly sensitive to both the changing security environment and public opinion, and who adeptly recognized the shifting domestic "rules of the game" that Koizumi induced. The significance of this brief period is that it provided Japan the means for changing the traditional approach to North Korea it had inherited from the 1990s.

Chapter Four

Japanese–North Korean Relations, 2002–04

The Koizumi–Kim Summit of 2002

Koizumi Junichirō's year-long secret negotiations with North Korea to realize a summit finally bore fruit on 17 September 2002, when he became the first prime minister of postwar Japan to visit Pyongyang. There, he met Kim Jong Il, and the two concluded a historical bilateral agreement, the Pyongyang Declaration. The international community initially regarded Koizumi's visit as a "shining example of the success of Japan's recent foreign policy," as it opened official channels for diplomatic normalization that had long been a high priority for Japan.[1] Koizumi's initiative was perceived to be an important stepping stone for Japan, not only resolving one of the last remaining agenda issues of the Second World War legacy, but also achieving greater diplomatic leverage in the region.[2]

Koizumi and Kim met twice that day, and the mutual agreement they signed dealt comprehensively with all the historical and security-related issues that had hindered the normalization process in the past. The Pyongyang Declaration accordingly stated that the two governments would restart negotiations for diplomatic normalization the following month, Japan would initiate economic aid to North Korea once bilateral relations were normalized, and both parties would mutually cede their right of claim for properties and other assets from the prewar period. As well, North Korea promised to take appropriate measures to prevent the further occurrence of "unfortunate incidents that endanger Japanese citizens' lives and security," and to adhere to international agreements aimed at resolving the nuclear issue. Furthermore, North Korea agreed to extend its moratorium on ballistic missile launches to 2003, and to cooperate with Japan on general regional security talks.[3]

The declaration's most significant breakthrough, however, was Kim's open admission of North Korea's involvement in the *fushinsen* incidents and the abductions of Japanese citizens, confirming at last Japan's long-held suspicions. Although the words *fushinsen* and *rachi* (abduction) were not incorporated into the declaration, Kim confessed verbally to Koizumi during the summit that the *fushinsen* of December 2001 had in fact been a North Korean spy vessel. Concerning the abductions, Kim informed the Japanese that, of the thirteen confirmed Japanese victims, eight were dead and five were still living in North Korea.[4] After offering both his personal and official apologies to Koizumi, Kim added that both incidents had been conducted "voluntarily" by special units without his prior knowledge – that some operatives unfortunately had decided to act on "[overly] patriotic and heroic intentions" to win the hearts of Kim and the fatherland.[5] Kim's "frank" apologies for the unfortunate incidents as the head of state were then balanced by a clause in the Pyongyang Declaration that Japan, for its part, would apologize for "the pains and the sufferings inflicted on the people of the Korean Peninsula" by past Japanese colonialism.[6]

The contents of the declaration thus were a delicate compromise between both parties to save face while also genuinely seeking a workable solution to various "abnormalities" that had marred bilateral relations throughout the postwar period. One-quarter of the declaration consisted of an official Japanese apology for its past colonialism and the means by which the Japanese side would provide economic aid in the form of low-interest loans by the Japanese government and the Japan Bank for International Cooperation.[7] Another quarter, reflecting a non-negotiable Japanese position, constituted North Korea's open admission of past conduct that had seriously undermined the security and lives of Japanese citizens, and its promise to take all necessary measures to prevent future occurrences.[8] A sentence stating that such incidents happened "within the context of unfortunate and abnormal bilateral relations of the past" was added to absolve Kim Jong Il of some personal blame, but the official North Korean admission of responsibility for the incidents was supplemented by Kim's verbal apology to Koizumi during the summit and also broadcast on North Korean state television.[9] Although Koizumi strongly protested the deaths of eight of the Japanese abductees and, at the insistence of Deputy Chief Cabinet Secretary Abe Shinzō, returned to Tokyo without attending previously scheduled discussions on the signing of a bilateral peace treaty,[10] the Pyonyang Declaration in itself was a balanced and well-thought-out blueprint for a diplomatic breakthrough for both parties.

The Pyongyang summit illustrated what an ambitious prime minister's foreign policy initiative could achieve for Japan. There were, in fact, potential obstacles in the international environment, especially since the United States, Japan's most influential ally, continued to refuse to engage in bilateral talks with North Korea.[11] The US government, when informed at the last minute by Koizumi of his planned Pyongyang visit, briefed the Japanese about the North's possible nuclear weapons program, and expressed its "disquiet" about the idea of a summit in light of such a regional security threat. Koizumi nevertheless made a political decision to exercise more diplomatic freedom for Japan.[12]

Tanaka Hitoshi, then-director general of the Asian and Oceanian Affairs Bureau of the Ministry of Foreign Affairs (MOFA) and Koizumi's representative throughout the secret negotiations with the North, countered the accusation that the United States had been kept deliberately in the dark by asserting that Koizumi had personally informed President George W. Bush by phone and that he had also briefed Deputy Secretary of State Richard Armitage and Assistant Secretary of State for East Asian and Pacific Affairs James Kelly in late August, as soon as the plan for the summit was finalized.[13] He also admitted, however, that Koizumi's decision had been Japan's choice, made independently of international constraints: since the Japanese government had its own distinctively bilateral agenda with the North, it would be unreasonable for any outsider to assume that Japan must always coordinate with the United States its every move towards North Korea.[14]

Besides the "independent" process through which the preliminary negotiations had been conducted, Koizumi's summit with Kim Jong Il was also unprecedented in that the Japanese side finally succeeded in persuading the North Koreans to recognize the merit of better bilateral relations. As the preliminary negotiations progressed, North Korea gradually showed signs of yielding on the issues of Japanese colonialism and the abductions. The change in the North Korean stance was facilitated by the Japanese insistence on "drawing a big picture" to realize long-term mutual benefit.[15] The North Koreans were successfully persuaded that normalization would especially benefit them economically, although Japan would gain equally from the opening of the North Korean market and from the long-due financial return from Japan's heavy investment in the northern part of the Korean Peninsula before the Second World War.[16] In addition, the opening of "aid and development" programs after normalization was expected to provide business opportunities for associates of core factional members of the Liberal Democratic Party (LDP) in the recession-hit Japanese construction industry, as they would take part in infrastructure building in North Korea.[17]

However, the one single factor that most convinced the North to agree to the summit and subsequent declaration was Koizumi's willingness to act as a mediator between the United States and North Korea. Although Japan's offer of the "carrot" of economic incentives surely played a part in enticing Kim to reconsider North Korea's traditionally stubborn stance towards Japan, such considerations had not previously helped the normalization process, since the North had always deemed other issues – such as historical legacies and shifting regional security arrangements – as more important. But Kim undoubtedly found Koizumi's proposal to help the North communicate with the United States, its most significant military threat, a much more attractive incentive. At a time when regional tension was mounting as a result of President Bush's labelling North Korea a member of an "axis of evil" – and with North Korea responding in an equally direct fashion – Koizumi's political gamble to become a broker was an unprecedented example of a Japanese prime minister's skilful use of potentially unfavourable external circumstances to gain timely diplomatic leverage.[18] As Okonogi Masao, a distinguished Japanese scholar on North Korean affairs, notes, Koizumi's "self-driven approach to East Asian diplomacy [was] based on skillful use of the post-9/11 global situation."[19]

Koizumi's strategic insight and personal drive to achieve both regional stability and the resolution of bilateral historical legacies – colonialism, the abductions, and North Korean military threats – through the promise of mutual benefit was also apparent in his public statements right after his visit to Pyongyang. On 18 September 2002, he declared in a Tokyo press conference that, if both sides adhered to the "principles and spirits" of the Pyongyang Declaration, it would turn their bilateral relations from animosity to cooperation and directly promote Japan's national interest by mitigating threats. Concerning the abductions, Koizumi stated that improving bilateral relations was especially important so as to prevent similar incidents from occurring, and he asked for Japanese citizens' cooperation and support.[20]

The immediate reception of Koizumi's summit among experts was generally positive. For example, Iokibe Makoto, former president of the National Defense Academy of Japan, expressed high regard for Koizumi's political initiative. In February 2002, some six months prior to the Pyongyang visit, Koizumi invited Iokibe to share his personal insights on how Japan should approach North Korea. Iokibe, without any knowledge of the secret negotiations taking place at the time, advised Koizumi that "the Prime Minister's Office, unlike in the past, must take the initiative in negotiating with the North by mobilizing all possible policy tools to secure stability of Japan and East Asia, with a clear goal: persuading North Korea to be a respectable member of international society." Iokibe now understands the reason for Koizumi's invitation that day; Koizumi wanted to make sure that his cabinet-led secret negotiations were on the right track by feeling out expert opinions before the official announcement of his planned summit.[21]

The Pyongyang Declaration was not only beneficial for Japan's national interest, but also a historic success of postwar Japanese diplomacy that opened a new chapter for a more stable East Asian security environment.[22] In a drastic departure from the typical bilateral negotiations of the past, Japan, by signing official agreements with the North on cooperation in regional security and trust-building measures, succeeded with North Korea's consent in institutionalizing its legitimate right to participate directly in the security matters of the Korean Peninsula and East Asia.[23] Moreover, Koizumi finally persuaded the North to accept Japan's preferred formula for the normalization process – Japan's apologies for its past colonialism and its economic cooperation, as a new partner, to repay the legacy – rather than paying unconditional financial compensation, as North Korea had demanded in the past.[24]

Experts who had long witnessed North Korea's external behaviour were especially impressed by its actually acknowledging and apologizing for the abductions at the cost of openly self-contradicting its own previous denials.[25] Few observers expected Kim to express his remorse personally, and although some Japanese media were dissatisfied by the term *ikan* (remorse; *yugam* in Korean) used in Kim's statement and the Pyongyang Declaration, rather than *shazai* (apology), it clearly contained the nuance of the latter in standard diplomatic practice.[26] Considering that the abductions might have even constituted a *casus belli* under international law, and given the frustratingly limited realistic options that had been available to Japan,[27] Koizumi's head-on approach, involving personal political risk, to resolving this long-neglected issue by linking it to the official conditions for diplomatic normalization and future economic cooperation was highly regarded by most experts.[28]

All in all, the academic community in Japan considered the bilateral agreements to be a reasonable approach to a diplomatic breakthrough, and such voices were reflected in the mainstream media, at least in the months immediately following the summit. Now that the North Korean side had accepted most of the Japanese formula for normalization and the resolution of the abductions issue, expert voices advised Japan to adhere to what Koizumi had achieved without recklessly pushing things too far. Since it could not be denied that Japan had also "committed atrocities in Korea during the colonial period," it would be "morally problematic" to press further, as it might result in the loss of support of the international community for Japan's cause.[29]

The Post-summit Societal Discourse on North Korea

Discourse immediately following the summit

Japanese society's reception of the news about the summit was relatively balanced in the period immediately before and after Koizumi's Pyongyang visit. Despite increasing threats from North Korea, normalizing diplomatic relations with the North had long been considered a desirable goal for Japan. The public, therefore, generally expected that Koizumi's meeting with Kim should, for the present and future sake of both countries, result in "*sengo shori/kako no mondai no seisan* (the full resolution of historical issues from the prewar period)" if the two sides could somehow agree on how to proceed with normalization.[30] Reflecting the turbulent record of past bilateral negotiations and recent North Korean threats, the public did not necessarily draw a naively optimistic picture of the future prospects of bilateral relations. However, opinion polls conducted prior to the summit reflected that, once the opportunity had presented itself, the public cautiously supported Koizumi's initiative. In opinion polls conducted by *Asahi Shimbun* in late August and on 3 September 2002, 53 per cent of respondents expected positive results for bilateral relations from the summit, and 58 per cent supported Japan's formally normalizing diplomatic relations with North Korea.[31] A poll taken after the summit by the Cabinet Office in October 2002 confirmed these views, with 66 per cent of respondents in favour of diplomatic normalization and only 26 per cent opposed.[32]

After Koizumi's return from Pyongyang on 17 September, the immediate public response did not deviate from these pre-summit expectations. Almost all major newspapers and television media conducted special telephone opinion surveys on the day of the summit; their results showed that the public objectively evaluated the benefit of Koizumi's visit and expected it would have positive consequences for both bilateral and regional stability.[33] Likewise, opinion polls conducted on 20 September revealed that, even with the shock over the abductions issue, the majority of Japanese still considered diplomatic normalization to be necessary and Koizumi's agreement to reopen official negotiating channels to be the correct approach.[34] Major newspapers found that more than 80 per cent of the public had a good image of Koizumi as a politician. Moreover, the Koizumi cabinet had the support of 64 per cent,[35] a figure, according to *Yomiuri Shimbun*, significantly higher than the average, especially considering that 57.1 per cent of respondents were "political neutrals" without any formal or emotional attachment to a particular political party.[36] Besides the obvious breakthrough brought about by Koizumi's "courage," Japanese found it simply "refreshing" to see him visiting Pyongyang without consulting the United States. As one journalist reflected, "one reason why most Japanese people consistently supported the normalization of Japan–North Korea relations despite being angry about the abduction was Koizumi's forthright manner of advancing Japan's foreign policy independent of the U.S.,"[37] in contrast to the approach taken by past LDP-led cabinets.

The most noticeable aspect of media opinion polls during the period immediately following the summit, however, concerned the abductions. Even though the majority of the public supported Koizumi's initiative and the move towards normalization in principle, an even higher percentage of Japanese felt that North Korea's handling of the abductions issue by a verbal apology and a promise eventually to return the five survivors (and their children born in North Korea) was quite unacceptable. In an *Asahi Shimbun* poll, 76 per cent of respondents were severely critical of North Korea, and 90.6 per cent of respondents to a *Yomiuri Shumbun* poll felt that the Japanese government had to push for a Japanese-led investigation of the issue using diplomatic normalization as leverage.[38] Considering that the public had given Koizumi and the principles behind the Pyongyang Declaration a high score, and that the majority of the same respondents said their image of North Korea had not changed much after the summit,[39] it is highly revealing that the shock of the abductions issue clearly stood out in the public's mind even during this early phase of the post-summit environment. The contradictory reception towards the summit in general relative to the abductions issue indicated that, of all the bilateral sub-agreements in the declaration, the Japanese public's utter dissatisfaction with how the two governments had compromised on the abductions issue would have a potentially devastating effect on the smooth implementation of other bilateral agreements. That is exactly how bilateral relations would unfold as September passed and the shock of the abductions snowballed and overshadowed other aspects of the original agreements.

Based on the results of opinion polls conducted within a few days of the summit, the most reasonable interpretation of Japanese societal discourse towards North Korea would be as follows. In principle, the public highly appreciated Koizumi's courageous initiative to overcome the deadlock in bilateral relations and persuade Kim to sit at the negotiating table. As well, Koizumi had succeeded in reaching a mutually acceptable formula for resolving the prewar legacy of Japanese colonialism, in the form of economic cooperation and diplomatic normalization, in contrast to the previous dogged North Korean demand for an unconditional Japanese apology and compensation. In light of the Japanese public's suspicions about North Korea in recent years, most Japanese found Koizumi's achievements to be surprising. Therefore, although the public had already long regarded North Korea as a threat, it was willing to support Koizumi's attempt to end the turbulence in Japanese–North Korean relations and turn Japan's unstable neighbour into a more responsible actor through the sharing of formal diplomatic and economic links.

At the same time the Japanese public was utterly shaken by the realization that its suspicions about the abductions had proved to be true.[40] Although persuading Kim to admit openly to the abductions constituted Koizumi's most significant achievement – at least in the eyes of outside observers and Japanese academics – ordinary Japanese, now facing the truth about an act of state terrorism, felt perplexed as to how to make sense of this situation in the context of the broader Japanese–North Korean relationship. The perplexity soon enough turned to open anger as emotions mounted. In this complex state of affairs immediately following the summit, the Japanese public was forced to embrace a dual attitude towards North Korea: it accepted the Pyongyang Declaration and the idea of diplomatic normalization to be valid in abstract principle, but its emotional focus remained directly fixed on its already-negative image of the North, with suspicion and anger mounting daily.[41]

Paradoxically, Koizumi's achievement beyond anyone's expectations on the abductions issue eventually would overshadow both his broader blueprint for bilateral normalization and his other, equally significant, achievements. As the Japanese public's initial perplexity turned to anger, this shift, in which the societal atmosphere came to focus solely on the abductions issue, became the central theme in all North Korea–related discourse.

The political fallout from the abductions issue

At the most abstract level Japanese societal reaction to the abductions issue resembled US emotions following 9/11: ordinary people were simply shocked to recognize that their nation, and innocent and ordinary citizens just like them, had become the target of an "outside force."[42] As the public's initial objectivity in evaluating the summit started to give way to a focus on the abductions issue, perplexity over the nature of this North Korean crime gained momentum, drastically heightening anger towards the North. This, in turn, initiated a process by which the public's anger put pressure on subsequent Japanese government decisions to deviate from the bilateral framework upon which Koizumi and Kim had agreed.

As early as the first week following the summit, both the government and the media began to feel signs of societal anger mounting faster than anyone had expected. After North Korean officials briefed their MOFA counterparts about the tentative results of their own investigation of the abductions as part of the arrangement for the surviving victims' eventual return to Japan, an opinion poll revealed that 82 per cent of the Japanese public refused to trust any North Korean findings, while 72 per cent considered the North Koreans' handling of their own crime to be completely inadequate.[43] Under such circumstances the public's negative opinion of North Korea started to become a "wall of deterrence," hindering the government's ability to follow the agreed-upon steps of the Pyongyang Declaration, and both the government and the LDP were forced to be cautious in their North Korea–related statements to avoid criticism that they were being too conciliatory.[44] Societal concern and anger about the abductions issue, an understandably genuine emotional reaction at first, gradually became a "national obsession" that would "swamp debates about other crucially important aspects of the Japan–North Korea relationship."[45]

The Japanese government, while negotiating with the North, was aware of the change in the societal sphere after the summit. Some central figures in the Koizumi cabinet, such as Deputy Chief Cabinet Secretary Abe Shinzō and Vice Minister of the Cabinet Office Yoneda Kenzō – who had not been in the insider group prior to the summit – advocated a "diplomatic fight" for the sake of national security and the security of Japanese citizens, even at the cost of discarding the agreed-upon framework.[46]

As the months passed, the government and Koizumi thus found themselves in a dilemma. Having achieved a historic breakthrough with the summit, they would have preferred to resolve the remaining aspects of the abductions issue – the return of the surviving victims, their families, and the remains of the deceased, as well as additionally conducting a joint investigation – within the framework of the Pyongyang Declaration, while concurrently proceeding with other important negotiations related to diplomatic normalization, economic cooperation, and regional security. It was becoming apparent, however, that it would not be the government but the public that would maintain *shudō-ken* (leadership) and *kettei-ken* (decision-making power) on how the abductions issue would be handled.[47] Under pressure, the government was already shifting its negotiating stance concerning the abductions, but it was also aware of the consequences: North Korea, protesting that the Japanese side was breaking the agreed procedures, was gradually assuming a non-cooperative stance in return.[48] Special Advisor to the Cabinet Okamoto Yukio, in an interview with *Asahi Shimbun*, admitted that, in the face of the Japanese public's taking the abduction of their fellow citizens more "personally" than past North Korean provocations, it would be simply impossible for the government to reach a decision without fully incorporating public opinion.[49] As the governor of the Tokyo Metropolitan Government Ishihara Shintarō also argued, the abductions issue facilitated the resurgence of long-forgotten national *rentaikan* (oneness),[50] and it would be an underestimation to discard this "personalization factor" as irrelevant. The abductions issue, for the public, was no longer an incident that had happened to someone else, somewhere else, in the distant past.

Paradoxically, MOFA bureaucrats now found it somewhat easier to deal with their North Korean counterparts in additional post-summit negotiations, according to what some of them told Okamoto, since they could now simply assume a forceful manner to reflect domestic anger in Japan without having to take responsibility for the broader diplomatic consequences. During those difficult negotiations, however, Koizumi and most of the members of his cabinet continued to face the dilemma of having to choose between prioritizing the ever-worsening "people's preference" concerning the abductions and prioritizing the bilateral agreements.[51]

Reflecting the drastic shift in public opinion concerning the abductions, several abductions-issue-specific interest groups now rose to the forefront of societal and media attention – indeed, some analysts claimed that these organizations' lobbying and "intentional manipulation" of public opinion were the primary catalyst for societal anger. Three of these groups became the most widely covered, supported, and vocal interest organizations after the summit: the National Association of Families of Japanese Abducted by North Korea, otherwise known as Kazoku-kai (the families association); the National Association for the Rescue of Japanese Abducted by North Korea, more familiarly referred to as Sukuu-kai (the rescue association); and Rachi-Giren (Association of Diet Members for the Japanese Abductees).[52] It would be an oversimplification to argue, however, that societal anger generated by the shock of the abductions was fuelled solely by deliberate manipulation on the part of agents of particular interest groups. It is true that Sukuu-kai and Rachi-Giren, in particular, were politically motivated groups that were already better known for advocating a hardline stance towards North Korea to weaken (or even topple) the communist regime than for their immediate concern over the abductions. This was especially the case with Sukuu-kai, which was made up of various academics and social activists generally belonging to the right wing, and which had espoused various political agendas spanning all the way from Japan's military nuclearization to historical revisionism denying Japan's wartime atrocities.[53] For some members of the organization, therefore, the Japanese public's heightened anger towards North Korea, although focused on the abductions, was a rare and timely opportunity to push a broader and more nationalistic agenda into domestic politics and diplomacy. North Korea's admitting the abductions gave these groups an unprecedented justification for their existence and agenda, and their views began to have an extraordinary influence on media debates. Their influence was further inflated as a growing number of politicians, sensitive to the societal atmosphere converging with these groups, started to position the abductions as their central political concern, above any other North Korea–linked issues.[54]

The emergence of these groups in Japanese society cannot be explained fully without understanding both the sympathy that ordinary citizens expressed towards their fellow-citizen victims and their families and the resulting fury against North Korea. In this regard, the public's anger had a purely humanitarian origin, and therefore should not be misconstrued as Japan's suddenly adopting a xenophobic nationalism, even though certain groups indeed saw opportunities to influence the public in that direction.[55] As Tessa Morris-Suzuki has summarized, the most fundamental reason the abductions issue had an unprecedented influence on Japanese public opinion was exactly that "many ordinary people who had never been involved in politics or [non-governmental organizations] activism before rallied to the cause because they were genuinely moved at the terrible plight of the abductees and their families,"[56] not because of certain organizations' political drumbeat.

In the end, however, the genuine anxiety of the Japanese about the violation of the human rights of their fellow citizens and their altruistic sympathy towards the victims led to a societal current that supported and empowered Kazoku-kai, Sukuu-kai, and Rachi-Giren. The abstract anger and sympathy initially felt by ordinary citizens were indeed given more concrete expression by the arguments of these organizations, especially those of the most politically motivated anti–North Korea Sukuu-kai. Thus, discourse about North Korea started to convey a certain "storyline" encompassing the public's initial emotions about the abductions issue. As more concrete explanations of the nature and the origin of the abductions became widely presented in the media, frequent mention began to be made of specific political terms such as "sovereignty," "human rights," and "dictatorship." Although there is no quantitative way to gauge the extent of the abduction-linked organizations' influence in this process, one can nevertheless surmise that the public's drastic exposure to media debates and discussions about North Korea that included such organizations and other elites must have played a part in leading the direction of the discourse.

The main "storyline" concerning North Korea and the abductions that took shape from October 2002 and became widely accepted throughout 2003 was of a peaceful and democratic state's human rights – an integral part of *kokka-shuken* (national sovereignty) – being utterly violated by an individual-worshipping, criminal dictatorship located dangerously close to Japan. As a special editorial in *Yomiuri Shimbun* marking the fifty-first anniversary of the end of the Allied occupation of

Japan and the signing of the San Francisco Peace Treaty (28 April 1952) stated, for many Japanese the disclosure of the abductions was closely linked to how they understood the importance of national sovereignty. The anniversary of the day the Japanese recovered their lost rights as an independent state, the editorial suggested, should also be a "meaningful time to discuss the proper role of the state in protecting the lives and properties of its citizens, as the abduction issue now provided Japan with a clear example of a violation of its state sovereignty."[57]

The developing societal discourse was significant, however, not only because it incorporated the notion of "sovereignty." After all, previous North Korean provocations – missile launches and especially the *fushinsen* incidents – had also been discussed and understood by the public as examples of Japanese sovereignty being "toyed" with by the North. What distinguished the newest version of the sovereignty issue, as compared to previous incidents, was that it was the first time Japanese came to view the danger to their vital *shuken* in the form of "human rights."

Incorporation of the human rights factor in societal discourse in this context did not necessarily represent a heightened concern for the principle of human rights in general, since the Japanese public's understanding of rights was highly selective to the fate of fellow citizens.[58] Significantly, however, for the first time in Japan's postwar history, widespread emotions caused by the humanitarian tragedy of its citizens were linked to concerns about national security and sovereignty, especially as the public came to focus on "a particular external force which is seen both as radically threatening to national security and as violating key human rights."[59] To many Japanese, this "external force" was not just any state, but one of the most bizarre and eccentric dictatorships in the world, practising individual-worship within a closed system of governance. Along with heightened consciousness about national sovereignty and human rights, the strange nature of *rachihan kokka* (the state that practised abduction) thus further fuelled the growing animosity, as evident in newspaper editorials from October 2002 onward. Moreover, open support of diplomatic normalization increasingly flew in the face of the many Japanese who believed that, instead, further pressure should be exerted on the North now that it had now finally "confessed its crime."[60]

Even as intergovernmental negotiations concerning the return of the victims' families from North Korea and mutually acceptable means of conducting investigations were prolonged throughout 2003, the opinions of Japanese society became an ever-stronger obstacle to the normalization process. According to an opinion poll conducted in July 2003, for the first time since the Koizumi–Kim summit the proportion of respondents disapproving of normalization (46 per cent) was larger than the share approving it (44 per cent),[61] and in a September poll, the gap widened to 49 per cent against versus 38 per cent in favour.[62] That a substantial proportion of respondents still approved of normalization in mid-2003 meant that the public's initial acceptance of Koizumi's initiative was not yet wholly lost. Nevertheless, the societal trajectory was clear, and the claim of some that Japanese society's fixation on the abduction issue limited Japan's broader opportunity to play a leading role in the search for regional peace was increasingly becoming too "audacious against near-uniformity in emotional criticism of the North."[63] Indeed, by then, openly suggesting any concession to North Korea on any issue was tantamount to "political suicide" in Japan.[64]

As I have observed, the primary reason that the public's initial anger became a more politically focused discourse was the incorporation of three political themes – sovereignty, human rights, and the nature of the North Korean regime – into one coherent "storyline" concerning the abductions, with the potential to exert substantial pressure on the government, although, of the three themes, only concerns about "sovereignty" existed before the summit. Considering that the North Korean regime had always been a dictatorship and that the Japanese government and public alike, in full realization of its nature, had nevertheless preferred better relations in the past, it is interesting that the "dictatorship" metaphor became a new reason to put pressure on North Korea. It is thus reasonable to conclude that any one of the three discursive strands of the "storyline" concerning the abductions would not, on its own, have created the dominant discourse on North Korea, but the timely combination of the three, unprecedented in Japan's postwar history, made the negative discourse on the North persuasive and justifiable in the public's mind.

Additional implications: A "sense of victimhood"

Discourse concerning the abductions issue had another societal implication: closely linked to the ongoing trend after the summit, there was a subtle reinterpretation of mainstream, postwar narratives about the historical relationship between Japan and North Korea. As the initial euphoria over Koizumi's political success subsided and the public began to focus solely on the abductions issue, a number of prominent

Japanese scholars with "rightist" inclinations started to present their own interpretations of the cause of the issue. Professor Nakanishi Terumasa of Kyoto University, for example, found its origin in the way the Japanese had incorrectly understood the nature of Japanese–North Korean relations in the past, including those of the prewar era. He asserted that the true villain of the abductions was none other than Japan's leniency and sense of guilt towards its neighbours: that embracing a "wrong" historical notion of Japan as the oppressor in the past had allowed alleged historical "victims" – North Korea being the worst among them – to violate the rights of Japanese without being punished. Therefore, North Korea, through the abduction of innocent Japanese citizens, had taught Japan a valuable lesson that such a misconstrued historical perspective must be corrected.[65] Nakanishi concluded that the shock that ordinary Japanese felt at the disclosure of the abductions – "the amount of shock equivalent to what Americans must have felt in 9/11" – had demonstrated to the public that an erroneous "*shokuzai-ishiki/tsumi-ishiki* (sense of guilt and atonement)" was not simply a criminal act against one's own history, but a danger to state sovereignty and to the security of one's fellow citizens.[66]

The argument for linking mainstream interpretations of Japan's historical relations with its neighbours to the abductions was more than a political statement by a limited number of vocal, highly educated right-wing elites; it also had wider resonance among the public. It might not be readily clear to some outside observers how historical interpretations of prewar East Asia could be causally linked with the abductions in the minds of Japanese, so it would be understandable to express some doubts that such arguments even existed in post-summit Japan. Nevertheless, scholars, journalists, bureaucrats, and other figures who were closely monitoring the unfolding of North Korea–related discourse in Japan reported that the historical reinterpretation factor was subtly influencing the way the public, and even family members of the abductees, perceived the nature of the abductions. For example, Hasuike Tōru, former chief spokesman for Kazoku-kai and elder brother of abduction victim Hasuike Kaoru, claimed that the secretary general of Kazoku-kai, Masumoto Teruaki, whose sister allegedly died in North Korea in 1981, had made an uncommonly political statement[67] after the summit that, "as a result of Kim Jong Il's admission and apology for the abductions, Japan, at last, has been freed from the spell of '*kako no shokuminchi shihai no shokuzai* (always having to atone for past colonial rule).'"[68]

The argument that mainstream historical narratives that had prioritized Japan's atonement to its neighbours were to blame for the abductions had a certain persuasive appeal, since the abductions had resulted in the first instance of Japanese suffering in the postwar era caused by the deliberate act of a neighbouring state. In the background of public criticism of North Korea's immorality and Japan's past naivety was the overpowering societal realization that the abductions revelation had, in a day, turned Japan from a historic *kagaisha* (aggressor) into a *higaisha* (victim).[69] In short, the abductions issue effectively helped push the long-embraced "conscience of guilt" out of Japanese minds and towards North Korea.[70]

In the post–Cold War context, when Japan was struggling to find a "new national identity" that would restore social unity and a sense of purpose to the nation, the "victim mentality" stimulated by the abductions even had the "somewhat cathartic" effect of freeing Japan from the weight of historical accusations by its neighbours.[71] This effect seems especially evident when one considers that, around the same time, Japan was being criticized for its "lack of earnestness" in taking responsibility for the issue of "comfort women" (sex slaves) in the Japanese military during the Second World War; interpretations that North Koreans had also committed crimes against Japanese helped "even the score" in the minds of many.[72] Moreover, at a time when many Japanese were becoming "defensively nationalistic" about criticism from both Koreas and China of Koizumi's visit to the Yasukuni Shrine, the abductions issue provided an indirect target for their frustration.[73] In any case, the "*shūdanteki higaisha kanjyō* (collective victim mentality)" was a new phenomenon, as this mixing historical reinterpretation with North Korea–related issues had not existed in the mainstream public discourse before 2002.[74] This is not to suggest that the Japanese public as a whole fully and consciously accepted the arguments of right-wing scholars and activists: the government's official stance on prewar regional history did not shift during this period, and there was no major public outcry to adopt revisionist versions of history in Japan's diplomatic dealings with its neighbours. Rather, the collective victim mentality and the related reinterpretation of regional history illustrated that an environmental opportunity had allowed for the essence of some right-wing elements' claims, which had long been regarded as too extreme even in Japan, to be accepted more easily by broader societal audiences as a plausible version of historical narration than they had been in the past. It was similar to the process by which the public ended up supporting various abductions-specific organizations foremost out of humanitarian sympathy, even though most people did not fully share these groups' more extreme long-term political goals.

Heightening societal criticism of social elites

Public anger also resulted in severe criticism of certain Japanese politicians and bureaucrats for their past conduct concerning the abductions issue. Although North Korea was clearly the villain, the public increasingly came to view bureaucrats and the politicians of both the ruling and opposition parties as equally at fault for failing to be sufficiently assertive towards the North in the past.[75] Right from the day Koizumi returned from Pyongyang, MOFA and the headquarters of the major political parties, including the LDP, were bombarded with e-mails and telephone calls from ordinary citizens attacking their previously lenient stances.[76]

In the political realm, the most hard-hit parties were the Social Democratic Party and the Communist Party, two major representatives of the leftist elements of Japanese society that had also been traditionally sympathetic to North Korea. It could be argued that the two parties "dug their own graves," since, prior to Kim's admission of the abductions, they had accepted the North's denial at face value and even criticized Japanese politicians who pointed at possible North Korean involvement for making accusations without concrete evidence. After the summit, public anger swiftly shifted to the previous actions of the two parties, which came to be seen as having resembled "spokesmen" of the North; thus the credibility of their official statements related to anything North Korean evaporated. The two parties tried to control the damage either by publicly apologizing for blindly believing the North Koreans' denial or by explaining the rationale for their past behaviour. For example, Doi Takako, head of the Social Democratic Party, made an apologetic statement in October 2002, while Shii Kazuo, chairman of the Communist Party, argued in the media that the people's criticism that his party was a mere messenger of the North was unfounded and that the party had never officially stated that the abductions could not have taken place. Nonetheless, criticism of the two parties continued.[77]

Regardless of party affiliation, however, any politician who, whether in the past or after the summit, made public statements that lacked "sufficient emotional involvement" concerning the abductions came under criticism from the public and fellow Diet members for "weakening

Japanese diplomatic leverage" against North Korea by assuming a distant "third-person" perspective at this crucial moment for the Japanese nation.[78] Abe Shinzō, for example, claimed that anyone who criticized public reaction to the abductions as "too extreme" was, in all practicality, "siding with North Korea."[79] Under the circumstances, when even mild statements could be branded as "not sympathetic enough," any involvement in North Korean affairs after the summit could suddenly become a political liability. As more politicians preferred either to jump safely onto the bandwagon of public anger or refrain from taking part in any North Korea–related activities altogether to avoid public and media attention, political organizations such as *Nicchō Yūkō Giin Remmei* (Federation of Japanese–North Korean Diet/Parliamentary Members for Mutual Friendship) ceased to function.[80]

With additional revelations about how the abductions had actually unfolded, an emotionally charged public targeted MOFA more severely than the political parties. After the summit, many Japanese perceived MOFA to consist of bureaucrats who had never been serious about protecting the security and welfare of their fellow citizens.[81] In this regard, the abductions issue took already-prevalent societal discontent about a secretive, "elitist bureaucracy" to a new level.[82] The media reported that many Japanese were especially angry about MOFA's consistently prioritizing issues belonging to the "big politics" of diplomatic normalization, by advising that the government offer incentives to North Korea – in the form of food aid, for example – while "assuming that the suspicion around Japanese abductions" was "an annoying obstacle to the realization of their grand foreign policy goal."[83] To the public, MOFA's "half-heartedness" in engaging the abductions issue was the primary reason for the prolonged suffering of the victims and their families. Abe wholly supported this reasoning, and emerged from obscurity to arrive at the forefront of Japanese politics during this period by aggressively participating in abductions-related debates. He considered MOFA's conduct to have been too passive, since "many Japanese diplomats had typically cared more about making North Koreans happy on diplomatic stages pre-arranged by their counterparts. And whenever North Koreans offered them a token reward for their cooperation, some MOFA bureaucrats indulged themselves in a false belief that it was a hard-won diplomatic achievement."[84] To Abe, MOFA's past dealings with North Korea in general and its stance towards the abductions in particular constituted an example of a fundamental pathology in postwar Japanese diplomacy.

As criticism mounted, societal anger towards MOFA spilled over into personal attacks on the officials who had been directly involved in diplomacy with North Korea. The main targets were Makita Kunihiko, director general of the Asian and Oceanian Affairs Bureau from 1998 until September 2001, and, especially, Tanaka Hitoshi, who succeeded Makita and had taken charge of the secret negotiations for the summit.[85] The October 2002 edition of the widely circulated weekly magazine *Shūkan Bunshun* labelled Tanaka a "class-A war criminal," and the same year Kazoku-kai and Sukuu-kai jointly sent him an open questionnaire to highlight his responsibility for "prolonging the resolution of the abductions issue in the past" and framing the issue to be of "secondary importance" to Japan.[86]

Considering that, without the summit, which Tanaka had been instrumental in realizing, the abductions issue probably would not have moved forward at all but would have remained a "suspicion," much of the public's accusations were unfair and unfounded. After learning of the victims' fate, however, public emotion was too involved with the issue, and Tanaka's somewhat methodical pursuit of diplomatic normalization, with a view to solving all North Korea–related issues comprehensively, was interpreted as a sign of his emotional detachment from the abductions. With public opinion already so well formed against him (a time bomb was even delivered to his house in September 2003), Tanaka found it difficult to defend his position that "diplomacy must be conducted in order to secure long-term security of one's own state in a comprehensive fashion and the abduction issue can also be resolved within this broader framework."[87] Since he knew that the societal atmosphere would further interpret such a statement as evidence of his "not taking the issue seriously," he was compelled to silence throughout this period.[88]

Media reaction

Although some politicians and bureaucrats faced acerbic criticism, the media were also not safe from scrutiny. The public bashed certain media outlets, especially *Asahi Shimbun,* monthly journals such as *Sekai,* and other magazines belonging to the "progressive camp" – understood in Japanese society as modestly "leftist/pacifist" – for insufficiently engaging the abductions issue. *Asahi Shimbun* and other progressive media traditionally had emphasized better relations with Japan's neighbours through Japan's sincere apology for and full acceptance of its historical responsibilities, citizen-centred democracy, and antimilitaristic pacifism – meaning adherence to the Constitution, limitations on the Self-Defense Forces (SDF), and resistance to a further strengthening of the United States-Japan military alliance. Therefore, these outlets had been somewhat sympathetic to the people of the North, and their past coverage of North Korea had indeed downplayed the plausibility of the abductions when the issue was still an open suspicion.[89]

In the post-summit environment, these media corporations increasingly faced public criticism similar to that directed at politicians and bureaucrats. *Asahi Shimbun* and *Sekai*, at least until early 2003, tried to parry the attacks by mixing downright apologies to the Japanese people with concurrent defensive explanations of the rationale behind their past coverage, but without much success. For example, on 27 December 2002, *Asahi Shimbun*, in a two-page article titled "Kenshō Kitachōsen Rachi Hōdō – Asahi Shimbun wa dō Tsutaetaka (Reviewing North Korea's abduction-related coverages: Asahi Shimbun's reports until now)," provided an extensive overview of how the newspaper had reported all North Korea–linked news since 1977.[90] Concerning the abductions issue, the newspaper defended its past "passivity" by asserting that, "since the incident, at that time, was neither official nor confirmed, we felt that reporting based on mere speculation could even result in the endangerment of the abduction victims possibly held in North Korea, and we therefore prioritized confirming the rumor first." In the end, nevertheless, *Asahi Shimbun* had to admit that its stance inevitably had produced a public impression that the newspaper had not been sufficiently engaged, and it officially apologized for causing such "misunderstanding."[91]

Sekai, a monthly journal read by more politically conscious readers, was also pressured to set the record straight. In a defensive article in which the journal tried to convince readers that it had never intended to downplay the gravity of the abductions, it also cautiously expressed concern about the ongoing "North Korea bashing" and the public's enthusiastic alignment with the trend. Specifically, the article suggested that a much more fundamental factor might be at work in the background – namely, the unchanging and persistent "distorted image of Koreans as troublesome, incomprehensible, complicated, and dangerous," which Japanese had embraced since the colonial period. *Sekai* claimed that the recent societal atmosphere, in which the journal's problematizing of such "distorted images" was regarded as typical "pro-North rambling," – and also the very fact that it had to publish a defensive article to explain its view of North Korea – illustrated the abnormal state of Japan in the post-summit environment.[92] One prominent journalist, Tahara Sōichirō, who faced criticism during this period for linking the abductions issue to Korean forced labourers during the colonial period,[93] similarly viewed the North Korea bashing as not merely a product of people's anger, but as part of a larger process that might be at work in the background, which some people with "*omowaku* (subtle intentions)" were using to change fundamental ideas about the Korean Peninsula and regional history.[94]

Despite such apologies and defensive articles, the public's already-established impression never fully subsided. The somewhat changed stance of *Asahi Shimbun, Sekai,* and other progressive media after the summit – that they also regarded North Korea's abductions of Japanese citizens to be an unforgivable crime and that Kim's regime must take full responsibility – was still regarded by many Japanese as pitiful "alibi making" in order to make up for past passivity.[95] To a large degree, such public scepticism was not without grounds, but it was also evident that these media sources, witnessing first-hand how the people's emotions towards North Korea had shifted drastically in such a short time, genuinely decided to place more weight on the abductions and to reflect societal sentiment. Editors and managers were indeed feeling guilty, as well as a clear disappointment in North Korea for "betraying" their sympathy; their guilt might even have forced them to counter their own mistakes by voluntarily adopting a tone that was relatively close to that of the conservative media and of mainstream public emotions towards the North.[96]

As was the case with public criticism of politicians and bureaucrats, media bashing was initiated by organizations such as Sukuukai and, to a lesser degree, Kazoku-kai. However, their criticism of some media outlets was able to maintain momentum after the summit precisely because the public fully backed and shared their irritation. Media corporations such as *Asahi Shimbun* and *Sekai* had to reply to these accusations defensively, not simply because the criticisms were initiated by famous figures, but also because they were aware that the public's anger supported those views. *Asahi Shimbun,* for one last time, argued in its New Year's editorial in 2003 that, despite legitimate public sympathy for the abduction victims and their families, the paper was nevertheless concerned about societal trends in the aftermath of the summit, in which diplomats were being labelled as "enemies of the state" and politicians were making extreme statements, even favouring war or nuclear armament against North Korea. Such an atmosphere, the editorial concluded, was making Japan resemble its authoritarian enemy in a way.[97] This was a bold statement that illustrated that the traditional "progressive" camp, although much weakened, could still raise its voice (with sufficient "courage") in non-monolithic Japanese society, even in the post-summit domestic environment.

As expected, however, this statement was critically received as a typical, leftist claim that undermined public consensus concerning the abductions. For example, in a public lecture on 25 January 2003, Abe Shinzō made an official statement that "such an editorial was hindering Japan's assertive negotiating position with respect to the North Koreans," and that *Asahi Shimbun,* in effect, was telling the Japanese people to forget about the abduction victims. It was very rare for a high-ranking cabinet official to criticize by name a particular newspaper's editorial, but Abe's view was largely shared among the agitated public.[98]

Such criticism was not limited to *Asahi Shimbun*; any media report or individual press statement that even remotely deviated from the stance of Sukuu-kai and Kazoku-kai was answered by thousands of critical and threatening e-mails every day, sent by ordinary citizens.[99] It is easy to surmise that, in the process, organizations related to the abduction victims became "sanctuaries" not to be touched, as the media quickly learned that annoying them also meant making an enemy of the Japanese public.[100] Those who monitored Japanese media after the summit observed that journalists were self-censoring and fastening onto the public's main trends, and that the media were being pressured into a situation resembling Noelle-Neumann's "spiral of silence" for those who chose not to join the mainstream.[101] The structure of the spiral of silence was complete by early 2003, as the media's self-monitoring of the contents of their abduction reports became the norm.[102] It was said that liberal journalists in general – and *Asahi Shimbun* editorials in particular – "always fold back [on themselves] two or three times,"[103] clear evidence of their loss of self-confidence and of their painstaking measures to dilute any potential source of public criticism. As Wakamiya Yoshibumi, the chair of the editorial board of *Asahi Shimbun* during this period, admits, any newspaper in a democratic country has to make sure that its arguments do not deviate too much from the opinions of the majority of its readers, as "too openly going against the trend for the sake of maintaining consistency in its political views could even be counterproductive for the newspaper's agenda in the long run." Newspapers, including *Asahi Shimbun,* while waiting for public fever to subside, had no choice but to emphasize that they were sympathetic to the majority's opinion, since any statement that did not share it, no matter how objective and rational, would be far from persuasive.[104]

In contrast, the more conservative media such as the weekly *SAPIO* and monthly *Seiron* (affiliated with the right-leaning *Sankei Shimbun*), known for their strongly negative views on North Korea, experienced increased sales, especially among the younger generations in their twenties and thirties.[105] Magazine stories about North Korea were published at a phenomenal rate, and everyday television news offered almost saturation coverage of every imaginable negative aspect of the North. In addition, *manga* – a highly approachable means of casual information transfer for ordinary Japanese – was also used successfully to educate the public about Kim Jong Il's despotic image; one such title sold half a million copies in its first three months of publication, "more than all books ever published in English about Korea put together."[106]

Most media experts in Japan recognized the prevalent societal atmosphere, which discouraged diverse interpretations of the coverage of North Korea after the 2002 summit, as a clear case of the "*kyū-wari genshō* (90 per cent phenomenon)," a not-so-common trend in which the absolute public majority strongly supports a particular idea and ends up further reinforcing the direction of the discourse.[107] Thus, after the initial shock of the abductions disclosure had sunk in by the end of 2002, all media coverage of North Korea came to be more or less of "one voice," planned and broadcast on the premise that expressing anything other than hatred towards North Korea and the anger of the Japanese public would be rejected by the people.[108] Although the pressure the Japanese media were facing was inevitable, it also led scholars of Japanese–North Korean relations and of mass media to worry that the media had generally failed to function in their role of providing objective journalism or to correctly grasp the complex political environment surrounding the bilateral interactions and to advise both the government and the public as to the best feasible options.[109]

A number of experts were especially fascinated by developments in media-society relations after the disclosure of the abductions. Among those who approached them theoretically, Tessa Morris-Suzuki's comparison of 9/11 to the shock brought by the abductions issue in Japan is highly relevant to understanding the Japanese media's conformity to societal pressure in the aftermath of the summit. Adopting the analytic framework used by Murray Levin in his 1971 work, *Political Hysteria in America: The Democratic Capacity for Repression*, Morris-Suzuki argues in her 2003 article, "The Politics of Hysteria: America's Iraq, Japan's

North Korea," that public anger about the abductions and the Japanese media's voluntary haste to conform and reflect this societal trend was an example of "pluralistic repression." It was "pluralistic" because, in a democracy, the press is free and obviously retains the right to criticize and question any socially dominant narrative of key events. There was also, however, a strong element of "repression" because, when there is a "*shihaiteki monogatari* (single enormously powerful dominant narrative)" about the key events of the day, critics who question it are liable to be "marginalized, ridiculed, decried as unpatriotic, and labelled an extremist" if they exercise that right too freely.[110] In the case of the "dominant narrative" concerning North Korea after the summit, the Japanese media indeed refrained from such questioning. As the mainstream narrative became ever more prevalent among the public, it was natural that other critical elements in journalism would also face pressure to self-censor or join the trend.

The explanatory powers of both the "spiral of silence" and the "pluralistic repression" models are empirically valid when applied specifically to Japanese media practices towards North Korea issues. Morris-Suzuki argues that, when "the key event of the day" is particularly related to national security or external actors, a strengthening of "the dominant narrative" sometimes even turns into a type of "hysteria." To her, Japanese societal discourse concerning North Korea generally and the abductions in particular is a primary example. As with 9/11, the "dominant narrative" of North Korea easily transformed into a powerful "national hysteria" in Japan because the people's fear and anger were not just a product of fantasy, but were built around a real act of violence or source of danger – a "core of truth," consisting of "*tsukai-mawashi no kiku jijitsu* (usable facts)" prone to contextual manipulation within the confines of that "truth."[111] As with many security threats involving an external actor, when the truth of outsiders' violence strikes "*taishū no kokoro no kinsen* (a receptive chord with the public)," a dominant narrative built around usable facts and the resulting hysteria also create a sense of national unity in the face of a commonly perceived threat.[112]

The Government's Response to the Changing Societal Discourse

Readjustment of the policy towards the abductions

With the hardening of public opinion against North Korea, the Japanese government quickly responded to the changing societal atmosphere.

Within a week of the summit (28 September 2002), Koizumi met with family members of the abductees to apologize publicly for the LDP's "insufficient dedication and handling of the issue" in the past. He promised that the abductions issue would be the government's *highest priority* and that, in the absence of further explanation and sincere cooperation by North Korea, the government would not proceed with diplomatic normalization.[113] The promise was announced again in early October as the government's basic policy.[114] Kōmura Masahiko, minister of foreign affairs in 1998 and 1999 and again in 2007 and 2008 and who led the foreign relations advisory group of the LDP that had recommended that Koizumi designate the abductions the government's top concern, recalled that intense public anger was the most significant background for the groups's recommendation.[115]

The first actual test for the Koizumi government to take societal anger towards North Korea seriously came in October 2002. Adhering to the bilateral agreements reached during the summit, North Korea announced on 10 October that the surviving five victims would "temporarily return" to Japan.[116] They arrived at Narita Airport, near Tokyo, on October 15 by a special charter flight organized by the Japanese government. The government also announced that the five would stay for about ten days, meet with their long-parted families, and go back to North Korea, where the victims' children still resided, on 26 October.[117]

The reason the Japanese government originally agreed to the victims' "temporary return" to Japan was that their children, who were all born in the North, believed they were North Koreans, and knew little of their parents' Japanese origin; they would be utterly shocked if they were simply told to "return" permanently to a country to which they had never been before. Therefore, the government assumed it would be reasonable for the five to return first to comfort their waiting families and relatives in Japan and to demonstrate to the public that they were well. Then they would return to the North to break the news to their children themselves, before everyone made one last trip back to Japan in the near future. A cabinet official confirmed this to Kazoku-kai when the victims arrived in Japan, telling the families and relatives, "this is a temporary return, and children are not accompanying this time. Whole families will come back next time though, and this is the agreement [with the North]."[118] The government even prepared allowances for the five to buy souvenirs to take with them when they returned to North Korea.[119]

Whether the Japanese government's agreement with the North was reasonable or not, it became clear that it had utterly failed to predict the public's reaction. Once the five abduction victims returned, there was a public outcry, understandably starting with the families and relatives belonging to Kazoku-kai, urging Koizumi to make the five remain permanently in Japan. The government, already sensitive to heated public opinion and strongly sympathetic to the victims' families, found itself in a difficult situation, having to prioritize the families' demands while running the risk of discarding the bilateral agreement if it gave in to public criticism.[120] As the media also sided with the public in their sympathy for the abductees and their families, it became apparent to government officials that returning the five to North Korea had become politically impossible.[121]

Within the Koizumi cabinet a debate raged. Chief Cabinet Secretary Fukuda Yasuo, along with Tanaka Hitoshi of MOFA, insisted that the five be sent back to North Korea for the time being, because MOFA had obtained the North's agreement on the basis of a "temporary return." Deputy Chief Cabinet Secretary Abe Shinzō countered that returning them "would be an abdication of a sovereign nation's responsibility" and that the abductees themselves should decide whether they wanted to go back or stay permanently.[122] It was not clear if the five victims themselves all preferred to remain in Japan – they never expressed their intention publicly throughout their stay, as it would have complicated the reunion with their children – but Kazoku-kai and the sympathetic public surely did. It was this societal atmosphere that was the background for the cabinet's subsequent adoption of Abe's position.[123] As Deputy Chief Cabinet Secretary Furukawa Teijirō observed, it was apparent to the wary government officials that, if they returned the five and then made no progress with the North, the Koizumi government surely would be forced to resign, as the abductees' families and the public would never forgive it.[124]

Inevitably, then, on 24 October, two days before the abductees' scheduled return to North Korea, the cabinet announced that it would allow them to remain in Japan. Furthermore, it demanded that the North allow their children and other family members to be reunited with the five abductees in Japan.[125] Even from the viewpoint of governmental officials, the decision to keep the victims and to make a new demand of North Korea was due to the Koizumi cabinet's being moved by public pressure – in "the direction of the wind."[126]

Predictably, Pyongyang denounced the Japanese government for "betraying its trust," and warned that it would postpone other scheduled bilateral talks agreed to during the summit.[127] North Korea eventually conceded to the five's permanent stay, however, saying that it would be up to those individuals to decide where they wanted to settle, and that the North Korean government would not intervene in their decision-making. Nevertheless its criticism of the Japanese government for breaking the agreement persisted, with the North arguing that Japan must understand the abductions in the context of past bilateral animosity, and that, if Japanese cared so much for human rights, they should show equal concern for their historical atrocities against Koreans.[128]

The decision to keep the five victims in Japan at the expense of the scheduled diplomatic normalization marked the Koizumi cabinet's passing of the first "test" imposed by the public. Although North Korea eventually yielded to the five victims' settlement, Pyongyang nevertheless rejected new Japanese demands to send the remaining family members still in North Korea, insisting that the victims themselves must persuade their children, as the North had no intention of getting involved in this matter once the Japanese government broke the original agreement. From this point on, Japanese–North Korean relations bogged down in a general stalemate, and the diplomatic momentum Koizumi originally sought was lost.

In the domestic realm, however, the cabinet's decision went down well with the Japanese public:[129] when asked to evaluate the government's stern stance towards North Korea in an *Asahi Shimbun* poll conducted in January 2003, 62 per cent of respondents said they thought of it as positive.[130] Although some media kept pressing the government on whether, in fact, it had originally agreed with the North Koreans that the visit was to be temporary (which it unquestionably had), the cabinet skilfully diverted such scrutiny by claiming that it had "coordinated" the victims' return without once mentioning the terms *ichiji-teki* (temporary) or *gōi* (agreement).[131] Considering the potential for extensive political blowback in case the media scrutiny got out of control and the interested public demanded more detailed answers, the government had to tread carefully through a political minefield for some time and wait for the media questioning to subside, even after the decision to keep the five victims had been announced.

Links to other security policies

The shock and anger caused by the disclosure of the abductions not only pushed the Koizumi government to adjust its policies concerning the issue itself; it also had a broader impact on the way the public understood Japan's domestic and international security policies. The abductions were regarded not simply as a bizarre state crime committed by a few foreign infiltrators in the remote past, but as the most symbolic embodiment of all security threats linked to North Korea. For example, an opinion poll conducted by the Cabinet Office in October 2002, right after the Pyongyang summit, found that, among all North Korea–related issues, ordinary Japanese showed the highest interest in the abductions (83.4 per cent), followed by the *fushinsen* (59.5 per cent), the North Korean nuclear program (49.2 per cent), and the Taepodong missile launches (43.7 per cent). The opinion poll was repeated a year later, in October 2003, and revealed that, although public interest in the abductions and *fushinsen* remained more or less constant (the former again topping the list with 90.1 per cent of respondents interested and the latter in fourth place at 58.7 per cent), societal concern for the North Korean nuclear program (66.3 per cent) and the ballistic missiles (61.1 per cent) had increased noticeably, even though, during this one-year period, there had been no particular developments on these two issues for Japan.[132] Representing such feelings, Minister of Defense Ishiba Shigeru commented in early October 2002 that the abductions issue had to be understood in the context of overall Japanese national security, and that it would be naive to expect a country that had kidnapped foreign citizens to be sincere about resolving other regional security issues such as ballistic missiles, the nuclear program, or the *fushinsen*.[133]

In the same vein, the National Police Agency, for the first time in its history, allocated a whole chapter to North Korean threats in its 2002 Public Safety/Security White Paper. Defining all past North Korea–related security threats such as the abductions and the *fushinsen* as ongoing, the paper argued that the nature of the "terrorist state" would never change. Predicting that *fushinsen* would again try to infiltrate Japanese waters, it concluded by advising the government that new legislation would be required to deter North Korea's spy activities.[134] It is now known that, in late September 2002, Japanese police also transferred the bulk of the personnel who had been assigned to intelligence-gathering missions concerning China and Chinese nationals to a new branch specializing in possible North Korean spy activities in Japan.[135]

Prefectural governments joined the police in advising the government to be more assertive in protecting national security. Prefectural assemblies of Fukuoka, Kumamoto, and Kanagawa submitted letters to Koizumi urging the central government to be firm in negotiating with the North, and the governor of Niigata Prefecture, from which most of the abductees had come, petitioned the government in June 2003 to halt the North Korean passenger ferry *Mangyongbong-92* – which had long been the only regular means of human movement between the two countries – from entering its harbour.[136]

Clearly, societal and political discourse on North Korea after the disclosure of the abductions carried much broader implications for national security in Japanese minds, and those who had vehemently resisted updating Japan's national security policies or institutions found it increasingly difficult to justify their cause after 2002.[137] As the societal threat perception of North Korea widened in scope, more government officials and LDP politicians raised concerns about *senshu-bōei*, Japan's exclusively defence-oriented security principle, and even members of the opposition Democratic Party of Japan (DPJ) in security subcommittees of the Diet followed suit, especially after Defense Minister Ishiba's comment.[138] After Ishiba once again commented in April 2003 that Japan needed to re-evaluate the *senshu-bōei* principle and its reliance on the United States for offensive capabilities, one hundred young Diet members belonging to both the ruling and opposition parties made an emergency public statement in support, urging Japan to obtain the minimal military capability to attack potential enemy targets abroad.[139] Kakiya Isao, formerly a professor at the National Defense Academy of Japan (NDA), presented his own interpretation of what an "exclusively defensive-oriented security principle" should now mean in the post-summit environment: if Japan ever conducted offensive military operations – for example, an infiltration of Japanese special commando units into North Korea –to rescue other (alleged) remaining abductees and their families, it should be rightfully interpreted as legitimate defensive conduct on the part of Japan.[140]

Professor Kitaoka Shinichi of the University of Tokyo – also Japan's former ambassador to the United Nations and a close advisor to Abe Shinzō – confirms that the abductions had much wider societal implications for the Japanese public's *mesen* (perspective or viewpoint) of pacifism in general. Although Japan as a whole still strongly upheld peace and non-aggression as the most sacred national principle, the abductions gave the Japanese people a timely opportunity to contemplate other North Korean threats. It easily convinced them during the process that the *senshu-bōei* principle by itself would not deter such threats as the nuclear program, ballistic missiles, or incursions by *fushinsen*. Although most policy-makers surely had been aware of this since the early 1990s, Kitaoka points out that, in the early 2000s, the North Korea factor triggered this realization among the wider public; North Korea, in this regard, contributed tremendously to lessen the Japanese public's long-held resistance to "realism" in national security.[141]

Professor Iokibe Makoto, former president of the NDA, also agrees that North Korea was the most influential factor in facilitating the public's questioning of the postwar "*junketsu heiwa-shugi* (dogmatic pacifism)." Although there had been previous public discussions on national security – especially during the First Gulf War – arguments that Japan must shift its pacifism "to contribute to the peace and security of the world" were still too abstract and not as convincing as the impact of actual, next-door threats presented by North Korea. Therefore, like Kitaoka, Iokibe claims that North Korea contributed to the rise of a more "*futsū no kankaku* (commonsense approach)" to national security debates in Japan. In response, several high-ranking officers of the SDF told Iokibe that they could not sleep with their feet towards North Korea because of their "gratitude."[142] (In East Asian culture, one never sleeps with one's feet facing an object or a person one is thankful to or reveres.)

The passage of emergency legislation

The heightening of the consciousness of the threat from North Korea among the public resulted in more than loud public statements about security preparedness by politicians. Now that the abductions had become linked to broader national security issues, the Japanese Diet finally passed *Yūji-hōsei/Yūji-kanren-hōan* (emergency legislation) on 7 June 2003 with close to 90 per cent approval, even from the opposition DPJ.[143] The legislation, in three parts, provided the legal framework for clearing roads for military vehicles and supervising evacuations, in order to help the SDF respond effectively to foreign attacks. It also centralized authority previously held by local governments, and imposed controls on the release of government information.[144]

Although deliberations on emergency legislation had been postponed indefinitely in May 2002 because of the potential danger to individual rights and civil liberties, the high percentage of support from Diet members barely a year later clearly indicates the changes through which Japan had gone. Since no new major security threat had materialized from North Korea or anywhere else during this period, it is reasonable to surmise that the shift in the security discourse after the

Pyongyang summit must have played a crucial role in the public's and politicians' new willingness to accept the legislation. DPJ politician Ubukata Yukio confessed: "Originally, one-quarter of the party members were against and another quarter were strongly in favour. The rest were willing to go where the 'wind' of the public attitude would lead them. But once the media reported that 70% of the ordinary citizens were in support, everyone quickly decided to follow the trend."[145]

In a special editorial for the one-year anniversary of Koizumi's visit to Pyongyang, *Yomiuri Shimbun* said that the overwhelming support for the emergency legislation in the Diet was the result of Japanese citizens' realizing that the dictatorship in North Korea was indeed a serious threat to Japan's peace and security.[146] North Korea had helped the public embrace a new "*kokka-ishiki* (national consciousness)," which held that it was common sense to prepare for terrorist targeting of a country's citizens and other contingencies, and that, since late 2002, such societal discourse had directly facilitated the deliberation of the legislation.[147] Maehara Seiji, then a rising star in the opposition DPJ and minister of foreign affairs from September 2010 to March 2011, who took the leading role in his party's support for the legislation, similarly asserted that North Korea–related issues had required more realistic security policy initiatives by both the ruling party and the opposition.[148]

The abductions issue also fundamentally undermined the political influence of the Social Democratic Party and other left-leaning political organizations. As these parties, which traditionally had blocked any emergency bills out of concern for civil liberties, were effectively doomed, the post-summit environment provided an additional boost for the legislation to be passed without hindrance. For the Socialists, who were being severely criticized by the public for their traditional pro–North Korea position and naive acceptance of Pyongyang's past denial of its involvement in the abductions, not being able to block the legislation was the least of their worries. Although the party – surely still a legitimate political organization in a non-monolithic democratic state – somehow maintained the loyalty of its (fast-diminishing) social support base, it won only six seats in the 2003 general election; even the head of the party, Doi Takako, humiliatingly lost hers.[149]

Not just the Socialists, but all politicians facing the 2003 election were forced to realize that public perceptions about North Korea had gone through a quantum shift in a year, and that a pro-North stance had no future in Japanese politics. It is, therefore, not an understatement to argue that North Korea shaped Japanese electoral politics from 2002.[150] All major parties added the abductions issue to their official election platforms, and competed to appeal to voters with their hardline stance and support for a more realistic security framework against North Korean threats.[151] Individual candidates, aware that they were under close scrutiny by the voters, were pushed into making assertive statements concerning North Korea, even if it had very little to do with the actual, everyday politics of their constituencies.[152]

Conclusion

Koizumi's visit to North Korea and the signing of the Pyongyang Declaration, at least in its original intention, was a groundbreaking diplomatic victory in the history of postwar Japan. Through his own personal initiative and by accepting political risks that previous prime ministers had eschewed, Koizumi decided to engage all issues that were hindering Japanese–North Korean diplomatic normalization head on, and succeeded in winning previously inconceivable concessions from Kim Jong Il.

The way Koizumi conducted his North Korean diplomacy up to his visit to Pyongyang could also be understood as an example of his "taboo breaking" – dramatically departing from the Japanese government's traditional approach to North Korea. The Japanese public, at least before the anger of the abductions became widespread, supported his ambition to resolve all North Korea–linked problems obstructing better bilateral relations in a single masterstroke. The media generally also praised his decision to conduct a more "independent" foreign policy that prioritized the needs of Japan.

However, societal anger resulting from the disclosure of the abductions – which was much more severe than the government's initial prediction – subsequently diluted the meaning of the original achievements, and the Koizumi cabinet was eventually pressured to adjust its post-summit negotiating stance, as illustrated by the government's decision to break its previous agreement with the North and keep the five abduction victims in Japan. Although evidence suggests that Koizumi intended to pursue both the resolution of the abductions issue and diplomatic normalization concurrently within the original context of the Pyongyang Declaration, in the post-summit environment he faced diminishing viable choices and subsequently had to accommodate the drastically anti–North Korea societal atmosphere.

One important consequence of the anger towards North Korea stemming from the abductions was the subtle emergence of a historical victim mentality among many Japanese. Although this "victimhood discourse" after the summit progressed somewhat elusively and gradually underneath the more visible diplomatic interactions between the two countries, many observers, especially in Japan, did not fail to catch the nuanced shift in the traditional aggressor-victim narrative that had characterized the history of the two states. Another indirect, but equally important, implication of the rising anti-North sentiment was heightened overall national security consciousness on the part of the Japanese that led to freer discussions of other hardline policy options and the eventual passing of the emergency legislation.

Throughout this period, in the midst of the societal momentum, some Japanese elites adeptly and successfully used public anger towards North Korea as a means to push their larger security agenda, but it would be an oversimplification to interpret this trend as the manipulation of the public by a small number of opinion leaders and politically motivated organizations. Instead, the public discourse concerning North Korea in the aftermath of the summit suggests that the public's anger, which originally stemmed from humanitarian concerns over the fate of fellow citizens, created, as a byproduct, a domestic environment in which some elites could more easily persuade the societal sphere of their other security and historical agendas concerning North Korea, with the Japanese media – also very conscious of the clear domestic trend – functioning as intermediaries.

As we shall see in the next chapter, this domestic environment was the context in which the proposals for unilateral sanctions against North Korea gradually would take form, even without, of course, the foreknowledge that the North would conduct another ballistic missile test in 2006.

Chapter Five

Japanese–North Korean Relations, 2004–06: Debates about Unilateral Sanctions

Proposals to impose sanctions on North Korea for that country's various provocative acts had their earliest origin in the immediate aftermath of the 2002 Pyongyang summit, but they gradually came to the fore of Japanese national discourse as negotiations with the North concerning the abductions dragged on throughout 2003. Although Prime Minister Koizumi Junichirō tried to break the stalemate by revisiting Pyongyang in May 2004, the ever-worsening frustration on the part of the Japanese had reached a point where sanction proposals were already being legislated in the Diet.

Despite Koizumi's apparent personal desire to maintain the framework of the Pyongyang Declaration even up to the end of 2004, by then the prospects for diplomatic normalization had faltered for good, as Japanese investigation of DNA from one of the deceased abductees' cremated remains, provided by North Korean authorities, found it to be that of someone else. This crucial turning point in the abductions issue provided further legitimacy for implementing sanctions bills, and Koizumi – in a drastic deviation from his original plan – eventually had to admit that sanctions would be a justified option for Japan in light of bilateral developments and the domestic environment.

In this chapter, I demonstrate that the detailed plans for unilateral sanctions against North Korea that eventually would be implemented in 2006 were formulated earlier through strong societal and political interaction, and were imposed in a form that was virtually identical to the one that had been envisioned in 2004. Further, the process by which plans for the sanctions crystallized in 2004 was guided almost solely by worsening public opinion concerning the abductions, rather than by the prospect of a future military threat from North Korea, and quite separately from the unfolding of the Six Party Talks on the North Korean nuclear program, which took place over the same period.

Koizumi's Second Visit to Pyongyang and the "Return" of the Abductees' Families

Japanese public anger towards North Korea, which started in 2002, maintained its momentum into 2004. Koizumi's second visit to Pyongyang, in May 2004, was aimed at bringing the abductees' remaining family members (the children and one American husband) from North Korea, at convincing the public that the abductions issue was at least moving somewhere, and at providing the government with justification to proceed with the long-delayed diplomatic normalization. Despite Koizumi's gamble, however, his trip would not be sufficient to overcome the stalemate over the abductions or to mollify Japanese society's image of North Korea.

Indeed, domestic anger over the abductions issue was much more severe than Koizumi had initially anticipated. All through 2003, he was under substantial pressure somehow to make headway on the issue, to convince the public of the need to resume bilateral talks, and to put the Pyongyang Declaration back on track for the sake of Japan's long-term interests.[1] Therefore, when the North Koreans secretly contacted Hirazawa Katsuei – a key, well-known member of the Association of Diet Members for the Japanese Abductees (Rachi-Giren) and a close aide of Koizumi's – for an unofficial talk in Beijing in December 2003, Koizumi grasped the opportunity and agreed that a high-ranking Japanese government official should visit North Korea at the nearest possible opportunity to retrieve the remaining family members as the first step to reinvigorating the stalled negotiations.[2] In yet another example of bypassing the normal diplomatic channels of the Ministry of Foreign Affairs (MOFA) for coordinating foreign policy matters, Koizumi again relied on his close supporters to gauge North Korean intentions and the most likely reaction of the Japanese public prior to making his decision.

Whatever he concluded about the public's likely reception, Koizumi decided, after several months of unofficial contacts with the North, that spring 2004 would be a good time to play his new card. The initial coordination with the North did not require Koizumi, but only someone at the ministerial level; nevertheless, he decided on 14 May 2004 that he would visit Pyongyang once more and take a personal political risk, despite the open opposition of the chief cabinet secretary, the deputy chief cabinet secretary, and the secretary-general of the Liberal Democratic Party (LDP).[3]

Accordingly, on 23 May, Koizumi made his way to Tokyo's Haneda Airport for a trip to North Korea. As expected, he returned the same day with five children of the abductees, after meeting with Kim Jong Il in a second round of summit talks. At first the Japanese media focused on the children's return and North Korea's new promise to launch another follow-up investigation to reveal the truth behind the (allegedly) deceased abduction victims. It also came to their immediate attention, however, that, in return, Koizumi had agreed to deliver 250,000 tons of food and US$10 million worth of medical goods to North Korea within a month or two by coordinating with international aid organizations. Moreover, he had promised that his government would do its best to prevent discrimination against ethnic Koreans with official or informal ties with the North, which had been inflamed by societal anger towards North Korea.[4] Koizumi, in effect, was positioning himself to reopen the normalization process and salvage the stalled implementation of the Pyongyang Declaration by concurrently giving North Korea additional incentives and, he hoped, containing public antipathy towards the North by providing the Japanese media new images of the abduction victims and their children happily reunited.

Although the government consoled itself after Koizumi's return that it had somehow cleared the "minimum line" required to persuade the public, from that day on it was forced to face ominous indications that neither the public nor politics shared that view. The National Association of Families of Japanese Abducted by North Korea (Kazokukai) and other abduction-related organizations voiced a strong protest against the government's "concessions," and domestic political actors, even within the LDP, kept silent, noting that public opinion was seemingly indifferent to Koizumi's limited achievement.[5] From the day Koizumi returned from Pyongyang, it was apparent that the public would not "appreciate" the agreements he had reached with the North, although the majority did not openly protest against them either, as news of the children's reunion with their parents and adaptation to their new homes in Japan filled the media.

In this regard, although Koizumi did not lose much political ground, he also failed to achieve the breakthrough he had hoped. In the midst of such a cool societal reception, Koizumi must have felt fortunate that at least the public and the media did not criticize him as harshly as the government had feared they might. This was because, in another demonstration of his populist tendency, Koizumi had deliberately broadcast, through all major Japanese media, his personal briefing to Kazoku-kai of the result of the summit, only hours after his return from Pyongyang. As expected, the family members of the abduction victims vehemently criticized him on national television without thanking him for retrieving the children. Despite unwavering public sympathy for the families, however, to everyone watching television, Koizumi's being verbally abused without having a chance to defend himself was a bit much, and it immediately spurred further societal sympathy, this time towards Koizumi, as the public felt that Kazoku-kai's treatment of him was understandable, but "unfair."[6] Thus, by portraying himself as a loyal and sincere but helpless servant of the families and the public, who had tried his utmost to resolve the abductions issue but unfortunately had failed to achieve an end that was satisfactory to them, Koizumi at least succeeded in damage control during this potentially devastating political crisis.

Some have asserted that the true purpose of his second visit was not necessarily to put bilateral relations back on track, but to benefit Koizumi and the LDP in the upcoming elections for the upper house (Sangiin) of the Diet in July 2004, by strengthening his image as someone dedicated to the resolution of the abductions issue.[7] It is doubtful, however, if Koizumi actually would have considered the return of the children as a definite means of winning the election, since his move was a double-edged sword that could either end positively, or – as it almost turned out – prove to be an unnecessary gamble and worsen his position right before the election. Therefore, rather than a calculation for the election, it is more plausible that Koizumi actually prioritized reaching a diplomatic breakthrough, by engaging the issue that held the key to that very goal. He must have felt tremendous pressure to pull bilateral relations out of stalemate, and the only means by which he could achieve that was to produce a visible result on the abductions issue, regardless of the election, since a clear majority of the public – 86 per cent, as one opinion poll in June 2004 indicated – still held the abductions to be the most important topic in Japanese foreign policy.[8] In another poll, conducted in July, when asked if Koizumi's second summit and the "return" of the children had any impact on their voting during the election, 58 per cent of respondents answered that it had not.[9]

Whatever his true motives, Koizumi did not win much by the second summit, although he did not lose much either. Bringing back the victims' children with full, live television coverage certainly did not result in a wider public acceptance of diplomatic re-engagement with the North. Although there were brief hopes immediately following the summit that the children's return would mark the start of the resolution of the abductions issue, the lack of further positive developments allowed the public to maintain its fixation on the injustice done to Japanese citizens by the North.[10]

The Origin of the Unilateral Sanctions Legislation

Significantly the sanctions option was first proposed and supported by political parties and members of the wider public, *not* by the bureaucracy or the cabinet. As the public became increasingly convinced that a full resolution of the abductions issue would not materialize unless certain pressure was applied to North Korea, societal support for sanctions, as they had originally been envisioned, came to dominate mainstream debate by 2003. During this process, the North Korea discourse that had developed after 2002 – that Japan's traditional postwar national security stance vis-à-vis its neighbours was problematic, and that Japan was a political entity democratically and economically superior to North Korea in every sense – also gave the idea of unilateral sanctions a distinct Japanese character and content as the debate progressed. In this domestic context, those among the public and political parties who favoured unilateral sanctions against North Korea would see their ideas develop into official Diet proposals, culminating in the passage of formal legislation in 2004, although the sanctions were not imposed immediately afterwards.

The early proposals

That the idea of applying unilateral sanctions did not originate with Koizumi's government is understandable, considering that he was still cautiously hopeful that the Pyongyang Declaration could be salvaged. Although some members of his cabinet, such as Ishiba Shigeru and Abe Shinzō, raised their voices in favour of pressuring Kim Jong il and weakening his political base, they did so in their capacity as members of Rachi-Giren and as individual LDP politicians, since even ministers appointed by Koizumi enjoyed differences in opinion.

Nonetheless, two months after the October 2002 decision by the Japanese government, under public pressure, to keep the returned abductees in Japan, more Diet members began to align themselves with Ishiba and Abe. Politicians knew that supporting the idea of sanctions would enhance their tough image in the eyes of the Japanese people. As more members took the initially vague but potentially beneficial idea seriously, the National Security Committee of the lower house (Shūgiin) of the Diet held a meeting on 10 December 2002 to discuss the option. What is interesting is that, rather than the debate's being confined to committee members, various consultants and witnesses from domestic think tanks and North Korea–related organizations were invited to offer their own ideas and expertise. One of them, Satō Katsumi – head of both the newly popular National Association for the Rescue of Japanese Abducted by North Korea (Sukuu-kai) and the right-leaning Modern Korea Institute – was invited by the LDP as a presenter. Concerning the abductions, Satō asserted that putting solid pressure on North Korea in order to *topple the regime* would be necessary if Japan were to expect the issue to be resolved, and that Kim Jong Il must not be regarded as a counterpart in any diplomatic negotiations. When the committee, intrigued by his blunt argument, questioned how he proposed to achieve that end, Satō claimed that stopping all movement of money, goods, and people between the two countries, by banning North Korean freighters and passenger liners from entering Japanese harbours, would result in "the demise of Kim's regime within three months."[11] Satō's suggestion was the earliest example of a concrete proposal from the non-governmental sector on how Japan should develop the "pressure option."

Interestingly, on 13 December, just three days after the committee hearing, rising young LDP politicians in both the lower and upper houses – such as Yamamoto Ichita and Kōno Tarō – launched a Diet policy study group called Tai-Kitachōsen Gaikō Kādo wo Kangaeru-kai (Association for Considering Foreign Policy Cards against North Korea).[12] Although it is hard to know with certainty how much the association's aim was influenced by Satō, it went on to formulate its own "foreign policy cards" of unilaterally stopping both trade and money transfers between the two countries. In addition to a ban on North Korean ships, the association also discussed the possibility of revising Japan's lax foreign exchange laws, since some Korean residents who supported the North were using them to their advantage when sending hard currency to support Kim's regime.[13]

Thus, although the first arguments in favour of pressuring North Korea to resolve the abductions issue originated from think tanks and

LDP politicians, a domestic atmosphere hostile towards the North allowed the idea to permeate easily into public discourse and develop into an even stronger version after 2003. The options of banning North Korean ships and revising foreign exchange laws appeared in the media with increasing frequency, and the term "economic sanctions" replaced "foreign policy cards" in both the political and public spheres. Again, it is difficult to trace quantitatively exactly how ideas originally proposed by the head of Sukuu-kai and the LDP's Kangaeru-kai influenced the subsequent trajectory of the sanctions discourse. It is certain, however, that, by the beginning of 2003, all sanctions discussions in the media and among political parties, prefectural governments, and the general public had adopted the position that banning key North Korean vessels and updating foreign exchange laws were the most realistic and readily imposable means at Japan's disposal. From this early stage, in public discourse, "unilateral economic sanctions" thus would denote these two options in one set piece.

The banning of North Korean vessels from entering Japanese harbours won wider publicity first, since some of these ships – especially the ferry *Mangyongbong-92* – were already well known. Once the National Police Agency announced in January 2003 that the vessel could have functioned in the past as a command centre for North Korean spies in Japan, media support for the ban became even more widespread.[14] Prefectural governments – especially the assembly of Niigata, since the *Mangyongbong-92* regularly docked at Niigata harbour – also ardently supported the argument, and declared that *fushinsen*, after all, were not the only North Korean "mystery/spy ships" that Japan should be worried about. They urged the central government that, at the very least, inspections of the vessel once it had entered Japan must be tightened.[15] Although the idea of banning North Korean vessels was confined at first to the well-known *Mangyongbong-92*, by mid-2003 it was expanded to cover all North Korean ships – mostly small freighters numbering about four hundred a year – bringing marine products and mushrooms to Maizuru in Kyoto and Sakai, in Tottori Prefecture, and leaving with used automobiles.[16]

In May and June 2003, societal support for another pillar of the "pressure option" – the revision of foreign exchange laws – also gained momentum. The public was more convinced than ever that blocking Japanese goods from flowing into North Korea could not be complete unless the capital transfer of so-called pachinko money to Pyongyang by pro-North, ethnic Korean residents in Japan was strictly controlled.

Throughout 2003 both proposals attained wider public understanding, and societal discourse in support of them became the mainstream. By the end of that year, the Japanese media realized that there was already a "national consensus in principle" among the political sphere and the public concerning the validity of pressuring North Korea.[17] It is not surprising, then, that the LDP decided to consider the two foreign policy pressure cards as potential Diet legislation in the near future, with public, prefectural, and media backing.[18]

Sanctions legislation in 2004

The Japanese government's official explanation for its initial reluctance to introduce sanctions legislation was that a strategy of "*atsuryoku to taiwa* (pressure and dialogue)" would be a more skilful way to send dual messages to North Korea: while Koizumi personally offered to talk to Kim Jong Il, domestic support for sanctions would remind the North of the consequences of not responding sincerely to Japanese demands.[19]

In retrospect the claim is logical, and it would have entered the government's calculation at some level. However, it certainly does not sit comfortably with the fact that the prime minister made two trips to the North, at substantial political risk, and even promised additional incentives in exchange for the abduction victims' children. A more logical interpretation is that, although Koizumi still preferred the Pyongyang Declaration as the framework through which to negotiate without the "sanctions card" – notably because his design would have been even more difficult to achieve with possible North Korean retaliation – he nevertheless also had to succumb to rising domestic support for sanctions, and thus overlooked the activities of his fellow LDP politicians.

Ever since the disclosure of the abductions in 2002, Deputy Chief Cabinet Secretary Abe Shinzō – among those fellow LDP politicians – had established himself as the head of the hawkish voices against North Korea. He never openly disagreed with Koizumi's North Korea policies, and Koizumi, in turn, retained Abe in his cabinet. However, Abe succeeded in winning enormous popularity among the public by insisting on applying direct pressure to Kim's regime, even though some of his claims consequentially deviated from his boss's true intentions. Since animosity towards North Korea was growing, Abe's strong statements simply rang true with the public, which led Kazoku-kai and Sukuu-kai to lend their unanimous support to Abe as well.[20] Therefore, once the sanctions debate got under way, he came to the forefront of the politicians who favoured legislation, confidently assuring the public that "time will work to our advantage," since North Korea's economic difficulties inevitably would force it to surrender to the Japanese resolution.[21]

Though an adept populist politician, in retrospect Koizumi failed to appreciate correctly the extent of Abe's popularity, as he also had failed to anticipate the likely societal reaction to the disclosure of the abductions in 2002. Therefore, in 2003, regardless of what he had in mind for the resolution of the diplomatic stalemate, Koizumi showed signs of leaving Abe alone to pursue the North Korea agenda. It is likely that, by retaining the popular Abe in the cabinet and preventing a public disagreement over the government's North Korea policy, Koizumi aimed to keep the public on his side.[22] Koizumi's difficult position was especially apparent during the sanctions debates. Although, as the head of the cabinet, Koizumi at least restrained Abe from initiating any definite move to impose sanctions during the 2003–05 period, his hierarchical control was not always evident, and Abe was increasingly allowed a free hand to pursue the abductions issue and sanctions legislation in his own style.[23] Koizumi's "yielding" to Abe demonstrates that, although he had originally won his popularity and prime ministership by skilfully using the media and public perceptions to his advantage, his foreign policy strategy from 2003 on, in contrast, was tilted more towards observing the mainstream domestic mood first before taking a political path that reflected the majority domestic discourse.[24]

The LDP did not overlook Abe's rise in domestic politics. Anticipating that the huge popular support for Abe would benefit the party during the general election for the lower house scheduled for November 2003, the LDP "promoted" him to secretary-general of the party. Abe, in turn, launched a "manifesto" promising sanctions on North Korea. Other parties – the Democratic Party of Japan (DPJ) and the New Komeito Party (better known simply as Kōmeitō) – quickly copied him, incorporating in their manifestos their own plans for sanctions in order to benefit from the source of Abe's popularity.[25]

The election ended with the LDP's winning a solid majority in the lower house. This satisfactory result further consolidated Abe's position in the party, and it was clear to LDP members that he would be the most likely candidate to be the next prime minister. Koizumi, for his part, went along with the atmosphere within the party by showing signs of further tacit tolerance of Abe's aggressive policy initiatives.[26]

The new secretary-general then declared that he would take full personal responsibility for passing legislation on the revision of foreign exchange laws; by December 2003, the executive council of the LDP was already regarding his statement as a *fait accompli*.[27]

On 29 January 2004, *Gaikoku Kawase/Gaikoku Bōeki-hō Kaisei-an* (Amendment of Foreign Exchange and Trade Laws) enabling Japan unilaterally to stop the transfer of capital and goods to North Korea, passed a plenary session vote in the lower house.[28] On 1 February the LDP, DPJ, and Kōmeitō agreed to cooperate in passing the bill in the upper house as well;[29] it was duly realized eight days later. Although the ban on North Korean vessels had been the first of the "pressure cards" and had been discussed in domestic debates for a slightly longer period, the foreign exchange ban was given the first "go," evidently because it was simpler to amend already-existing laws than to draft a whole new bill from scratch. Reflecting the sanctions supporters' thorough preparation, however, drafting a new bill did not take much time. On 17 February the LDP officially adopted the final draft of a "Law Prohibiting Particular Vessels from Entering Japanese Harbours," and on 4 March the LDP, DPJ, and Kōmeitō once again agreed to support its passage through the Diet.[30]

By this point Diet discussions were snowballing to expand the scope of the sanctions bills beyond the two options originally envisioned in December 2002. To complete the ban on the movement of people between the two countries, the Diet, in addition to targeting North Korean vessels, started to consider the possibility of rejecting the issuing of re-entry permits to particular *eijyū gaikokujin* (foreigners with permanent-resident status) – the majority of them ethnic Koreans – by revising the immigration control laws.[31] Rare for the largest opposition party, the DPJ was more than willing to support the proposal; in fact, it went even further than the LDP, announcing in March 2004 that it was independently analysing the prospect of banning all North Korean airliners as well as ships, thus virtually closing the border both at sea and in the air.[32] Since there were almost no direct flights between the two countries in the first place, the effectiveness of this proposed measure would be dubious at best. However, the DPJ's ready cooperation with the LDP when it concerned North Korea illustrates well how all of the political parties were influenced by the discursive trend in favour of the sanctions, and how they were under constant pressure to demonstrate their willing participation to the public. As we shall see later in the chapter, these latter two proposals would be incorporated into the actual unilateral sanctions implemented in 2006.

In an opinion poll conducted in February 2004 by *Yomiuri Shimbun*, 78 per cent of respondents welcomed the revised foreign exchange laws, and 80 per cent supported the draft bill on North Korean vessels entering Japanese harbours. In fact, the poll found that the majority of Japanese felt that even stronger sanction measures were desirable.[33] Media of both left and right political inclinations also accepted this public voice as a legitimate reaction by the people whose national sovereignty and human rights had been violated; they admitted that, by this point, it would be simply natural for Japan to show its resolution by demonstrating to the North Koreans that it was ready to impose pressures of Japan's choosing at any time.[34]

An article published by the monthly magazine *Seiron* in January 2004 is highly representative of the time when the momentum for sanctions legislation was at its peak. *Seiron*, jointly with Sukuu-kai, sent open questionnaires to all 480 members of the lower house of the Diet asking for their opinions on the two proposed sanctions bills as "the resolute means to fully resolve the abductions issue" and for their public recognition of whether or not the abductions were indeed "unforgivable state terrorism." The members' answers to each question were published verbatim with their name, affiliated party, and regional constituency fully disclosed as a useful reference for voters. The way the opinions were collected and published, needless to say, led most respondents to support the sanctions bills and to declare that the abductions were a state crime. What is especially intriguing, however, is that, while Abe obviously answered "strongly support" to all questions, Koizumi – possibly reflecting his "dilemma" just prior to the second Pyongyang visit – did not reply to the questions on sanctions.[35]

On 14 June 2004 the second pillar of the proposed sanctions, the bill on North Korean vessels, passed the Diet as *Tokutei Senpaku Nyūkō Kinshi Tokubetsu Sochi-hō* (Special Legal Measures Prohibiting Particular Vessels from Entering Japanese Harbours).[36] Now that both pillars of the original sanctions proposals were officially legislated, it was clear that, despite Koizumi's second Pyongyang visit barely a month earlier, his gamble to reinvigorate the Pyongyang Declaration had not paid off. On the contrary, from September – the second anniversary of his first trip to Pyongyang – the pressure on Koizumi to use the legal means now at Japan's disposal intensified through the constant statements by LDP, DPJ, and Kōmeitō politicians. Rachi-Giren, for its part, also supported the parties' demands by proposing that the two-year anniversary would be the perfect time to impose unilateral sanctions in order to *"rescue all abduction victims still held in North Korea."*[37] Opinion polls taken during October and November illustrated the same trend, with a substantial majority of respondents (65 to 68 per cent) still agreeing with the need to impose sanctions.[38]

The Final Dissolution of the Pyongyang Declaration Framework

For the obvious reason that one cannot expect to normalize diplomatic relations and impose sanctions at the same time, Koizumi, even after his second visit to Pyongyang, maintained his distance from the domestic legislation against North Korea. Some have argued that his caution stemmed more from his experiences with the North, in that he expected that sanctions would have only a limited effect on the Kim regime, and could even force Japan to deal with the consequences of a possible North Korean declaration of war.[39] Indeed, others in Japan echoed Koizumi's pessimism that sanctions unilaterally imposed by Japan would have little effect in any case without the support and participation of neighbouring states.[40] In addition, even politicians who had pushed the sanctions legislation in the Diet could not explain, when asked, how exactly (and through what process) the sanctions would result in the return of the abductees still held in the North – who allegedly were dead according to the North Koreans, but were presumed to be still alive by the Japanese public and government.[41] Koizumi, however, remained hopeful that the framework to which he and Kim Jong Il had agreed in 2002 could be put back on track if there were some progress on the abductions issue. In fact, as late as July 2004, Koizumi was still openly expressing his personal desire to normalize bilateral relations before his term as president of the LDP ended in September 2006.[42] In December 2004, however, Koizumi's hopes were effectively shattered by another incident related to the abductions.

The last straw: The Yokota Megumi DNA incident

It is likely that Koizumi believed that the retrieval of the abductees' children and the North Koreans' promise during his second Pyongyang visit to conduct follow-up investigations (although not a joint Japanese–North Korean investigation) would constitute some improvement of the abductions issue, and clear the lowest hurdle for renewing bilateral negotiations. As a part of the agreement, North Korea handed over what it claimed to be the cremated remains of Yokota Megumi, the youngest victim, who had been abducted in 1977 at age thirteen on her way back from school and, according to Pyongyang's claim, had committed suicide in the North in 1994.

In the best of scenarios, Megumi's ashes, even as a painful reminder of tragedy, should have become a symbol of North Korea's new willingness to cooperate with Japanese demands. They might even have helped to reinvigorate the normalization process by at least validating the results of past North Korean investigations. "Proving" that Megumi and other victims had indeed died would not have mitigated public anger, of course, but for those on both sides who were desperately looking for a breakthrough in the abductions deadlock, undeniable proof of Megumi's death could have helped silence wide speculation about her alleged current whereabouts. Once the public, however grudgingly, had accepted that evidence, a more "realistic" resolution of the abductions issue would have been possible.

The events that unfolded once the cremated remains arrived in Japan could not have been more different from such expectations. On 8 December 2004 Japanese authorities reported that a careful DNA examination had revealed that the remains were not Megumi's.[43] Although there were debates, especially from outside Japan, concerning the credibility of the examination results,[44] what is significant is not the scientific process through which the conclusion was derived but its empirical consequences in Japan.

Japan was stunned by the official report, probably as much as in 2002, when the abductions were first disclosed. Public anger immediately reached a new height, and domestic pressure to use the sanctions measures that had already been prepared won immediate and widespread support in both the Diet and the societal sphere. A day after the report was released, the LDP announced its detailed scenario for imposing unilateral economic sanctions, fully using both pieces of legislation that had passed the Diet earlier. The LDP plan was divided into five "levels": level 1 would begin with Japan's freezing humanitarian aid (food and medical supplies); level 2 would impose strict restrictions on sending money to North Korea; level 3 would wholly ban money transfers, as well as the trade of certain predesignated goods; level 4 would ban particular North Korean ships from entering Japanese harbours; and, finally, level 5 would expand level 4 to all North Korean vessels.[45] Level 1 was more of an expression of Japanese determination, since there had been almost no large-scale humanitarian aid since 2002, as well as a declaration to the North that, under current circumstances, Japan had no intention of implementing the aid that Koizumi had promised during the second summit. On the other hand, the other levels clearly illustrated how the sanctions legislation would be put to use.

The North Korean fabrication of Megumi's cremated remains and the LDP's timely five-stage countermeasures facilitated an uproar in public opinion and domestic politics alike in favour of unilateral economic sanctions, with major newspapers expressing their full support for the LDP's plan and Kazoku-kai urging Koizumi to impose sanctions immediately and criticizing the government for procrastinating.[46] A *Yomiuri* opinion poll on 14 December showed that 74 per cent of respondents supported Japan's immediate imposition of unilateral sanctions.[47]

Koizumi's shift towards unilateral sanctions

The DNA result shocked the Koizumi government to the core. For Koizumi himself, it was the turning point where he had to admit that normalizing relations with North Korea under the framework of the Pyongyang Declaration was impossible.[48]

Although it is difficult to pinpoint exactly when Koizumi changed his mind, the tremendous public uproar in the aftermath of the release of the DNA report proved to him beyond a doubt that it would be prudent to embrace a new direction. It is plausible that his personal humiliation of being betrayed by the North also played a significant part in this change. Whether from his personal conviction or from his ability as a populist politician to sense the discursive atmosphere, Koizumi, in the latter half of December 2004, started making statements that were more clearly in line with public emotions: pressuring the North was not just understandable, but necessary.[49] As mentioned earlier, Koizumi had let Abe take the initiative on the abductions issue, even as the cabinet as a whole kept its distance from Abe's measures, to maintain the impression that he and Abe were not necessarily pursuing contradictory strategies and to maintain public support. In this regard, Koizumi's shift after the DNA incident is an equally vivid example of his consciousness of majority preferences as a politician whose power largely depended on public support.

On 17 December, just nine days after the DNA test results were announced, came the first indication of the shift in Koizumi's policy towards North Korea. During a summit meeting with South Korean president Roh Moo Hyun, Koizumi said that "pressure [on North Korea] is necessary," which was widely interpreted in Japan as a "change of heart" by Koizumi from his previously cautious stance.[50] The stage on which Koizumi made his point is significant, since it was to the head of a South Korean government that had inherited former president Kim Dae Jung's "Sunshine Policy" of reconciliation and mutual coexistence with North Korea and thus was not fond of Japanese pressure on other Koreans. Moreover, many South Koreans in government and society alike were suspicious that the sanctions were a deliberate "precedent" for Japan's bigger hidden agenda: more aggressive regional foreign policy.

Koizumi's new expression of understanding for sanctions was not confined to this statement. On 30 January 2005 he again announced that "it is simply natural that voices urging the government to impose economic sanctions are overwhelming, considering the extent that North Korea has ridiculed the state and the citizens of Japan."[51] As a follow-up measure, the Diet's special committee on the abductions issue demanded that the government put unilateral sanctions into effect at the earliest possible opportunity, adding that the request was a "representation of the Japanese people's determination."[52] "Representation" it truly was: in February Koizumi received a petition, signed by five million people, demanding economic sanctions against North Korea.[53]

The North Korean Nuclear Issue Takes International Centre Stage

By the beginning of 2005 there was a broad consensus in the Japanese government, the Diet, the media, and among the public on the need to exert pressure on North Korea, and that normalizing diplomatic relations with the North within the original framework of the Pyongyang Declaration was a lost cause. Then, in February, North Korea officially announced that it possessed nuclear weapons, reinforcing the long-held concern that it constituted the most direct threat to Japan's national security.[54] Japan did not immediately impose sanctions, however – they would come only a year later, when a North Korean missile once again fell into the sea near Japan. Why were they not imposed in 2005?

The origin of the sanctions was, beyond doubt, the abductions issue. Since the abductions were a symbol of the evil nature of and threats associated with North Korea, the issue had broader implications for the public's perception of other North Korea–related problems. Therefore, although the sanctions option was first proposed and supported by the public as the result of the abductions, it was natural to argue that it could be applied to other North Korean issues as well.[55] Japan was thus already prepared, both logically and legally, to impose sanctions when North Korea made the nuclear weapons announcement. That it did not do so provides clues as to how the Japanese public had understood the nuclear issue, compared to other, more up-close-and-personal threats such as abductions and ballistic missiles. North Korean threats that, by their nature, visibly affected Japan's territorial and maritime sovereignty or (especially) the security of Japanese citizens had always been prioritized in the emotions of the Japanese.[56] An ongoing nuclear program in a foreign country – even North Korea – on the other hand, was comparatively more "distant, abstract, and arid," at least to the public: there was no "human-ness" to the story.[57] As an article in *Yomiuri Shimbun* explained, "amid the uproar over the fate of Japanese abductees, the Japanese public [was] in no mood to concentrate on the arcane details of North Korea's nuclear program."[58] Here lie the limitations of some contemporary analyses that focus on the nuclear issue as the driving force behind Japanese policy-making towards North Korea: the nuclear threat surely reinforced already-prevalent societal anger over the abductions issue, but it was neither the origin nor the main cause of hardened policies.

Of course, governmental and bureaucratic policy circles would have given all issues equal consideration. However, their aim to tackle comprehensively both the abductions issue and the nuclear issue at the same level, within the framework of the Pyongyang Declaration, had always been countered by the emotional current among the public and by Diet politicians who wished to jump on that emotional bandwagon. The government, as a result, yielded to domestic opinion and ended up giving the abductions clear precedence over other issues.[59] As Korea–Japan relations expert Izumi Hajime points out, there was a clear discrepancy of preferred focus between the government and the public from the beginning, since the "*ippan-teki shakai ishiki* (typical societal understanding)" of the nature of North Korean problems lacked awareness of international-level strategic considerations.[60] As Abe – representing such "typical societal understanding" – once asserted, it was natural that Japan prioritize the abductions above any other agenda item, "as Japan cannot expect or rely on help from others, since, for outsiders who have not experienced such tragedy, the kidnapping of one's own citizens by a foreign country is nothing more than '*taningoto* (somebody else's problem).'"[61]

Public opinion surveys conducted annually in October by the Cabinet Office further illustrate the prevalence of "typical societal understanding": the extent to which the abductions overshadowed other North Korea–related issues, including the nuclear threat. Asked to rank all such issues according to their level of concern, in 2003, 90.1 per cent of respondents placed the abductions at the top of their list, followed by nuclear weapons (66.3 per cent) and ballistic missiles (61.1 per cent). In 2004 the order remained the same: 88.3 per cent for the abductions, 56.6 per cent for nuclear weapons, and 56.2 per cent for missiles. Again, in 2005, 87.6 per cent saw the abductions as the biggest concern, followed by nuclear weapons (63.9 per cent), and missiles (52.2 per cent). Thus, although concern about the nuclear and missile threats experienced slight ups and downs, the abductions always remained at the top during this period, even after the North Korean nuclear announcement in 2005. What is even more surprising is that, in the October 2006 poll, taken after the first North Korean nuclear test, the abductions remained the top priority in the minds of respondents (86.7 per cent), although the proportion concerned about the nuclear threat jumped to 79.5 per cent.[62]

Of course, it would be an oversimplification to argue that the nuclear threat had no connection to the unfolding of Japanese security policies. Indeed, one plausible reason Japan refrained from imposing unilateral economic sanctions after the nuclear announcement was that the Japanese government saw a new opportunity to exert additional pressure on North Korea in a multilateral setting – namely, the Six Party Talks (SPT) – to resolve both the nuclear and the abduction issues. Therefore, although the establishment of the talks might have indeed played a role in delaying the imposition of sanctions in 2005, the delay still does not substantiate the claim that Japanese policies towards North Korea were governed by the nuclear factor. Participating states certainly considered the resolution of the atomic threat to be the central agenda of the SPT, but the Japanese public and media overwhelmingly regarded even this international institution as a stage on which to pressure North Korea concerning the abductions, and constantly leaned on the Japanese government to raise the abductions issue in the SPT and to win support for the Japanese cause among the other participants. Subsequent Japanese behaviour in the SPT further illustrates the extent to which the abductions issue guided – and limited – the government's position, even in multilateral settings. While the SPT progressed, Japanese media reports overwhelmingly focused on whether the Japanese representatives were raising the abductions issue sufficiently vigorously – indeed, the negotiations on the nuclear issue itself received only secondary attention in most domestic SPT coverage.[63]

A number of scholars have argued that, by urging the other parties to incorporate the abductions issue into the main agenda of the SPT – often in contravention of US requests to refrain – Japan made the already-delicate negotiations even less likely to reach agreement on the nuclear problem, and gave the North Koreans a pretext to deliberately impede progress when they were at a disadvantage.[64] As a result, South Korea and China also expressed displeasure that Japan was holding up the main discussion.[65] The Japanese delegation, therefore, faced a difficult tactical position: it had little choice but to be firm about putting the abductions issue on Japan's priority agenda to avoid a domestic political blowback, but the government was also fully aware that North Korea would use Japan's move to isolate it at the negotiating table and prevent the other participants in the SPT from forming a unified front against the North on the nuclear issue by highlighting Japan's introduction of an additional problem to an already-volatile multilateral framework.[66]

There is, of course, an alternative explanation for Japan's behaviour – one preferred by Japanese government officials – that points to the importance of normal diplomatic practices, rather than domestic pressure, in international negotiations. Since the SPT were originally established to resolve "comprehensively" the regional instability created by North Korea (the nuclear issue being the primary issue), a multilateral agreement among the participants to offer the North incentives to dismantle its nuclear program and arsenal naturally would require an acceptable environment in which each of the participants had first resolved all of its bilateral concerns with the North. In other words, although the main agreement in the SPT would be made at the multilateral level, acceptable preconditions for each participant to offer the North a "carrot" still needed to be met bilaterally, based on their differing relations with the North Koreans. According to this logic, it was thus natural for Japan to raise the abductions issue, irrespective of domestic pressure, as it undoubtedly constituted the most important bilateral hurdle to overcome if Japan were to offer the North incentives under the SPT.[67]

From this line of thinking, Japan's incorporation of the abductions issue into the talks was, in fact, a diplomatic victory. Japan and North Korea signed the Pyongyang Declaration in the first place because Japan succeeded in persuading the North that both countries would benefit from a "grand peace in the Korean Peninsula," and that bilateral diplomatic normalization would be a prerequiste for achieving that end. This was the reason that the Japanese government formulated the "*ōkina chizu* (big roadmap)," which included cooperation between Japan and North Korea to resolve comprehensively both the nuclear and abductions issues as a necessary process for achieving diplomatic normalization.[68] From Japan's point of view, therefore, diplomatic normalization, the nuclear issue, and the abductions issue constituted a "single package." Although the SPT had been initiated with the limited goal of achieving a nuclear-free Korean Peninsula, from Japan's perspective they constituted an important component of the broader goal of realizing a grand peace in Korea. Therefore, the other two parts of the package – the abductions issue and diplomatic normalization – had to be discussed along with the nuclear issue if North Korea expected Japan to deliver all its promised commitments to the North as outlined in the Pyongyang Declaration. Since the other participants in the SPT were fully aware of Japan's position, they inevitably would be forced to encourage the North to respond sincerely to Japan's demands if the talks were not to be stalled by deadlock over the abductions. Making the abductions issue an integral part of the agenda in a multilateral setting was thus a logical and strategic choice by the Japanese government to exert additional pressure on North Korea with international support.[69]

Although this explanation – that Japan persisted in making the abductions issue a bilateral condition for reaching a multilateral agreement – might be rational in terms of international diplomatic norms, many Japan observers were not conviced that it was the real reason for the Japanese delegation's particular agenda setting. After all, Japan not only raised the abductions issue in the bilateral setting; it did so consistently during general negotiations involving other participants in the SPT, with Japanese delegates including statements about the abductions in their opening statements at every round of the talks, as they obviously could not "afford to remain silent."[70] Thus, domestic pressure has been more widely interpreted as the real cause of Japan's insistence on winning international support for the abductions issue, rather than strategic calculations regarding the direction of the nuclear crisis.[71]

Viewed in this context it is not surprising that the nuclear announcement in 2005 did not have sufficient domestic impact for sanctions to be imposed automatically. For that to occur, an official justification readily understandable by the Japanese public would need to have been derived from new, negative developments in the abductions issue or in other issues of equally direct concern to the public, since the nuclear issue was of comparatively secondary interest to domestic audiences.[72]

Abe Shinzō's official statement as the newly appointed chief cabinet secretary on 2 November 2005 is a telling example of the consistency of the abductions issue as Japan's primary concern, independent of the SPT. Soon after the signing on 19 September of the first joint statement of the SPT, which had been negotiated with great difficulty, Abe again warned North Korea that Japan was ready to impose sanctions unilaterally at any time if the North failed to react sincerely to Japanese demands concerning the abductions.[73]

North Korea Policy, 2004–06, before the Second Missile Launch

Koizumi's second visit to Pyongyang, by which he hoped to put diplomatic normalization back on track by retrieving the abduction victims' remaining family members, was a bold political gamble that failed to produce the desired result. Despite the minor achievement in 2004, public anxiety over the lack of real progress concerning the abductions – meaning a full reinvestigation involving Japanese officials as well as the "return of all surviving victims" who North Korea claimed were deceased – continued to grow. The steady escalation of public animosity towards North Korea from 2003 on gave birth to a new discourse about the use of Japanese economic might as leverage. Evidence suggests that Koizumi, even though he initially distanced himself from the proposal and subsequent sanctions legislation, eventually succumbed to the domestic atmosphere in support of sanctions, especially after the Yokota Megumi DNA incident in December 2004. Steady domestic support for unilateral economic sanctions was maintained largely independent of progress in the SPT.

As Shinoda Tomohito argues in his model of Koizumi's decision-making, even public opinion led by well-informed and educated citizens does not guarantee good judgment in foreign policy. However, since a democratic government cannot neglect the public, it is therefore desirable that the prime minister and his cabinet provide strong political leadership in foreign policy, while investing equal energy in the process of persuading the public of the correctness of their strategy.[74] Koizumi's original approach to North Korea reflected his understanding of this duality in policy-making. He had pursued a comprehensive resolution of all North Korea–related problems by trying to normalize bilateral relations and enhance Japan's position in the regional security order through the framework of the Pyongyang Declaration. At the same time, he devoted energy to the difficult task of persuading Japanese citizens and politicians, hostile to the North as a result of the abductions, of the need for rational strategic thinking, while also expressing his sympathy and political dedication to domestic emotions.

These efforts at persuasion did not bear fruit in the end, however, and Japanese foreign policy-making towards North Korea from 2002 onward would become one of the most prominent examples of governmental design stalling in the face of overwhelming domestic pressure. North Korea, in this regard, significantly facilitated the "popularization" and "democratization" of foreign policy-making in Japanese politics. As Fujiwara Kiichi of the University of Tokyo asserts, the abductions issue was "perhaps the first example in postwar Japan" in which public opinion significantly altered the course of diplomacy, as it surely crippled Koizumi's "major pet project" – diplomatic normalization as "his hallmark achievement."[75] The base of his political power was deeply embedded in domestic popularity, but the emotional nature of the North Korean problem, as understood by the public, and North Korea's insincerity, as demonstrated by the Megumi DNA issue, contributed to limiting Koizumi's policy options by the end of 2004. In addition, the same domestic mechanism gradually would shift the de facto leadership in policy-making towards the North from Koizumi to his subordinate Abe during the sanctions' legislative process.

The passing of the two sanctions bills in 2004, even without their actual implementation, was a significant event. The idea that unilateral economic sanctions could be imposed legitimately on a neighbouring state for failing to respond to Japanese demands was unprecedented in postwar Japan. The legislation, regardless of the actual effect that the sanctions would have on the North Korean regime, demonstrated that Japan would stand firm on its "principles" as a sovereign state when faced with a clear injustice.[76] But most of all the construction of the sanctions legislation was unique for the level of overwhelming public engagement in support of it, in contrast to the typical image of Japanese foreign policy's being formulated by elite bureaucrats insulated from the public.

At the same time, however, the legislation should not be oversimplified as an example of Japan's embracing a new, assertive foreign policy doctrine based on brute force. Considering the extent of the overwhelming public anger that supported the move to legislating sanctions as the abduction issues dragged on, it is interesting that the bills crystallized in the particular form that they took without going even further. The legislation was, despite its significance, designed to ban the movement of capital, goods, and people between the two countries by closing North Korean access to Japan, not by actively blocking North Korea from the outside. Theoretically, in light of the sheer momentum at the time, Japan certainly would have been capable of legislating even more severe forms of pressure – perhaps even bordering on military sanctions such as a naval blockade or demonstrative naval exercises in the vicinity of North Korea – as a matter of "principle" and as long as it was ready to accept the consequences.

The very fact that the legislation was confined to the economic and societal spheres of the domestic realm without stepping into the more controversial area of power projection illustrates the multifaceted nature of the sanctions discourse. Although the idea of unilateral sanctions itself was unprecedented, the limited action the legislation proposed implies that the idea still fell short of a fundamental deviation from the postwar principles that restrained Japan from the use of force as a legitimate form of conducting foreign policy. In short, the sanctions legislation of 2004 symbolized a significant change, but one that was bounded within the continuation of Japan's overall postwar principles and foreign policy norms.

Throughout 2005 Japan continued to pressure North Korea with the threat of economic sanctions. Many in the Diet, the media, and among the public expected North Korea to tremble and eventually to yield merely at the threat of sanctions, without Japan's actually having to implement them. The North, however, did not yield, and in 2006 came another shock.

Denouement: The Second Taepodong Launch and the Imposition of Unilateral Economic Sanctions

On 5 July 2006 North Korea conducted another multistage ballistic missile exercise, the first since the 1998 launch. From the early morning and throughout the day, North Korea launched seven missiles from Musudan-ri towards its eastern seaboard. Six were identified as conventional, short-range antiship missiles, but the third, launched at 4:59 am, was a Taepodong-2,[77] which plunged into the sea off Russia's Maritime Province, a few hundred kilometres from the western seaboard of Hokkaidō.[78]

Although the missile had not flown over Japan, as had the earlier missile in 1998, and the actual threat it had posed was comparatively less provocative and direct, the Japanese government's response was swift: on the same day it announced the imposition of unilateral sanctions on North Korea. The unprecedented speed with which the government reacted later amazed experts who had been used to endless interministerial coordination and buck passing in typical Japanese foreign policy-making. It is now known that all the key figures in the Koizumi cabinet had met – after receiving the latest intelligence report on the North Korean movement – an hour before the first missile was launched, and had already reached a decision on the detailed components of the sanctions by 7:30 am.[79]

The announcement was divided into twelve parts, with the first nine stating how Japan would conduct the sanctions by domestic means and the latter three urging other states and international organizations – the United States, the United Nations Security Council, the participants in the Six Party Talks, and members of the Group of Eight major industrial economies – to cooperate with Japan and participate in pressuring the North.[80] The first nine clauses, besides the obvious verbal condemnation of the launch and of North Korea's development and export of missile technology, also included

- an immediate six-month ban on the entry of the North Korean ferry *Mangyongbong-92* into any Japanese harbour;
- a ban on the entry of North Korean government officials into Japan, along with heightened security and immigration checks for anyone who had travelled to the North;
- the cessation of the issuance of re-entry permits to ethnic Korean residents in Japan who had affiliations with the North (mostly the officials of Chōsen-Sōren) once they had left Japan;
- the cancellation of Japanese government visits to North Korea and a call for citizens to refrain from travelling to the North for personal and business reasons; and
- a ban on North Korean flights making a stop at any Japanese airport.

In addition, one clause expressly indicated that these measures were only the beginning, and that the government was already considering the imposition of stronger measures – a ban on foreign exchange, capital transfers, and trade – depending on the North Korean reaction.[81]

The domestic reception to the first imposition of unilateral sanctions was supportive, as even the Communist and Socialist parties quickly expressed their consent. In fact, while Chief Cabinet Secretary Abe responded to journalists' questions about the actual effectiveness of the measures by saying that "expressing Japan's firm resolution is what counts the most," the head of Rachi-Giren, Hiranuma Takeo, was still criticizing Koizumi's "past lukewarm policies favouring diplomatic normalization" for delaying what should have been realized much earlier.[82]

Also, in a drastic departure from Japan's posture in 1998, when it had to be content with a UN press release that merely raised concerns about the first Taepodong launch, this time the Japanese government took the initiative, as promised in the three latter portions of the July 5 announcement. Japan demanded that the UN Security Council pass a formal resolution condemning the launch as a serious threat to international peace and security and urging members to join the Japanese sanctions, and submitted its own draft resolution on 7 July – the first time Japan had proposed a UN resolution calling for sanctions against a neighbouring state.[83]

Although the Security Council resolution that eventually passed on 15 July did not include a clause requiring UN member states to take part in sanctions as Japan had hoped – most likely because of Chinese and Russian restraints – it nevertheless clearly condemned the North Korean action and encouraged all UN members to refrain from exchanging with the North military technologies related to weapons of mass destruction.[84] Even though the resolution was not as assertive as Japan had demanded, the Japanese government interpreted its passage as having given Japan's sanctions policy international approval, as the North had openly rejected the "will of the international community" – indeed, the North Korean ambassador to the UN left the Security Council meeting in protest in the middle of the proceedings.[85] At least the resolution was more direct and severe than the 1998 press statement, and this time Japan undeniably had taken the most active role throughout the process in persuading the Security Council to pass the resolution.

On 17 July the Japanese government once again requested that all UN member states participate in sanctions against North Korea, and announced that it would soon take additional measures to ban money transfers to the North.[86] Then, on 19 September, the government announced that, to step up the pressure, Japan was imposing measures legally based on the "Amendment of Foreign Exchange and Trade Laws" that had been passed in 2004, which included a ban on sending cash to the North and a freeze on all North Korean assets in Japan. Effective immediately, the financial accounts of fifteen North Korean companies and one individual trading with Japan were frozen.[87] Coincidentally, the LDP's presidential election took place a day later. Abe, who had led the call for the imposition of sanctions from the beginning, won an easy victory, as expected, and replaced Koizumi as the head of the party. The timing of the election made it hard to deny that the North Korean missile launch and Abe's subsequent demonstration of leadership on the sanctions question were the key to his victory.[88]

Considering the swiftness with which Japan imposed the detailed, twelve-point sanctions on the very day of the missile launch, as well as other follow-up measures in subsequent months, the usefulness of the thoroughly prepared policy options that were already at the government's disposal becomes apparent. MOFA indeed admitted to the media that they were part of an already-existing policy "menu" that could be drawn upon immediately when the need arose.[89] The 2006 sanctions were not a spontaneous Japanese reaction to the missile launch itself. Rather, they were the application of already-prepared punitive measures originally thought out for a different issue – the abductions – but with the same target state. As Abe himself admitted, all plausible scenarios for sanctions had already been considered much earlier by a Diet task force (established by his initiative) when the primary national concern was bringing back the abduction victims' children from North Korea (in 2004). The Taepodong-2 launch in 2006 merely made the implementation of sanctions timely and suitable.[90] Abe also pointed out on numerous occasions that Japan's unprecedented initiative at the UN Security Council was natural, as "we are the most threatened party by the North Korean actions and Japan alone is suffering from the big issue called the abductions."[91]

North Korean provocations did not end with the Taepodong-2 launch. On 9 October 2006, a day before the anniversary of the founding of the Korean Worker's Party, North Korea conducted its first underground nuclear test deep in the mountainous region of the central part of the country. Although it was assumed, correctly, that the international reaction in the UN would be much more severe than it had been in July, Japan nevertheless unilaterally raised the level of its already-effective sanctions on 13 October without waiting for a new Security Council resolution. Now the closure of Japanese harbours was extended to all North Korean ships, trade – especially imports from the North such as mushrooms and marine products such as clams – was further restricted, and the freeze on cash flows and assets was increased through the expanded application of the foreign exchange and trade laws. Moreover, immigration control laws were also further applied to prohibit not only the government and Chōsen-Sōren officials but all North Korean passport holders from entering Japan.[92] The restriction on trade would become a full ban by November, and Japan, interestingly, took special care to prohibit the export of twenty-four luxury items, including jewellery, cosmetics, and perfumes, to Pyongyang.[93]

On 14 October, as expected, the UN Security Council passed a new resolution that strongly condemned the North Korean atomic test, and requested – but again did not require – that member states inspect North Korean cargoes in order to prevent the movement of technologies and parts related to weapons of mass destruction.[94] As in July, Japan took the lead in pressuring the North by unilaterally strengthening the sanctions it had already imposed, and by deliberately trying to influence the direction of debates in the UN through the example of its own policy initiatives. In this regard it was clear that the imposition of additional unilateral sanctions in October was not another separate punishment by Japan for the nuclear test per se; rather, it was a direct extension of the policy momentum that had already been initiated in July and which simply had gained a timely extra push.

Chapter Six

Conclusion

Provocations of Japan by North Korea between 1998 and 2006 led to the imposition of unilateral economic sanctions on the North by Japan in 2006. Key elements in Japan's changing relations with North Korea over this period were the evolution of the Japanese public's discursive orientation towards the North and the interaction between Japan's societal sphere and the Japanese government. In this concluding chapter, I review the North Korean provocations that led to sanctions; the Japanese domestic reaction to those incidents, which facilitated changes in the broader societal discourse among both the general public and the mass media and a re-evaluation of Japan's traditional security policies and its "apologetic" and "reconciliatory" stance towards its neighbours; and the structural changes that took place within the Japanese government, especially the coming of Koizumi Junichirō, that resulted in the greater sensitivity of political decision-making and foreign policy to changing societal moods. Finally, I present some thoughts on the likely future of relations between Japan and North Korea.

The Origin and the Nature of the Sanctions

Repeated North Korean provocations between 1998 and 2006 stirred Japanese security consciousness. These provocations came in the form of multiple *fushinsen* (mystery/spy ship) incidents, the bizarre entry of Kim Jong Il's son, Kim Jong Nam, into Japan, and, most of all, the official admission by North Korea during the 2002 summit between Koizumi and Kim Jong Il of the North's abductions of Japanese citizens. These provocations were unlike other international-level incidents in the post–Cold War period. Other events – such as the First Gulf War – had given Japanese policy-makers a wakeup call to re-evaluate Japan's security principles, but had largely failed to invite the public's committed and consistent participation in that re-evaluation. Unlike any distant war or act of terrorism, however, the threats from North Korea – in particular as they affected Japan's maritime and territorial sovereignty and the safety and security of Japanese citizens, as demonstrated by the abductions issue – caused Japanese to take an unprecedented hard look at their country's security policy, especially towards neighbours.

During the period from 1998 to 2006, the Japanese public thus rethought Japan's traditional, postwar self-limitation on the use of the "sovereign right of the nation" against its neighbours, which was a direct extensions of the Peace Constitution and Japan's postwar pacifist and antimilitaristic tendency to resolve international (and especially regional) disputes diplomatically, without relying on forceful, punitive measures. Indeed, North Korea's actions demonstrated to the Japanese public that this self-limitation was anachronistic in its original, dogmatic form. Although such an argument was nothing new – nationalist politicians and others belonging to the "rightist" camp had long been advocates of this position – the highly illustrative and proximate nature of the "North Korea factor" gave this line of thought more domestic legitimacy from 1998 on. As the public became increasingly convinced that Japan's timid diplomatic stance was at the core of its inability to prevent North Korea's abuse of its postwar security institutions, actual examples of North Korean breaches of Japanese sovereignty and the abductions of Japanese citizens gave strength to public discourse that favoured the use of national power to prevent and punish such actions.

The public discourse also facilitated a subtle shift in the way many ordinary Japanese embraced the mainstream historical narration of Japan's relations with its neighbours in the prewar era, which, in turn, had also influenced Japan's postwar regional diplomacy. In contrast to the equally subtle but prevalent understanding ingrained in the postwar Japanese societal disposition, wherein there was always a grain of a "victim mentality" concerning the country's prewar relations with the United States and other Western powers, Japan as a whole had largely accepted and officially admitted its role as the "aggressor" in regional history.[1] In conjunction with the increasing might of China and criticisms by Japan's neighbours concerning other historical issues, the North Korean provocations facilitated a surge in the "victim mentality" among substantial portions of the Japanese public, who now applied it to Japan's relations with its neighbours, especially North Korea.

Therefore, the domestic environment from 1998 onward – and especially after 2002, when the abductions were disclosed – made it easier to scrutinize Japan's official historical narrative in which it had been the past aggressor.

In addition, the Japanese mass media played a crucial role at the societal level. Contrary to those who suggest that they always portray things the way the government wishes, the mass media have been largely pluralistic throughout the postwar period, and have informed Japanese citizens of all aspects of domestic and international phenomena from diverse perspectives. However, although the media have enjoyed significant societal prestige and influence as reliable sources of information on political and diplomatic issues, they have also been highly susceptible to the influence of domestic discursive currents. Such currents have served as indicators of how to frame and present coverage on issues of high interest – including publicized foreign policy matters – to viewers and readers.

Naturally, such a media environment reinforced ongoing trends in the societal discourse concerning North Korea from 1998 on, by providing a public stage on which societal anger towards the North could gain focus and momentum. In turn, Japanese media outlets realized how the mainstream public viewed North Korea, and they promptly went with the domestic "current," although whether this was voluntary or reluctant depended on a media corporation's traditional stance towards North Korea and its position within the left-right domestic political cleavage. This media trend to jump on the bandwagon was at its peak from 2002 onward, as the abductions issue started to replace all other previous North Korea issues in the public's mind. Between 2002 and 2006 the media mostly performed the role of confirming the already-prevalent societal discourse that advocated pressure on North Korea, as by then all previous North Korea–related threats and provocations were incorporated into a single, mutually reinforcing "package" around the abductions issue.

The nature of the Japanese government while societal discourse on North Korea unfolded must be analysed in the same context. The Liberal Democratic Party (LDP) regained the prime ministership after the political turmoil of the immediate aftermath of the post–Cold War period had briefly shifted political leadership into the hands of other parties. The LDP's recovery was initially realized in the form of a coalition with the New Komeito Party and the New Conservative Party, but within that coalition, the dominant status of the LDP was undisputed.

As this new political balance took hold, the emergence of Koizumi as prime minister in 2001 further facilitated an environment in which the LDP cabinet could formulate foreign policy with relative freedom from the pressures of other coalition allies and traditional LDP factional considerations. Koizumi won his position by his populist tendency to reach out directly to ordinary citizens through his adeptness at using the mass media, and his image as a new type of politician – one bold enough to make political decisions on his own initiative – was widely supported by the constituency and the new generation of Diet members.

Koizumi's rise and the nature of his political power led to a style of decision-making that put more powerful policy initiatives in the hands of the prime minister at the cost of bureaucratic and LDP factional considerations. Since Koizumi's power base strongly depended upon public support, the nature of his prime ministership gave popular preferences and societal atmosphere a significant influence on the government's decision-making process in both domestic and foreign policy areas. Understandably, this structural political change had crucial implications for how the government's policies towards North Korea would unfold. Koizumi's bold initiative to be the first prime minister while in office to meet Kim Jong Il and his agreeing with Kim on the 2002 Pyongyang Declaration exemplified his political risk taking. Despite his personal willingness to normalize bilateral relations with the North and the public's initial support of his courageous attempt, societal anger raised by the disclosure of the abductions subsequently forced him to abandon the agreed-upon framework of the Pyongyang Declaration.

Developments at the international, societal, and political levels between 1998 and 2006 thus mutually reinforced one another. At the international level, accumulating North Korean provocations visibly convinced the public of the image of North Korea as the most direct threat to Japanese security. At the societal level, the resulting public shock and re-evaluation of Japan's traditional foreign policy posture led to a hardened domestic discourse towards North Korea, further facilitated by the media's jumping on board with respect to public opinion. And at the political level, a concurrent, structural power shift made public preferences more influential in foreign policy decision-making, and rising populist politicians – including, of course, Koizumi – were pressured to incorporate changing security discourse into their subsequent North Korea policies. Given this context, it is unlikely that the imposition of unilateral economic sanctions in 2006, immediately following the second Taepodong missile launch, would have been realized in the form they took in the absence of the particular interactions of these three levels.

Rather than a rationally calculated and long-term national strategy, the sanctions were the unintended consequence of domestic societal factors that grew out of eight years of various provocations by the North and that compelled the Koizumi government to change the trajectory of its planned approach to North Korea. Government policy experts alone never dominated the process through which sanctions were proposed in 2002–03, legislated in 2004, and implemented in 2006. Rather, it could be argued, the extent of the interaction among the public, the media, and the government is perhaps the most vivid example of Japanese foreign policy's being influenced by non-governmental societal discourse in postwar Japan.

The Future of Japanese–North Korean Relations

Kim Jong Il died in December 2011, but the North Korean regime continues under his son, Kim Jong Un, and the potential for a resolution of the abductions issue and other North Korea–related security issues that bar the normalization of bilateral relations remains uncertain. The Japanese government has been appointing *Rachi-mondai Tantō-shō* (ministers of the abductions issue) to handle the case specifically at the ministerial level, but without effect on the North. Japanese sanctions against North Korea have been in place for more than eight years, but they have failed to produce the results envisioned by the original policy-makers, who expected the North either to collapse or to yield to Japanese economic might. Even if the Kim regime were to collapse in the future, it surely would not be because of the sanctions, even though their supporters in Japan argue otherwise.

Admittedly, the attitude of Japanese society currently seems calmer towards the North than during the saturated media coverage of the abductions issue that occurred between 2002 and 2006, most likely because the public's threat perception has largely shifted to China in recent years. Abductions fever, although still alive, has lost some of the momentum it once had. Although the security and historical discourses facilitated by the abductions issue are still strongly valid, the public also seems somewhat fed up with sensational daily media coverage of the issue itself, which has partially lost its exciting "entertainment value."[2]

This does not mean, however, that the Japanese and North Korean governments, even if they wanted to, are free to pursue diplomatic normalization or another bilateral agreement similar to the Pyongyang Declaration without worrying about domestic repercussions in Japan. Even if the absolute amount of media coverage of North Korea has decreased, the negative image of the North among the public is still closely tied to the stalemate on the abductions issue, and the Japanese government, no matter which party is in power, cannot take unnecessary political risks unless there is a major breakthrough. Therefore, all cabinets since 2002 have had to refrain from "budging from a principled stance" in accordance with the still-pervasive societal atmosphere.[3] Experts have long realized that this "*kokunai shohiyō no taigai seisaku* (foreign policy principle for domestic consumption)" is maintained in the absence of a realistic analysis of the situation and has already proven to be ineffective.[4] Yet, since April 2007, Japan has continued to renew sanctions every six months despite their dubious effect, in a frustrating attempt to resolve the abductions issue above others.[5]

The Japanese definition of what exactly would constitute a "resolution" has also prevented a major breakthrough in the abductions issue. Ever since the issue came to dominate domestic discourse on North Korea, the Japanese government, the abductions-related interest groups Sukuu-kai and Kazoku-kai, and the media have agreed that the absolute minimum requirement the North would have to meet to put bilateral negotiations back on track would be Pyongyang's acceptance of a transparent reinvestigation that allowed Japanese officials access to locations, documents, and persons related to the issue.

What is problematic is that such a reinvestigation is largely regarded in Japan, at least officially, as an initial step towards bringing *all* abductees and families back to Japan alive, meaning those already repatriated plus those the North claims are deceased. In the midst of surging societal anger after the disclosure of the abductions, and especially after the release of DNA results related to the Yokota Megumi case in 2004, the government, under pressure from interest groups and the public, subsequently had to formulate policies based on the societal assumption that North Korea was hiding the real fate of the victims, and that those who were supposedly dead were likely to be still alive. Although it is highly unlikely that many policy-makers privately share this supposition, societal discourse in Japan still largely adheres to it, and the government, at least officially, has had to incorporate it in dealing with the issue. Therefore, even if North Korea were to launch a transparent and sincere reinvestigation, the Japanese public might not believe the result even if it turned out that victims not yet repatriated to Japan had indeed died.[6]

In this regard, in May 2014, Japan and North Korea agreed that the latter would set up a "special investigation committee" to reinvestingate the abductions issue, and the former, in turn, would start lifting parts of the ongoing sanctions in gradual stages, depending on the sincerity and the contents of the initial report presented by the committee.[7] But this latest reinvestigation is already proving to be a bumpy process: the two parties met again in July 2014 to work out the details,[8] but in September the North announced it would delay the first report, which originally had been scheduled to be presented to Japan in late summer or early autumn. Chief Cabinet Secretary Suga Yoshihide added that, based on North Korea's behaviour so far, the initial probe for the abductees might even take another full year;[9] nonetheless the Japanese government pledged in January 2015 to continue to push Pyongyang to report its findings as soon as possible.[10] As of this writing (July 2015), no such report has surfaced.

Moreover, uncertainty around the exact number of persons actually abducted further complicates the resolution of the issue. Although the Japanese government initially recognized twelve as the official figure, it has also admitted that there could be more. The government maintains a list of so-called *tokutei shissōsha* (special missing persons), prepared in conjunction with Sukuu-kai, but the list is flexible, and neither the government, nor Sukuu-kai, nor Kazoku-kai has been able to establish the exact number of those who might have ended up in North Korea.[11] In September 2014, the National Police Agency added another 23, bringing the figure to 883.[12]

As long as the resolution is officially understood in the Japanese domestic context as the rescue of *all* abductees – including those allegedly deceased but presumed alive, as well as the highly flexible number of "special missing persons" – it is unlikely that the issue will ever be resolved in the form that Japan has demanded. As in the previous decade, however, the Japanese government is constrained in its policy flexibility, and it has to maintain its official position while facing still-unpredictable public reaction. As far as Japan's relations with North Korea are concerned, the utmost priority has never changed in the public's mind. For better or worse, this consistent societal force will continue to frame Japan's interactions with the North. An October 2014 Cabinet Office survey of three thousand adults showed that, when asked to rank which issue associated with Japanese–North Korean relations they were most concerned about, 88.3 per cent of respondents chose the abductions issue, followed by the missile threat (55.6 per cent), the nuclear issue (54.0 per cent), and North Korea's political system (37.3 per cent). Only 24.1 per cent were interested in the possibility of bilateral diplomatic normalization.[13]

Furuya Keiji, the current minister in charge of the abductions issue, has said that his government is still determined to bring "all of the abductees" back to Japan. When asked how realistic it would be to expect the North to explain the whereabouts of more than eight hundred missing Japanese, he said that "the ball is in [the North's] court." Speaking on condition of anonymity, another senior government official close to Prime Minister Abe Shinzō added that the key to the resolution of the abductions issue is still "public reaction," saying, "it all depends on whether the public is satisfied with Pyongyang's explanation or not."[14] Abe himself, now in his second term as prime minister, also publicly reaffirmed in September 2014 that resolving the abductions issue is a top priority for his administration.[15]

Some experts of Korean affairs in Japan have voiced the opinion that Japan must formulate a more achievable goal and approach the North with more realistic policy guidelines if the deadlock between the two countries is to be overcome.[16] Although this argument seems to be gaining more support in the policy sphere, it would still be like opening Pandora's Box for politicians to suggest openly the need for a more realistic diplomatic target that incorporated the possibility of some abductees' deaths, as nobody can predict the likely reaction of the Japanese public to such an approach.

Even if the Japanese government were somehow to reach internal consensus on a more negotiable diplomatic target, it would have to make a strategic choice as to how to balance other North Korea–related issues against the abductions issue in bilateral negotiations, and there seems to be no concrete agreement in this regard. Since Japan is currently imposing sanctions for both bilateral (the abductions) and multilateral (ballistic missiles and the nuclear program) threats posed by North Korea, even though the pressure for sanctions undoubtedly was first envisioned to persuade the North to resolve the former, some Japanese experts claim that Japan is bound to be further frustrated if it continues to chase two hares of a different nature – the bilateral and the multilateral issues – at the same time by giving equal priority to both. Since the bilateral portion at least has the possibility of progress through future direct negotiations between Japan and North Korea, and since the abductions issue still constitutes the foremost priority in the minds of Japanese citizens where the North is concerned, separating bilateral and multilateral issues and focusing on a breakthrough in the former, these experts argue, would be a more prudent and realistic approach for Japan.[17]

The opposing camp asserts that both bilateral and multilateral North Korean issues have been multifaceted from the very beginning, and thus cannot be separated. North Korea is not only dealing with Japan, and it is naive to assume that progress in one area would lead to an equal breakthrough in the other, since the North, more than any other related party, has preferred to seek a "comprehensive resolution" involving all concerned states, especially the United States. From this perspective, the problem is not that Japan is chasing two hares of a different nature – indeed, chasing both is the correct approach – but that Japan has concentrated too much on one at the expense of the other instead of giving equal attention to both. According to this position, what Japan needs, especially for the resolution of the abductions issue, is to go back to the strategy that Koizumi envisioned when he agreed to the Pyongyang Declaration. This would involve seeking agreement on all bilateral and multilateral security concerns in one comprehensive package deal, as well as promoting regional and international participation in the process. Paradoxically, only by reframing the abductions issue as part of this broader framework, as was originally intended during the Koizumi–Kim summit in 2002, and only by giving equal consideration to all North Korean threats would it be possible for Japan to expect headway on the abductions.[18]

No one can foretell with certainty how bilateral interactions will unfold in the near future, as any development related either to the abductions or to other North Korea–linked issues is certain to produce unexpected repercussions for the nature and the direction of the current deadlock between the two countries. One fact, however, is currently valid, and is likely to remain so in the near future: Japanese policies towards North Korea will continue to be linked strongly to the resolution of the abductions issue – however Japan defines "resolution" – even though North Korea continues to pose a serious military threat to the region with its ever-expanding missile and nuclear capabilities. Under the current circumstances, the full realization of diplomatic normalization between the two countries likely will require a substantial amount of time, as Japanese diplomacy towards the North is one foreign policy area where the Japanese public retains its undeniable position as the main participant. Any development involving North Korea surely will remind the Japanese public of the anger that overwhelmed society between 2002 and 2006, and thus any real, long-term progress on relations with the North will not be feasible without Japanese societal consent.

Implications for the Debate on Revising the Constitution

The rise of the abductions issue in Japanese domestic politics has had repercussions beyond the sanctions debate. Indeed, the issue has secured the central position in Japanese citizens' understanding of Japanese–North Korean relations. The abductions have also had an indirect – but nevertheless profound – impact on other domestic political debates, particularly on revising the Constitution.

Relations between Japan and South Korea have also been affected by the abductions issue. Policy and societal changes taking place in Japan during the height of the abductions fervor caused the South Korean government and public to become increasingly suspicious that Japan was using the issue's momentum to legitimize a "hidden agenda." In particular, Japan was suspected of seeking to discard its postwar pacifist foreign policy principles by deliberately stirring and magnifying its victim mentality in order to flex its muscles at its neighbours once again. This South Korean suspicion was answered by Japanese suspicion of South Korea, as the Japanese government and public felt that South Korea, immersed in its "Sunshine Policy" in dealing with North Korea, was being too lenient towards the North and overly "pan-Korean nationalistic." The Japanese government and public were thus disappointed when South Korea did not readily agree to form a unified front against the North on what the Japanese public saw as a grave humanitarian crisis in East Asia.[19]

The most vivid repercussions of the abductions issue, however, have been its indirect impact on the national security discourse and the controversy surrounding revising the Japanese Constitution. The debate about constitutional revision has a long histrory, but the North Korea–related issues of the late 1990s and early 2000s had the powerful effect of bringing the constitutional debate to the fore of public attention, as the North Korea factor was used by "rightists" to propagate dissatisfaction with Japan's postwar security institutions in general. The issue was particularly made use of during the peak of the abductions issue fervor, when it was claimed that the Constitution, especially

Article 9, the "Peace" clause, which forced Japan to be overly "pacifist" and "antimilitarist," was the true villain behind the incident.[20] Indeed, some family members of the abduction victims belonging to Kazokukai were deliberately called on by constitutional revisionists and asked to make speeches denouncing Article 9 as the main hindrance to the resolution of the abductions issue.[21] In February 2004 former prime minister Nakasone Yasuhiro[22] claimed that, unlike in the 1980s, when LDP cabinets could not even schedule an official meeting to discuss constitutional amendment openly, the time had now ripened to discuss the possibility as a legitimate political agenda item.[23]

Rightists were not alone in linking constitutional revision to the North Korean threat. Opinion polls during the period, especially from 2003, show that a slight majority favoured revision, which the media widely interpreted as an example of Japanese citizens' increased embrace of "realism."[24] Even scholars of "leftist" inclination – who are opposed to amending the Constitution – came to accept the domestic reality that more Japanese citizens now desired that something be done about the gap between the security reality and the idealistic principles – what Sakamoto Yoshikazu has called the "prescribed standard" – upheld in the current Constitution.[25]

Nonetheless, during the early to mid-2000s, the increased support for constitutional revision was largely led by rightists who used the public's anxiety over North Korea and general national security vulnerability to beat the drum for their long-held dissatisfaction with the Constitution – especially Article 9.[26] The rightists' advocacy of revision has been a powerful factor in contemporary Japanese society ever since, and they indeed have had success in mobilizing broader societal support for their aims. Considering that the regional repercussions of Japanese constitutional change along rightist lines would not be confined solely to Japan's stance towards North Korea, it is natural that the international community should be wary about the spread of the rightists' ideas in Japan – concerns that Japan's neighbours should communicate clearly to the Japanese public.

Many of the rightists' claims about the alleged negative effects of the current Constitution are based on extreme and emotionally charged reactions to external factors and the denial of Japan's numerous positive postwar achievements – what Soeya Yoshihide calls "*gyaku-funsha kaiken-ron* (reverse-thrust constitutional amendment debates)." A far healthier approach to a movement led by rightists would be wide citizen participation in an open debate about constitutional revision that included fair consideration of Japan's postwar achievements under its current institutions, as well as a realistic assessment of Japan's national security in a changing external environment.[27] Therefore, much like the Japanese public's posture during the process leading up to the unilateral sanctions legislation, increasing societal support for constitutional revision should not be interpreted simply as Japanese citizens' agreeing wholly with, or taking at face value, the ideological claims of the rightists. Many who support constitutional revision do so because they believe that the supreme law of the nation should reflect the "modern sensibility" of people in the twenty-first century.[28]

At the time of this writing, the administration of Prime Minister Abe – who is widely regarded to be one of the most prominent rightists by many in and out of Japan – continues to advocate for revision. In July 2014 his cabinet announced a new interpretation of the Constitution that would allow the Self-Defense Forces (SDF) to conduct activities related to "collective self-defence," an issue that is highly controversial as it is linked directly to the debate surrounding Article 9. Abe, however, has long considered it necessary in order to implement Japan's current national strategy of a "proactive contribution to peace."[29] Yet, despite Japanese society's increasing willingness to be pragmatic in evaluating Japan's security environment, and despite its more accepting attitude with regard to constitutional revision, opinion polls conducted before and after the July 2014 announcement show that there is no guarantee that the public will blindly support Abe's conservative government in bringing about fundamental changes to Japan's postwar security orientation. For example, a nationwide survey conducted by *Kyodo News* in January 2014 after Abe first officially announced his intention to review the country's self-restrictions on collective self-defence showed that 53.8 per cent of respondents were opposed to the move while 37.1 per cent favoured it.[30] A Nikkei poll taken right after the July cabinet announcement still showed that 50 per cent opposed the new interpretation while 34 per cent supported it, reflecting the ongoing debate about Japan's postwar political identity and uncertainty about the Abe administration's long-term security objectives.[31] These results are highly indicative of the complex societal discourse continuing in Japan today; even though a substantial number of citizens might favour constitutional revision, they are still uncomfortable with the notion that security principles might be altered in haste or without sufficient domestic discussions, when they could potentially have far-reaching consequences.

The remaining time of the current Constitution, therefore, is not concrete. As of 2015 the Abe administration and the ruling LDP have proposed three additional points to be included in any revision: an "emergency situation" clause that potentially could limit individual rights during large-scale disasters or security-linked emergencies; a "fiscal discipline" clause to prevent a national financial burden from being passed on to future generations; and an "environmental rights" clause that would highlight the clear responsibilities of the government and the people for environmental protection.[32] With the exception of the "emergency situation" clause, the proposals are non-security in nature and in line with the general societal preference for updating the Constitution to better reflect the needs of the twenty-first century. The security-linked Article 9, however, will certainly be the point of greatest contention in any revision debate.

In February 2015 Prime Minister Abe announced his desire to start the process of constitutional revision as soon as the summer of 2016, since an LDP victory in the scheduled upper house election in 2016 could grant him the two-thirds majority in both houses of the Diet that would be required to approve his move to hold a public referendum on the revision. Relatedly, immediately after the news of the deaths of two Japanese hostages at the hands of the Islamic State shocked the nation, Abe stated again in the Diet that Japan should amend Article 9 and ease the legal restrictions on Japan's military in order to allow the SDF to engage in "police actions overseas" to free hostages and protect Japanese citizens.[33]

Although Abe used the abductions issue in the previous decade to lead the Japanese public to re-evaluate the country's posture towards North Korea and push for the first Japanese unilateral sanctions, it is unlikely that the shock of the horrifying executions of Japanese citizens by a terrorist organization would be equally sufficient to sustain societal momentum for a revision of Japan's security stance. Both incidents have "human face" elements, but the different number of victims involved, the difference in the geographic proximity of the two incidents, the voluntary nature of the latest victims' departure from Japan, and, most of all, the public's awareness of – and familiarity with – Abe's adeptness at opportunistically linking timely occurrences to his key agenda all make it less than certain that the majority of Japanese citizens will find his February 2015 statement a convincing argument.

At the end of the day, concerning national security, Japanese widely believe that even those who favour amending the Constitution would prefer that it clearly state that the legitimate existence and activity of the SDF falls under a clause concurrently emphasizing Japan's ongoing commitment to "pacifism."[34] One can surmise, however, that "pacifism" here no longer connotes the dogmatically antimilitaristic use of the term as it was first incorporated into the Constitution after the Second World War; rather, the new definition of pacifism reflects the influence of a more realistic assessment of national security among the majority of the public, much as we saw in the sanctions debate. It must also be noted, however, that more Japanese have come to embrace "active" or "proactive" pacifism because the public increasingly supports the notion that clearly stating the legitimate status and mission of the SDF in a revised Constitution would be more effective in ensuring democratic control of the military and in better enabling Japan to contribute openly to peace-building activities abroad without inviting misconceptions from overseas.[35]

In this regard, although one can never be certain how it will ultimately play out, the current speed and determination with which the Abe administration is pushing for constitutional revision – while making justificatory discursive links to various ongoing national and human security challenges – certainly does not ensure unanimous public support. Such support would be especially uncertain if Japanese society were to feel that the government was not sufficiently addressing, through domestic debate, the various rationales of those who wish to revise the Constitution and the diversity of their visions for the future of post-revision Japan. At this point, therefore, outside observers should recognize that the often-overlooked citizen-led public discourse on constitution revision – "*goken-teki kaiken-ron* (constitutional amendment debate upholding the principles of the current Constitution)"[36] – must be separated from their understanding of the discourse led by rightists. Even if, on the surface, they both seem to pursue the same goal, in reality they differ in their vision of what a new Constitution should look like.

Notes

1. Introduction

1 Throughout the main text, the names of East Asians will be provided in the local "last name first" fashion, but endnotes and bibliographic entries will adhere to the standard North American style.

2 *Asahi Shimbun*, 1 September 1998, 1.

3 Editorial, *Asahi Shimbun*, 18 September 1998, 5.

4 Japan, Ministry of Foreign Affairs, *Bluebook 1999*, online edition (Japanese version), part 1, chap. 1, section 2(2). Tokyo. Available online at http://www.mofa.go.jp/mofaj/gaiko/bluebook/99/1st/index.html.

5 Narushige Michishita, "Kitachōsen no Misairu Gaikō to Kakkoku no Taiō [North Korea's missile diplomacy and each state's responses]," in *Kiki no Chōsen Hantō: Gendai Higashi Ajia to Nihon* [Korean Peninsula in crisis: Contemporary East Asia and Japan], ed. Masao Okonogi (Tokyo: Keio University Press, 2006), 78–9; Editorial, *Asahi Shimbun*, 4 December 1999, 5; Editorial, *Yomiuri Shimbun*, 15 December 1999, 3; Editorial, *Asahi Shimbun*, 8 March 2000, 5; Editorial, *Yomiuri Shimbun*, 7 October 2000, 3.

6 *Asahi Shimbun*, 5 July 2006, 1–2; *Yomiuri Shimbun*, 6 July 2006, 1–2.

7 *Asahi Shimbun*, 5 July 2006, 1–2; *Yomiuri Shimbun*, 6 July 2006, 1–2; *Asahi Shimbun*, 6 July 2006, 1; *Asahi Shimbun*, 17 July 2006, 1; Japan, Ministry of Foreign Affairs, *Bluebook 2007*, online edition (Japanese version), chap. 2 (1). Tokyo. Available online at http://www.mofa.go.jp/mofaj/gaiko/bluebook/2007/pdf/pdfs/2_1.pdf.

8 *Asahi Shimbun*, 17 July 2006, 1; *Yomiuri Shimbun*, 17 July 2006, 3; Editorial, *Yomiuri Shimbun*, 24 July 2006, 3; *Asahi Shimbun*, 19 September 2006, 1; Editorial, *Yomiuri Shimbun*, 20 September 2006, 3; Editorial, *Yomiuri Shimbun*, 13 October 2006, 3.

9 *Yomiuri Shimbun*, 7 July 2006, 3; *Asahi Shimbun*, 17 July 2006, 1.

10 Takehiko Yamamoto, "Structural and Functional Vulnerabilities in Multilateral Export Control Regimes: A Japanese Perspective" (paper presented at the 2nd International Symposium of the Japan Atomic Industrial Forum, "How to Harmonize Peaceful Uses of Nuclear Energy and Non-Proliferation? Considering the Future of Nuclear Energy Development from Asia," Tokyo, March 2001); Kazuya Sakamoto, "Dokuritsukoku no Jōken [The conditions of an independent state: Japanese diplomacy in the 1950s]," in *Sengo Nihon Gaikōshi* [History of postwar Japanese diplomacy], ed. Makoto Iokibe (Tokyo: Yuhikaku ARMA, 1999), 93–4.

11 Hiroshi Nakanishi, "Jiritsuteki Kyōchō no Mosaku [Exploring the idea of 'independent cooperation': Japanese diplomacy in the 1970s]," in Iokibe, *Sengo Nihon Gaikōshi*, 180–1.

12 Kōji Murata, "Kokusai-Kokka no Shimei to Kunō [The mission and trials of the emerging international state: Japanese diplomacy in the 1980s]," in Iokibe, *Sengo Nihon Gaikōshi*, 221.

13 In Japanese academia, the term *disukōsu* is often used, in case a distinction between the two is required.

14 The most widely used definitions of "public opinion" in North America are: (1) an aggregation of individual opinions that can be obtained by polls of randomly selected samples; (2) a reflection of the majority beliefs and values of citizens and the equivalent of "social norms"; (3) individual opinions that are cultivated, crystallized, and eventually communicated by interest groups such as political parties, trade organizations, corporations, activist groups, and so on; (4) a simple projection of what journalists, politicians, pollsters, and other "elites" believe; and (5) a mere fiction, "phantom," and rhetorical construction only used by newspapers and television. See Carroll J. Glynn et al., *Public Opinion*, 2nd ed. (Boulder, CO: Westview Press, 2004), 19–32.

15 Ikuo Kabashima, Toshio Takeshita, and Yoichi Serikawa, *Media to Seiji* [Media and politics] (Tokyo: Yūhikaku ARMA, 2007), 116–17.

16 *Yomiuri Shimbunsha* Yoron Chōsashitsu, *Nihonjin no Iken 150* [150 opinions of the Japanese] (Tokyo: Chiseidō, 1982); cited in Masao Matsumoto, *Yoron (Seron) Chōsa no Yukue* [The future course of public opinion polling] (Tokyo: Chūōkōron Shinsha, 2003), 170.

17 Open Source Center Media Aid, "Japan – Media Environment Open; State Looms Large," 18 August 2009; available online at http://www.fas.org/irp/dni/osc/japan-media.pdf.

18 Asahi Shimbunsha Yoron Chōsashitsu, *Nihonjin no Seiji Ishiki: Asahi Shimbun Yoron Chōsa no 30 nen* [Political attitude of the Japanese:

Thirty years of *Asahi Shimbun*'s public opinion polling] (Tokyo: Asahi Shimbunsha, 1976). Cited in Matsumoto, *Yoron (Seron) Chōsa no Yukue*, 170.

19 *Iken no kazamuki* can be literally translated as "the wind-direction of opinion," and *kūki* as "air" or "atmosphere" (Kabashima, Takeshita, and Serikawa, *Media to Seiji*, 134–5). One of the most widely read works on the topic of *kūki* in Japanese society is Shichihei Yamamoto, *Kūki no Kenkyu* [Study of kūki] (Tokyo: Bungeishunjū, 1983).

20 Kabashima, Takeshita, and Serikawa, *Media to Seiji*, 35–7. One of the studies includes a survey conducted by Ikuo Kabashima in 1990. The questionnaires were answered by the leaders of the Liberal Democratic Party, opposition parties, major corporations, agricultural interest groups, labour unions, and civil movements. Bureaucrats and other social intellectuals also took part in the survey. See also Susan J. Pharr, "Media as Trickster in Japan: A Comparative Perspective," in *Media and Politics in Japan*, ed. Susan J. Pharr and Ellis S. Krauss (Honolulu: University of Hawai'i Press, 1996), 19.

21 Kabashima, Takeshita, and Serikawa, *Media to Seiji*, 39, 49–50.

22 Christopher W. Hughes, *Japan's Re-emergence as a "Normal" Military Power* (New York: Routledge, 2006), 59.

23 Masayuki Tadokoro, "Change and Continuity in Japan's 'Abnormality': An Emerging External Attitude of the Japanese Public," in *Japan as a "Normal Country"? A Nation in Search of Its Place in the World*, ed. Yoshihide Soeya, Masayuki Tadokoro, and David A. Welch (Toronto: University of Toronto Press, 2011), 68.

24 Kabashima, Takeshita, and Serikawa, *Media to Seiji*, 119.

25 John Creighton Campbell, "Media and Policy Change in Japan," in Pharr and Krauss, *Media and Politics in Japan*, 187.

26 Kabashima, Takeshita, and Serikawa, *Media to Seiji*.

27 Joji Watanuki, *Politics in Postwar Japanese Society* (Tokyo: University of Tokyo Press, 1977), 105.

28 See note 19 on the use of the term *kūki*.

29 Kabashima, Takeshita, and Serikawa, *Media to Seiji*, 131–3.

30 See, for example, Kaori Hayashi, "Masumedia Jānarizumu wo Shihai suru 'Saidai Tasū no Saidai Kōfuku' no Saidai Fukō [The absolute tragedy of the 'absolute happiness to absolute majority' principle governing mass media journalism]," *Ronza* (July 2008): 26–31.

31 Ellis S. Krauss, "The Mass Media and Japanese Politics: Effects and Consequences," in Pharr and Krauss, *Media and Politics in Japan*, 369.

32 Hideo Ōtake, *Nihon-gata Popyurizumu – Seiji e no Kitai to Genmetsu* [Japan-style populism: Hope and disillusionment towards politics] (Tokyo: Chūōkōron Shinsha, 2003), 237.

33 Ibid. *Yokonarabi taishitsu* literally means a "tendency to stand in a single horizontal line."

34 Kabashima, Takeshita, and Serikawa, *Media to Seiji*, 131–3. The "spiral of silence" metaphor will be dealt with in more detail in Chapter 4.

35 Tomohito Shinoda, *Koizumi Diplomacy: Japan's Kantei Approach to Foreign and Defense Affairs* (Seattle: University of Washington Press, 2007), 15.

36 Tomohito Shinoda, "Becoming More Realistic in the Post–Cold War: Japan's Changing Media and Public Opinion on National Security," *Japanese Journal of Political Science* 8 (2007): 175.

37 Linus Hagström and Jon Williamsson, "'Remilitarization,' Really? Assessing Change in Japanese Foreign Security Policy," *Asian Security* 5, no. 3 (2009): 249.

38 Ibid.

39 Kabashima, Takeshita, and Serikawa, *Media to Seiji*, 185–7.

40 Yoshibumi Wakamiya, former chairman, Editorial Board, *Asahi Shimbun*, columnist, *Asahi Shimbun*, and Guest Professor, University of Tokyo, interview with the author, 17 December 2009.

41 Kabashima, Takeshita, and Serikawa, *Media to Seiji*.

42 Matsumoto, *Yoron (Seron) Chōsa no Yukue*, 13–14, 130.

43 Michishita, "Kitachōsen no Misairu Gaikō to Kakkoku no Taiō," 87.

44 Ibid., 87–90.

45 Ibid., 87–8.

46 Hajime Izumi, "Dealing with North Korea: Time for Japan to Reengage," *Japan Echo* (February 2008), 39.

47 Editorial, *Yomiuri Shimbun*, 15 February 2005, 3.

48 The "West" here denotes English-speaking academia in North America and some parts of Europe, where analyses of Japanese politics and foreign policy are based mainly on the application of the major theoretical traditions of international relations. Although most English-language literature on this topic is published in North America and the United Kingdom, there has been a noticeable increase in the number of relevant publications from other European institutions since the 1990s. There are also many Japanese and other Asian scholars researching within this theoretical academic tradition. In this book, all these sources are categorized as "Western."

49 The Yoshida Doctrine, formulated in the immediate post–Second World War period by then Prime Minister Yoshida Shigeru, helped Japan to concentrate on the task of national rebuilding by seeking economic, political, and security guarantees from its new ally, the United States. By integrating its security with that of the United States and relying on US protection

with a minimum commitment to military expenditures of its own, Japan could focus its national energy on joining the capitalist Western bloc with its export-based economy during the Cold War, with the sponsorship of the United States. See Glenn D. Hook et al., eds., *Japan's International Relations, Politics, Economics, and Security*, 2nd. ed. (London; New York: Routledge, 2006), 32, 34. Another "national principle" of the postwar period is Japan's well-known Peace Constitution. The Constitution has been, and still is, the main symbol of Japan's transformation from a militaristic state into a pacifist, antimilitaristic democracy. Article 9, the so-called Peace Clause, is especially well publicized. It states: "the Japanese people forever renounce war as a sovereign right of the nation and the threat or use of force as a means of settling international disputes." Furthermore, "the right of belligerency of the state" is not recognized in the Constitution, as it bans Japan from maintaining land, sea, and air forces, as well as other war potential (Hook et al., *Japan's International Relations*, 558–9).

50 Kenneth B. Pyle, *Japan Rising: The Resurgence of Japanese Power and Purpose* (New York: Public Affairs, 2007); Richard J. Samuels, *Securing Japan: Tokyo's Grand Strategy and the Future of East Asia* (Ithaca, NY: Cornell University Press, 2007).

51 Kenneth B. Pyle, "Profound Forces in the Making of Modern Japan," *Journal of Japanese Studies* 32, no. 2 (2006): 417.

52 Samuels, *Securing Japan*, 208–9.

53 Ibid., 4–5.

54 Michael J. Green, *Japan's Reluctant Realism: Foreign Policy Challenges in an Era of Uncertain Power* (New York: Palgrave, 2001), 6–8.

55 Ibid., 3, 6–8, 33–4.

56 Hughes, *Japan's Re-emergence*, 14, 18–19.

57 Ibid., 18–19.

58 Peter J. Katzenstein, *Cultural Norms and National Security: Police and Military in Postwar Japan* (Ithaca, NY: Cornell University Press, 1998); Thomas U. Berger, "From Sword to Chrysanthemum: Japan's Culture of Anti-militarism," in *East Asian Security*, ed. Michael E. Brown, Sean M. Lynn-Jones, and Steven E. Miller (Cambridge, MA: MIT Press, 1996); idem, "Norms, Identity, and National Security in Germany and Japan," in *The Culture of National Security: Norms and Identity in World Politics*, ed. Peter J. Katzenstein (New York: Columbia University Press, 1996).

59 For example, Peter J. Katzenstein, "Japanese Security in Perspective," in *Rethinking Japanese Security: Internal and External Dimensions*, ed. Peter J. Katzenstein (New York: Routledge, 2008), 18.

60 Berger, "Norms, Identity, and National Security"; Andrew Oros, *Normalizing Japan: Politics, Identity, and the Evolution of Security Practice* (Stanford, CA: Stanford University Press, 2008), 1, 6–7.

61 Oros, *Normalizing Japan*, 5, 10, 45; idem, "Listening to the People: Japanese Democracy and the New Security Agenda," Commentary C07–3 (Washington, DC: Maureen and Mike Mansfield Foundation), available online at http://mansfieldfdn.org/program/research-education-and-communication/asian-opinion-poll-database-commentary/listening-to-the-people-japanese-democracy-and-the-new-security-agenda/.

62 Thomas U. Berger, "The Pragmatic Liberalism of an Adaptive State," in *Japan in International Politics: The Foreign Policy of an Adaptive State*, ed. Thomas U. Berger, Mike M. Mochizuki, and Jitsuo Tsuchiyama (Boulder, CO: Lynne Rienner, 2007), 261.

63 Thomas U. Berger, "Japan's International Relations: The Political and Security Dimensions," in *The International Relations of Northeast Asia*, ed. Samuel S. Kim (Lanham, MD: Rowman & Littlefield, 2003), 136–7, 161.

64 For realism, see Hans J. Morgenthau, *Politics among Nations: The Struggle for Power and Peace* (New York: McGraw-Hill, 1993). For "neo" realism, see Kenneth Waltz, *Theory of International Politics* (New York: McGraw-Hill, 1979); John J. Mearsheimer, *The Tragedy of Great Power Politics* (New York: W.W. Norton, 2003); and Robert Gilpin, *War and Change in World Politics* (Cambridge: Cambridge University Press, 1981). For a general overview of the realist paradigm in international relations, see Scott Burchill, "Realism," in *Theories of International Relations*, 2nd ed., ed. Scott Burchill et al. (New York: Palgrave Macmillan, 2001), 70–102.

65 For an overview of constructivism in international relations, see Alexander Wendt, *Social Theory of International Politics* (Cambridge: Cambridge University Press, 1999); Christian Reus-Smit, "Constructivism," in Burchill et al., *Theories of International Relations*, 209–30; and Emanuel Adler, "Constructivism and International Relations," in *Handbook of International Relations*, ed. Walter Carlsnaes, Thomas Risse, and Beth A. Simmons (London: Sage, 2005), 95–118.

66 Berger, "Pragmatic Liberalism of an Adaptive State," 267–8.

67 Oros, *Normalizing Japan*, 3.

68 Ibid., 1.

69 Oros, "Listening to the People."

70 Pyle, *Japan Rising*, 356; Katzenstein, "Japanese Security in Perspective," 19.

71 Samuels, *Securing Japan.*, 58.

72 Christopher W. Hughes, "The Political Economy of Japanese Sanctions towards North Korea: Domestic Coalitions and International Systemic Pressures," *Pacific Affairs* 79, no. 3 (2006): 455–81.

73 Hyung Gu Lynn, "Vicarious Traumas: Television and Public Opinion in Japan's North Korea Policy," *Pacific Affairs* 79, no. 3 (2006): 483–4, 507.
74 Heigo Satō, "A Japanese Perspective on North Korea: Troubled Bilateral Relations in a Complex Multilateral Framework," *International Journal of Korean Unification Studies* 18, no. 1 (2009): 54–92; Brad Williams and Erik Mobrand, "Explaining Divergent Responses to the North Korean Abductions Issue in Japan and South Korea," *Journal of Asian Studies* 69, no. 2 (2010): 507–36; Anthony DiFilippo, "Still at Odds: The Japanese Abduction Issue and North Korea's Circumvention," *UNISCI Discussion Papers* 32 (May 2013): 137–70; Atsuhito Isozaki, "Japan–North Korea Relations: The Abe Administration and the Abduction Issue," *Samsung Economic Research Institution (SERI) Quarterly* (July 2013): 67–72; Richard J. Samuels, "Kidnapping Politics in East Asia," *Journal of East Asian Studies* 10, no. 3 (2010): 363–95.

2. Relations after the First Missile Launch

1 Akio Watanabe, "Japanese Public Opinion and Foreign Affairs: 1964–1973," in *The Foreign Policy of Modern Japan*, ed. Robert A. Scalapino (Berkeley: University of California Press, 1977), 143; Yoshihide Soeya, "The Misconstrued Shift in Japan's Foreign Policy," *Japan Echo* (June 2006), 17. For example, one of the former chief editors of the liberal-progressive monthly *Sekai* comments that the magazine, launched after the war and based on principles of "peace and social justice" and "harmony and solidarity with the peoples of East Asia," enjoyed a huge popularity at the time since it "struck a chord among the Japanese people who deeply regretted Japan's role in the war"; see Motohiro Kondō, "The Rise and Fall of Intellectual Journalism," *Japan Echo* (June 2005), 49.
2 Watanabe, "Japanese Public Opinion and Foreign Affairs," 114–15.
3 Makoto Iokibe, "How Japan Has Fulfilled Its Postwar Responsibilities," *Japan Echo* (December 2005), 45–50.
4 Editorial, *Asahi Shimbun*, 3 May 2000, 2.
5 Watanabe, "Japanese Public Opinion and Foreign Affairs," 111–12.
6 Andrew Gordon, "Society and Politics from Transwar through Postwar Japan," in *Historical Perspectives on Contemporary East Asia*, ed. Merle Goldman and Andrew Gordon (Cambridge, MA: Harvard University Press, 2000), 281–2.
7 See, for example, Yoshibumi Wakamiya, *Sengo Hoshu no Ajia-kan* [The post-war conservative view of Asia] (Tokyo: Asahi Senshō, 1995), 202–22.
8 Akitoshi Miyashita, "Where Do Norms Come From? Foundations of Japan's Postwar Pacifism," *International Relations of the Asia-Pacific* 7 (1, 2007): 115–16.

9 Makoto Iokibe, President of the National Defense Academy of Japan, interview with the author, 18 December 2009.

10 Hideo Ōtake, *Nihon Seiji no Tairitsu-jiku* [The axis of political controversies in Japanese politics] (Tokyo: Chūōkōron Shinsha, 1999), 7–9.

11 Robert A. Scalapino, "Perspectives on Modern Japanese Foreign Policy," in Scalapino, *Foreign Policy of Modern Japan*, 393.

12 Berger, "From Sword to Chrysanthemum," 318. The results of opinion surveys are from Watanabe, "Japanese Public Opinion and Foreign Affairs," 116. Based on *Mainichi Shimbun* polls, only 3 per cent of respondents in June 1968 thought there was a likelihood of an attack; the figures were 5 per cent in October 1969 and 4 per cent in April 1972.

13 Matake Kamiya, "Gunjiryoku e-no Kyohi Hannō wo Kokufuku surunoga Senketsu-da [The first priority must be to overcome the adverse reaction to military power]," *Chūōkōron* (July 2003), 54–5.

14 The work of former Japan Defense Agency (now Ministry of Defense) bureaucrat Takuya Kubo is a primary example. See Takuya Kubo, *Kokubōron: 80 nendai Nihon wo dō Mamoruka* [On national defence: How to defend Japan in the 1980s] (Kyoto: PHP Kenkyūjyo, 1979).

15 William Grimes, "Institutionalized Inertia: Japanese Foreign Policy in the Post–Cold War World," in *International Relations Theory and the Asia-Pacific*, ed. John G. Ikenberry and Michael Mastanduno (New York: Columbia University Press, 2003), 359–60.

16 Yōichi Funabashi, *The Peninsula Question: A Chronicle of the Second Korean Nuclear Crisis* (Washington DC: Brookings Institution Press, 2007), 66–7.

17 Matake Kamiya, "Japanese Foreign Policy toward Northeast Asia," in *Japanese Foreign Policy Today: A Reader*, ed. Takashi Inoguchi and Purnendra Jain (New York: Palgrave, 2000), 247.

18 Kōji Murata, "Japanese Domestic Politics and the U.S.–Japan–ROK Security Relationship," in *The Future of U.S.–Korea–Japan Relations: Balancing Values and Interests*, ed. Tae-Hyo Kim and Brad Glosserman (Washington, DC: Center for Strategic and International Studies, 2004), 140; Balbina Hwang, "Seoul's Policy towards Pyongyang: Strategic Culture and the Negligibility of Japan," in *North Korea Policy: Japan and the Great Powers*, ed. Linus Hagström and Marie Söderberg (Oxford: Routledge; European Institute of Japanese Studies, Stockholm School of Economics, 2006), 65.

19 Murata, "Japanese Domestic Politics," 146. Notice that the survey was taken after the first North Korean nuclear crisis of 1994.

20 Hajime Izumi, "Chikakute Tōi Rinjin [Close, but far-off neighbour]," in *Sengo Nihon no Taigai Seisaku* [Postwar Japanese foreign policy], ed. Akio Watanabe (Tokyo: Yūhikaku Senshō, 1995), 180–1.

21 Kazuhiko Togo, *Japan's Foreign Policy 1945–2003: The Quest for Proactive Policy* (Leiden, Netherlands: Brill Academic, 2005), 184.
22 Green, *Japan's Reluctant Realism*, 117.
23 Shūzō Yamakoshi and Tomohisa Hirai, "Media Hōdō to Seron Chōsa ni miru Nihon no Jiko Imēji [Japan's self-image based on media coverage and public opinion polls]," in *Imēji no Naka no Nihon – Sofuto Pawā Saikō* [Japan as an image: Reconsidering Japan's soft power], ed. Y utaka Ōishi and Nobuto Yamamoto (Tokyo: Keio University Press, 2008), 48.
24 Togo, *Japan's Foreign Policy 1945–2003*.
25 Hideo Ōtake, *Koizumi Junichirō Popyurizumu no Kenkyū – Sono Senryaku to Shuhō* [Koizumi's populism: The strategies and techniques] (Tokyo: Toyo Keizai Shimposha, 2006), 202–3.
26 Togo, *Japan's Foreign Policy 1945–2003*, 185.
27 Ōtake, *Koizumi Junichirō Popyurizumu no Kenkyū*, 206–7.
28 Ibid., 202; Green, *Japan's Reluctant Realism*.
29 Green, *Japan's Reluctant Realism*; Pyle, *Japan Rising*, 294.
30 *Asahi Shimbun*, 1 September 1998, 1.
31 Editorial, *Yomiuri Shimbun*, 3 September 1998, 3.
32 Editorial, *Asahi Shimbun*, 18 September 1998, 5; two weeks later, the US government concluded that it was a failed satellite launch.
33 *Asahi Shimbun*, 1 September 1998, 1.
34 Editorial, *Asahi Shimbun*, 25 March 1999, 5.
35 Editorial, *Asahi Shimbun*, 25 March 2000, 5.
36 Editorial, *Yomiuri Shimbun*, 1 April 1999, 3.
37 Funabashi, *Peninsula Question*, 7; Hughes, *Japan's Re-emergence*, 44.
38 *Yomiuri Shimbun* Editorial Committee, *Yomiuri vs. Asahi – Shatsetsu Taiketsu Kitachōsen Mondai* [*Yomiuri* versus *Asahi* editorials on North Korean issues] (Tokyo: Chūōkōron Shinsha, 2002), 166–7; Editorial, *Yomiuri Shimbun*, 1 April 1999, 3.
39 Editorial, *Yomiuri Shimbun*, 1 January 1999, 3; Editorial, *Yomiuri Shimbun*, 3 May 1999, 3. At this time, the term *shuken* (sovereignty) made increasing appearances in the coverage of North Korean issues.
40 *Yomiuri Shimbun* Editorial Committee, *Yomiuri vs. Asahi*, 147–8.
41 Editorial, *Yomiuri Shimbun*, 22 May 2000, 3.
42 Tarō Asō and Shōichi Watanabe, "A Talk with the Foreign Minister," *Japan Echo* (October 2006), 9–12.
43 Editorial, *Asahi Shimbun*, 28 August 1999, 5.
44 Editorial, *Yomiuri Shimbun*, 18 June 2000, 3.
45 See, for example, Editorial, *Yomiuri Shimbun*, 1 September 1998, 3.

46 See, for example, Editorial, *Yomiuri Shimbun*, 3 September 1998, 3; Editorial, *Yomiuri Shimbun*, 12 September 1998, 3; and Editorial, *Yomiuri Shimbun*, 5 February 1999, 3.
47 See, for example, Editorial, *Asahi Shimbun*, 1 September 1998, 5; Editorial, *Asahi Shimbun*, 5 September 1998, 5; and Editorial, *Asahi Shimbun*, 22 September 1998, 5.
48 See, for example, Editorial, *Asahi Shimbun*, 25 March 1999; and Editorial, *Asahi Shimbun*, 25 March 2000, 5.
49 Editorial, *Yomiuri Shimbun*, 25 March 1999, 3.
50 Togo, *Japan's Foreign Policy 1945–2003*, 188.
51 Michishita, "Kitachōsen no Misairu Gaikō to Kakkoku no Taiō," 88.
52 Makoto Iokibe, "Reisengo no Nihon Gaikō [Japanese diplomacy in the post–Cold War period]," in Iokibe, *Sengo Nihon Gaikōshi*, 253. Akihiko Tanaka illustrates the legal, political, and organizational constraints that typical postwar prime ministers had to embrace in policy-making until the 1990s; see Akihiko Tanaka, "Domestic Politics and Foreign Policy," in Inoguchi and Jain, *Japanese Foreign Policy Today*, 4–7.
53 See, for example, Editorial, *Yomiuri Shimbun*, 1 September 1999, 3.
54 *Asahi Shimbun*, 1 September 1998, 1.
55 Green, *Japan's Reluctant Realism*, 126.
56 Michishita, "Kitachōsen no Misairu Gaikō to Kakkoku no Taiō," 90.
57 This multilateral framework was established after the first North Korean nuclear crisis in 1994 to pressure the North to freeze and eventually to dismantle its nuclear program while the member states provided a light water reactor.
58 Editorial, *Yomiuri Shimbun*, 3 September 1998, 3.
59 Editorial, *Asahi Shimbun*, 21 October 1998, 5.
60 Michishita, "Kitachōsen no Misairu Gaikō to Kakkoku no Taiō," 78–9.
61 Editorial, *Yomiuri Shimbun*, 27 December 1998, 3.
62 Michishita, "Kitachōsen no Misairu Gaikō to Kakkoku no Taiō," 86.
63 Editorial, *Yomiuri Shimbun*, 1 September 1999, 3.
64 Editorial, *Asahi Shimbun*, 25 March 2000, 5.
65 Hughes, "Political Economy of Japanese Sanctions," 472.
66 Editorial, *Asahi Shimbun*, 4 December 1999, 5; Editorial, *Yomiuri Shimbun*, 4 December 1999, 3.
67 Ibid.
68 As we shall see from Chapter 4 on, prior to the official admission by Kim Jong Il during Koizumi's visit to Pyongyang in 2002, the North Korean abduction of Japanese citizens had not been an official issue in Japanese–North Korean bilateral relations. Even after *Sankei Shimbun* had reported in

1980 on the "suspicious circumstances" surrounding the disappearance of several Japanese, the Japanese government and society in general considered the *giwaku* (suspicion) to be mere media speculation and treated it as "nothing more than a conspiracy theory" (Funabashi, *Peninsula Question*, 7). Therefore, although the Japanese side occasionally and half-heartedly raised the issue on behalf of certain elements of the Japanese public involved in the issue and asked for North Korean cooperation in investigating the disappearances, many Japanese policy-makers passively believed that, even if the allegations of North Korean involvement were true, the issue would have to be resolved politically in the final phase of the diplomatic normalization process (Editorial, *Yomiuri Shimbun*, 8 March 2000, 3). A family member of an abductee recalls that, prior to 2002, most government officials and bureaucrats actually thought the suspicion to be a Japanese-made fabrication, and they tried to avoid the topic as much as possible when contacting the North Koreans, as they strongly embraced the image of the North as "untouchable" and "eerie"; see Tōru Hasuike and Masakuni Ōta, *Rachi Tairon* [Abduction debates] (Tokyo: Ohta Shuppan, 2009), 33, 82. The most dramatic, but almost wholly unnoticed, example of this passivity in linking the abduction suspicion to the normalization process prior to 2002 is the private statement of former LDP prime minister Mori Yoshirō to former British prime minister Tony Blair on 20 October 2000, in which Mori confessed that, while in Pyongyang in 1997, he proposed to the North Koreans off-the-record that, if the North Korean involvement were indeed true, the two governments could still arrange for the abductees to be transported secretly to Beijing, Paris, or Bangkok. The "missing persons" – not abductees – then could somehow "re-emerge from those foreign cities as having lived there." Although the practicality of this option was highly dubious, some Japanese policy-makers actually considered it at one point as a secret compromise to help the North Korean government save face by providing a way out. See Editorial, *Asahi Shimbun*, 22 October 2000, 2; Editorial, *Yomiuri Shimbun*, 24 October 2000, 3.

69 *Yomiuri Shimbun*, 8 April 2000, 3.

70 Editorial, *Yomiuri Shimbun*, 4 December 1999, 3; Editorial, *Yomiuri Shimbun*, 15 December 1999, 3.

71 Editorial, *Asahi Shimbun*, 8 March 2000, 5.

72 Editorial, *Yomiuri Shimbun*, 8 April 2000, 3.

73 Funabashi, *Peninsula Question*, 34.

74 Editorial, *Yomiuri Shimbun*, 19 September 2000, 3; Editorial, *Yomiuri Shimbun*, 7 October 2000, 3.

75 Editorial, *Yomiuri Shimbun*, 13 November 2000, 3.

76 Editorial, *Yomiuri Shimbun*, 22 May 2000, 3.

3. Relations prior to Koizumi's Visit to Pyongyang

1 *Asahi Shimbun*, 5 May 2001, 1; Funabashi, *Peninsula Question*, 61.
2 Editorial, *Asahi Shimbun*, 5 May 2001, 2.
3 *Asahi Shimbun*, 5 May 2001, 1.
4 Richard J. Samuels, "New Fighting Power! Japan's Growing Maritime Capabilities and East Asian Security," *International Security* 32 (Winter 2007/08): 96; idem, *Securing Japan*, 148.
5 Editorial, *Yomiuri Shimbun*, 23 December 2001, 3.
6 It was presumed that the *fushinsen* sank as a result of its crew having activated a self-destruct mechanism to avoid being captured; see *Asahi Shimbun*, 24 December 2001, 1.
7 Ibid.
8 For example, Editorial, *Asahi Shimbun*, 5 May 2001, 2; Editorial, *Yomiuri Shimbun*, 5 May 2001, 3.
9 Editorial, *Yomiuri Shimbun*, 5 May 2001, 3.
10 Samuels, *Securing Japan*, 67–8, 81; Murata, "Japanese Domestic Politics," 146.
11 Murata, "Japanese Domestic Politics," 146. The survey result is taken from *Yomiuri Shimbun, Nihon no Yoron* [Japanese public opinion] (Tokyo: Kobundō, 2002), 210.
12 Hosup Kim, Masayuki Tadokoro, and Brian Bridges, "Managing another North Korean Crisis: South Korean, Japanese, and U.S. Approaches," *Asian Perspective* 27, no. 3 (2003): 67–8.
13 Samuels, "New Fighting Power!" 97.
14 Editorial, *Yomiuri Shimbun*, 23 December 2001, 3.
15 Samuels, "New Fighting Power!" 107–8.
16 Editorial, *Yomiuri Shimbun*, 3 May 2002, 3.
17 Shintarō Ishihara and Shinzō Abe, "Kangan-Kokka tono Ketsubetsu no Toki [It is time to say farewell to the country run by eunuch bureaucrats]," *Bungeishunjū* (August 2003), 114.
18 Ōtake, *Koizumi Junichirō Popyurizumu Kenkyū*, 2–4.
19 Ibid.
20 Kabashima, Takeshita, and Serikawa, *Media to Seiji*, 243, 249.
21 Ibid., 245.
22 Ibid., 219, 241.
23 Ibid., 254; Ōtake, *Nihon-gata Popyurizumu*, 225, 231.
24 Editorial, *Asahi Shimbun*, 2 July 2001, 2.
25 Margarita Estévez-Abe, "Japan's Shift toward a Westminster System: A Structural Analysis of the 2005 Lower House Election and Its Aftermath," *Asian Survey* 46, no. 4 (2006): 650–1.

26 Samuel Popkin and Ikuo Kabashima, "Introduction: Changing Media, Changing Politics," *Japanese Journal of Political Science* 8 (April 2007): 4. Young politicians among these Koizumi-supporting LDP Diet members are known in Japan as "Koizumi's children."

27 Estévez-Abe, "Japan's Shift toward a Westminster System," 651.

28 The cabinet includes the prime minister and the body of the cabinet secretariat, led by the *Kanbō Chōkan* (chief cabinet secretary) and three *Naikaku Kanbō Fuku-chōkan* (deputy chief cabinet secretaries). See Shinoda, *Koizumi Diplomacy*, 10, 13.

29 Ibid., 144; and T.J. Pempel, "Japanese Strategy under Koizumi," in *Japanese Strategic Thought toward Asia*, ed. Gilbert Rozman, Kazuhiko Togo, and Joseph P. Ferguson (New York: Palgrave Macmillan, 2007), 112.

30 Estévez-Abe, "Japan's Shift toward a Westminster System," 632–51.

31 Makoto Iokibe et al., "Reviewing Japan's Diplomatic Track Record," *Japan Echo* (August 2006), 10.

32 Shinoda, *Koizumi Diplomacy*, 144, 147.

33 Hiroshi Nakanishi, "Reisen Shūengo no Nihon no Henyō – Naisei to Chiiki Gaikō [Transformation of post–Cold War Japan: Domestic politics and regional diplomacy]," in *Nihon no Higashi Ajia Kōsō* [Japan's "East Asia" concept], ed. Yoshihide Soeya and Masayuki Tadokoro (Tokyo: Keio University Press, 2004), 293.

34 Hitoshi Tanaka, *Gaikō no Chikara* [The power of diplomacy] (Tokyo: Nihon Keizai Shimbun Shuppansha, 2009), 216–17.

35 *Asahi Shimbun*, 24 December 2001, 2.

36 Samuels, "New Fighting Power!" 111. Samuels interprets the empowerment of the JCG as a result of the *fushinsen* incident as "the most significant and least heralded Japanese military development since the end of the Cold War," since it constituted "the transformation of the JCG into a de facto fourth branch of the Japanese military" (95).

37 Samuels, *Securing Japan*, 54.

38 See, for example, Editorial, *Yomiuri Shimbun*, 17 June 1999, 3.

39 Kazuhiko Togo, "Greater Self-Assertion and Nationalism in Japan," *Copenhagen Journal of Asian Studies* 21 (2005): 26.

40 Editorial, *Yomiuri Shimbun*, 26 January 2002, 3.

41 Editorial, *Yomiuri Shimbun*, 17 April 2002, 3.

42 For example, the generation of leading politicians born before the war, such as Nonaka Hiromu, Kōno Yōhei, Miyazawa Kiichi, and Katō Kōichi of the LDP.

43 Pempel, "Japanese Strategy under Koizumi," 114; Samuels, *Securing Japan*, 148.

44 Murata, "Japanese Domestic Politics," 143.

45 Of the forty-eight, sixteen were from the LDP, twenty-two from the DPJ, three from the New Komeito Party, three from the Liberal Party, two from the Social Democratic Party, one from the Conservative Party, and one was independent. See "Nijyū, Sanjyū Dai Kokkaigiin Chōsa ni Miru – Nihon ga 'Neo-con'-ka Suru [Observations from a questionnaire to the Diet members in the twenties and thirties – Japan turning 'neo-con']," *Weekly AERA*, 16 June 2003, 11–12.

46 Berger, "Japan's International Relations," 159.

47 Ibid.; *Yomiuri Shimbun*, 21 March 2002, 3; Editorial, *Yomiuri Shimbun*, 11 May 2002, 3.

48 Funabashi, *Peninsula Question*, 62; *Yomiuri Shimbun*, 5 May 2001, 3.

49 *Yomiuri Shimbun*, 5 May 2001, 3; *Asahi Shimbun*, 5 May 2001, 1. Thus, Koizumi partially accepted the claims of both MOFA and the National Policy Agency, as, in accordance with the former's advice, he released the group without official investigation, while also making the deportation fully public in order to appease the latter.

50 Funabashi, *Peninsula Question*.

51 *Yomiuri Shimbun*, 5 May 2001, 3.

52 The first secret negotiations are reported to have started in October 2001. The chief negotiator for the Japanese side was Tanaka Hitoshi, newly appointed director general of the Asian and Oceanian Affairs Bureau of MOFA. His North Korean counterpart was an unidentified high-ranking official with a direct link to Kim Jong Il, simply known as "Mr X" by the Japanese media. During the whole length of the negotiation process, Tanaka, under strict orders from Koizumi, reported to only four others in the entire Japanese government (Koizumi, Chief Cabinet Secretary Fukuda Yasuo, Deputy Chief Cabinet Secretary Furukawa Sadajirō, and Vice-Minister for Foreign Affairs Nogami Yoshiji), as an early media leak would have invited complications and the stalling of the negotiations all together. The current prime minister, Abe Shinzō, then a deputy chief cabinet secretary, was not invited to join this "insider" group. As even the minister of foreign affairs and other MOFA officials were left in the dark, Tanaka was severely criticized by the media after the summit meeting in September 2002. See *Yomiuri Shimbun* Political Section, *Gaikō wo Kenka ni shita Otoko – Koizumi Gaikō 2000 Nichi no Shinjitsu* [The man who turned foreign policy into a fight – The truth behind the 2000 days of Koizumi diplomacy] (Tokyo: Shinchōsha, 2006), 16–18. Tanaka himself, in his books, admits that the first meeting was in fact held in Dalian, China, in the fall of 2001. Understandably, however, he has never revealed the identity of his North Korean counterpart; see Tanaka, *Gaikō no Chikara*, 104–6; Sōichirō Tahara

and Hitoshi Tanaka, *Kokka to Gaikō* [The state and diplomacy] (Tokyo: Kōdansha, 2005), 25.

53 Funabashi, *Peninsula Question*, 7.

54 *Asahi Shimbun*, 24 December 2001, 1.

55 To trace the debate behind the recovery process sequentially, see the Editorials in *Yomiuri Shimbun* on the following dates: 22 January 2002, 3; 26 February 2002, 3; 9 May 2002, 3; 19 June 2002, 3; 4 September 2002, 3; and 7 September 2002, 3. See also Editorial, *Asahi Shimbun*, 12 September 2002, 2.

56 *Yomiuri Shimbun* Political Section, *Gaikō wo Kenka ni shita Otoko*, 22–3.

4. Japanese–North Korean Relations, 2002–04

1 Togo, *Japan's Foreign Policy 1945–2003*, 189.

2 Ibid.

3 *Yomiuri Shimbun*, 18 September 2002, 1.

4 Ibid.

5 Ibid. It was revealed that North Korean agents had abducted Japanese citizens during the 1970s and 1980s to be trainers for North Korean spies infiltrating South Korea disguised as Japanese, with necessary language skills and Japanese passports. Another reason was to provide Japanese spouses for Japanese who were semi-permanently residing in North Korea (for example, Japanese Red Army faction members who had hijacked the Japanese airliner Yodo-gō in March 1970 and sought asylum in North Korea). See *Yomiuri Shimbun* Political Section, *Gaikō wo Kenka ni shita Otoko*, 35; Haruki Wada et al., "Kyōdō Teigen: Tai Kitachōsen Seisaku no Tenkan wo [Collective proposal: Shift in North Korea policy is necessary]," *Sekai* (July 2008), 126. For a more detailed analysis of the relationship between the hijacking incident and the abductions, see Patricia G. Steinhoff, "Kidnapped Japanese in North Korea: The New Left Connection," *Journal of Japanese Studies* 30, no. 1 (2004): 123–42.

6 *Asahi Shimbun*, 18 September 2002, 1. The latter part dealing with Japan's apology, for unknown reasons, was dropped from *Yomiuri Shimbun* coverage of the same day.

7 *Yomiuri Shimbun* Political Section, *Gaikō wo Kenka ni shita Otoko*, 32.

8 Ibid.

9 Ibid., 33.

10 Hirotaka Watanabe, "Impediments to Relations with Pyongyang," *Japan Echo* (February 2007), 8.

11 Mike M. Mochizuki, "Japan's Changing International Role," in Berger, Mochizuki, and Tsuchiyama, *Japan in International Politics*, 12.

12 Pempel, "Japanese Strategy under Koizumi," 129; Hughes, "Political Economy of Japanese Sanctions towards North Korea," 463.
13 Tanaka, *Gaikō no Chikara,* 119–20.
14 Ibid., 118–19, 212.
15 Tahara and Tanaka, *Kokka to Gaikō,* 36–7.
16 "North Korea's Last Chance for a Diplomatic Solution: An Interview with Tanaka Hitoshi," *Japan Echo* (June 2007), 27.
17 Gavan McCormack and Haruki Wada, "Forever Stepping Back: The Strange Record of 15 years of Negotiation between Japan and North Korea," in *The Future of US-Korean Relations: The Imbalance of Power,* ed. John Feffer (Oxford, UK; New York: Routledge, 2006), 85.
18 This diplomatic leverage was maintained even after the 2002 summit. As we shall see later, one reason Kim Jong Il agreed to a second summit with Koizumi on 23 May 2004, despite the breakdown of bilateral relations as a result of Japanese society's anger over the abductions issue, was North Korea's expectation that Koizumi would still be willing to accept the role of intermediary between North Korea and the United States. During the second summit, Koizumi allegedly mentioned the example of Libya to persuade Kim of the benefits of dismantling its nuclear program. Kim replied that, as long as the United States maintained its "threatening posture" against North Korea, it would be impossible. However, Kim also added that, although the case of North Korea was different than that of Libya, he desired coordination with the United States and asked for Japan's assistance, to which Koizumi promised his cooperation. See *Yomiuri Shimbun* Political Section, *Gaikō wo Kenka ni shita Otoko,* 66–7.
19 Iokibe et al., "Reviewing Japan's Diplomatic Track Record," 10–11.
20 *Asahi Shimbun,* 18 September 2002, 5.
21 Makoto Iokibe, interview with the author, 18 December 2009.
22 Shinichi Kitaoka, "Tokushū Kitachōsen: Narazumono Kokka no Ummei – Sengo Nihon Gaikōshi ni Nokoru Seikō de Aru [Special coverage North Korea: The fate of the "rogue state" – Historical success in Japan's postwar diplomacy]," *Chūōkōron* (November 2002), 46.
23 Jong-won Lee, "Datsu-Reisen wo Mezashi, Nessen no Shusenjō wo Fusen Kyōdōtai ni [By overcoming the Cold War, we must pursue a peaceful cooperative body in the main battlefield of the 'hot war']," in *Nicchō Kōshō* [Japan–North Korea negotiations], ed. Sang Joong Kang, Jong-won Lee, and Naoki Mizuno (Tokyo: Iwanami Shoten, 2003), 43.
24 Ibid.; and Kitaoka, "Tokushū Kitachōsen," 49, 51.
25 Iokibe, Kokubun, Lee, Okonogi, and Yamauchi, op. cit., p. 16.
26 Kitaoka, "Tokushū Kitachōsen," 50.

27 Yutaka Kawashima, *Japanese Foreign Policy at the Crossroads: Challenges and Options for the Twenty-first Century* (Washington, DC: Brookings Institution Press, 2003), 81–2.

28 Ōtake, *Koizumi Junichirō Popyurizumu no Kenkyū*, 200.

29 Kitaoka, "Tokushū Kitachōsen," 51.

30 Editorial, *Asahi Shimbun*, 15 September 2002, 2.

31 *Asahi Shimbun*, 3 September 2002, 1; database of poll conducted by *Asahi Shimbun*, presented to the author by Yoshibumi Wakamiya (http://xs-tyr01.asahi-np.co.jp/yoronopen/servlet/MainServletQ1: accessed by Wakamiya on 10 December 2009). Among the 53 per cent who responded positively, 11 per cent were "highly optimistic" and 42 per cent were "somewhat optimistic."

32 Japan, Cabinet Office, "Gaikō ni Kansuru Yoron Chōsa [Official opinion poll concerning foreign relations of Japan]" (Tokyo, October 2002), available online at http://www8.cao.go.jp/survey/index.htmlQ2, accessed 26 July 2010.

33 Matsumoto, *Yoron (Seron) Chōsa no Yukue*, 135–6.

34 In an *Asahi Shimbun* opinion poll on 20 September, 59 per cent of respondents supported the principle of normalization and 58 per cent agreed with the government's decision to reopen negotiating channels. In a *Yomiuri Shimbun* poll on the same date, 20.5 per cent of respondents preferred normalization at the earliest possible opportunity and 68.4 per cent agreed with eventual normalization, but "not in haste." Also, 51.4 per cent of respondents – close to the result of the *Asahi Shimbun* poll – similarly evaluated the government's decision positively. Such trends continued up to October 2002, as an *Asahi Shimbun* poll conducted early that month found the same percentage of respondents (58 per cent) still favouring diplomatic normalization; database of poll conducted by *Asahi Shimbun*, presented to the author by Yoshibumi Wakamiya.

35 Nakanishi, "Reisen Shūen go no Nihon no Henyō," 294; *Asahi Shimbun*, 20 September 2002, 4; *Yomiuri Shimbun*, 20 September 2002, 2. Of respondents to the *Asahi Shimbun* poll, 37 per cent evaluated the summit positively while 44 per cent said it was "positive to a certain degree" (a total of 81 per cent). Of respondents to the *Yomiuri Shimbun* poll, 43.6 per cent gave Koizumi a high score for the summit and 37.6 per cent answered "somewhat positive" (a total of 81.2 per cent).

36 *Yomiuri Shimbun*, 20 September 2002, 2.

37 Funabashi, *Peninsula Question*, 7, 73.

38 *Asahi Shimbun*, 20 September 2002, 4; *Yomiuri Shimbun*, 20 September 2002, 2.

39 Ibid. (69 per cent of respondents to the *Asahi Shimbun* poll and 66.4 per cent of those to the *Yomiuri Shimbun* poll). It must be emphasized, however, that the Japanese people's original "reference point" to this question surely had already been negative, as a result of the previous Taepodong-1 and *fushinsen* incidents.

40 Shinzō Abe and Kenzō Yoneda, "Nihon Kakusei no tameni Wareware wa Nani wo Nasubekika [What we must accomplish in order to awaken Japan]," *Seiron* (September 2003), 74.

41 The tone of *Asahi Shimbun* – generally critical of government policies – that interpreted the plausible nature of the societal discursive stance towards North Korea right after the summit also concurs with the dual logic presented here. See Editorial, *Asahi Shimbun,* 18 September 2002, 2; and Editorial, *Asahi Shimbun,* 22 September 2002, 2.

42 Lee, "Datsu-Reisen wo Mezashi," 34.

43 Database of poll conducted by *Asahi Shimbun,* presented to the author by Yoshibumi Wakamiya.

44 See *Yomiuri Shimbun,* 20 September 2002, 2; and *Asahi Shimbun,* 28 September 2002, 3.

45 Tessa Morris-Suzuki, "The Politics of Hysteria: America's Iraq, Japan's North Korea," *Japan in the World* (13 February 2003), available online at http://www.iwanami.co.jp/jpworld/top.html, accessed 14 February 2004. The same article in Japanese can be found at "Hisuterī no Seijigaku – Amerika no Iraku, Nihon no Kitachōsen," *Sekai* (February 2003). The quote is from pp. 233–4 of the Japanese version.

46 Abe and Yoneda, "Nihon Kakusei no tameni Wareware wa Nani wo Nasubekika," 73–4.

47 *Asahi Shimbun,* 8 November 2002, 3.

48 Ibid.

49 *Asahi Shimbun,* 4 December 2002, 4. Hyung Gu Lynn similarly claims that the "vicarious traumas" felt by ordinary citizens strongly guided the government's subsequent North Korea policy; see Lynn, "Vicarious Traumas," 507.

50 Ishihara and Abe, "Kangan Kokka tono Ketsubetsu no Toki," 114.

51 *Asahi Shimbun,* 4 December 2002, 4.

52 McCormack and Wada, "Forever Stepping Back," 86. Both Kazoku-kai and Sukuu-kai (and, to a lesser degree, Rachi-Giren) had been influenced by researchers and public commentators from Gendai Koria Kenkyūjo (Modern Korea Institute, formerly known as the Korea Research Institute), established in Japan in 1961 (Kazoku-kai was established in March 1997 and Sukuu-kai in April 1998). Researchers from the Modern Korea Institute

consisted either of Japanese scholars formerly belonging to left-wing groups disillusioned by communism and North Korea during the Cold War, or of hawkish nationalists aiming to topple the North Korean regime and establish non-apologetic historical interpretations domestically. Although these organizations had always been active, the government and the general public had not been interested in, or were not aware of, their activities prior to the summit. For further historical background on these abduction-related organizations in Japan, see Tessa Morris-Suzuki, "Refugees, Abductees, 'Returnees': Human Rights in Japan–North Korea Relations," in *North Korea: Toward a Better Understanding*, ed. Sonia Ryang (Lanham, MD: Lexington Books, 2009), 129–55; James L. Schoff, *Political Fences and Bad Neighbors: North Korea Policy Making in Japan and Implications for the United States* (Cambridge, MA: Institute for Foreign Policy Analysis, 2006).

53 Tōru Hasuike, *Rachi: Sayū no Kakine wo Koeta Tatakai e* [The abduction: Toward a fight beyond the left-right hedge] (Kyoto: Kamogawa Shuppan, 2009), 96. To trace Sukuu-kai's linkage to other like-minded groups seeking to publish revisionist history textbooks for public schools, see Nobuyoshi Takashima, "The North Korean Abductions … and the Rewriting of Japanese History," trans. John Junkerman, *Japan Focus*; available online at http://www.japanfocus.org/-Takashima-Nobuyoshi/1600/article.html.

54 Morris-Suzuki, "Refugees, Abductees, 'Returnees,'" 140.

55 Ōtake, *Koizumi Junichirō Popyurizumu no Kenkyū*, 238.

56 Morris-Suzuki, "Refugees, Abductees, 'Returnees,'" 140–1.

57 Editorial, *Yomiuri Shimbun*, 27 April 2003, 3.

58 Morris-Suzuki, "Refugees, Abductees, 'Returnees,'" 135. For this reason, Morris-Suzuki distinguishes the ideology of human rights proper from the discussion of "human rights" in Japanese societal discourse related to the abductions, calling the latter "human rights nationalism." Human rights nationalism differs from our typical understanding of human rights by its selective focus on "particular humanitarian concerns that happen to overlap with national security concerns," despite its "extensive use of the rhetoric of human rights." If North Korea discourse in Japan had concerned human rights – not human rights nationalism – then other humanitarian concerns, such as the fate of North Koreans under Kim's regime or of Koreans during the colonial period, would have taken an equally central position in these discussions.

59 Ibid.

60 See the following in chronological order as representative of this discursive trend: Editorial, *Yomiuri Shimbun*, 16 October 2002, 3; Editorial, *Asahi*

Shimbun, 13 November 2002, 2; Editorial, *Yomiuri Shimbun,* 5 December 2002, 3; Editorial, *Asahi Shimbun,* 9 December 2002, 2; Editorial, *Asahi Shimbun,* 17 September 2003, 2.

61 *Asahi Shimbun,* 1 July 2003, 2.

62 Database of poll conducted by *Asahi Shimbun,* presented to the author by Yoshibumi Wakamiya.

63 Togo, "Greater Self-Assertion and Nationalism in Japan," 31–2.

64 David Fouse, "Japan's Post–Cold War North Korea Policy: Hedging toward Autonomy?" in *Japan in a Dynamic Asia: Coping with the New Security Challenges,* ed. Yoichiro Sato and Sato Limaye (Lanham, MD: Lexington Books, 2006), 150.

65 Terumasa Nakanishi, "Kitachōsen no Kaku kara Kokka to Kokumin wo Mamorerunoka [Can we protect our nation and our citizens from the North Korean nuclear threat?]," *Seiron* (December 2002), 53.

66 Terumasa Nakanishi, *Nihon no Kakugo* (Resolution of Japan) (Tokyo: Bungeishunjū, 2005), 29–31.

67 The statement was "uncommon" because, unlike Sukuu-kai and Rachi-Giren, Kazoku-kai's foremost concern, understandably, had always been the rescue of the members' families in North Korea. The association's relative political neutrality, in addition to the obvious individual tragedies of its members, was at the heart of the Japanese public's unanimous support and sympathy for Kazoku-kai after the summit.

68 Hasuike and Ōta, *Rachi Tairon,* 104.

69 Tanaka, *Gaikō no Chikara,* 213, 217–18.

70 Masao Okonogi, Professor, Department of Political Science, Faculty of Law, Keio University, interview with the author, 11 December 2009.

71 Funabashi, *Peninsula Question,* 73.

72 Yōichi Komori, "Chimmoku no Rasen, Arekara [After the spiral of silence]," *Sōgō Jānarizumu Kenkyū* (July 2005), 13.

73 Yoshibumi Wakamiya, *Tatakau Shasetsu* [Fighting newspaper editorials] (Tokyo: Kōdansha, 2008), 32.

74 Masaru Satō, "Minzoku no Wana – 'Ōkina Monogatari' Shūengo no Nashonarizumu [Trap of 'nation': Nationalism after the end of the 'grand narrative'']," *Sekai* (July 2005), 88.

75 Nakanishi, "Reisen Shūen go no Nihon no Henyō," 294.

76 Editorial, *Yomiuri Shimbun,* 19 September 2002, 3.

77 For Doi's apology and the cold social reception, see Editorial, *Yomiuri Shimbun,* 11 October 2002, 3. For Shii's defence of himself and his party, see his interview with *Yomiuri Shimbun,* 13 November 2002, 4. See also Editorial, *Yomiuri Shimbun,* 24 March 2006, 3.

78 Shinzō Abe and Yoshiko Sakurai, "Futatabi Tatsu! Dare ga Kono Kuni wo Mamorunoka [Rising again! Who will protect this country?]," *Seiron* (September 2008), 52.

79 Abe and Yoneda, "Nihon Kakusei no tameni Wareware wa Nani wo Nasubekika," 74.

80 Haruki Wada, "Ushinatta Kanōsei no Kaifuku wo [Lost opportunity must be restored]," *Sekai* (March 2003), 139.

81 Murata, "Japanese Domestic Politics," 147; Mochizuki, "Japan's Changing International Role," 9.

82 Eiji Oguma and Yōko Ueno, Iyashi no Nashonarizumu – Kusanone Hoshu Undō no Jisshō Kenkyū [A nationalism of "healing": An empirical analysis of the grassroots conservative movement] (Tokyo: Keio University Press, 2003), 16–41.

83 *Yomiuri Shimbun*, 18 September 2002, 3; Editorial, *Yomiuri Shimbun*, 18 September 2002, 3; Editorial, *Yomiuri Shimbun*, 24 April 2003, 3.

84 Shinzō Abe, *Utsukushii Kuni e* [Beautiful country Japan] (Tokyo: Bungeishunjū, 2006), 46.

85 Hughes, "Political Economy of Japanese Sanctions towards North Korea," 467.

86 Wada, Ushinatta Kanōsei no Kaifuku wo," 138.

87 Tanaka, *Gaikō no Chikara*, 138–9; Tahara and Tanaka, *Kokka to Gaikō*, 71.

88 Tahara and Tanaka, *Kokka to Gaikō*, 71.

89 After the 2002 summit, there was also criticism that they had downplayed the abductions issue by drawing a parallel between the North Korean abductions and Japanese abductions of Koreans during the colonial period. Since the historical contexts and circumstances in which those two separate incidents occurred vary, the simple parallelism employed by these media – probably with an original intention to highlight to the Japanese public the multifaceted nature of regional history and politics and that North Korea was not the only party to be blamed for such types of crime – actually backfired in the post-summit environment.

90 *Asahi Shimbun*, 27 December 2002, 12–13.

91 Ibid.

92 *Sekai* Editorial Office, "Chōsen Mondai ni Kansuru Honshi no Hōdō ni tsuite [Concerning our position on Korea-related issues]," *Sekai* (February 2003), 260–6.

93 See, for example, Kazuya Fukuda, "Tahara Sōichirō-shi no Rekishikan wo Tou [Questioning Mr Tahara's understanding of history]," *Bungeishunjū* (February 2003), 134–41.

94 Sōichirō Tahara, *Koizumi no Nihon wo Yomu* ["Reading" Koizumi's Japan] (Tokyo: Asahi Shimbunsha, 2005), 173.

95 Abe, *Utsukushii Kuni e*, 52; Ōtake, *Koizumi Junichirō Popyurizumu no Kenkyū*, 223.

96 Masao Okonogi et al., "Sōgō Tōron: Nicchō Pyongyang Sengen no Rekishiteki/Kokusaiteki Igi [Historical and international significance of the Pyongyang Declaration]," in Kang, Lee, and Mizuno, *Nicchō Kōshō*, 26; Tahara and Tanaka, *Kokka to Gaikō*, 74–5. Although *Asahi Shimbun* did not take a more assertive tone, only because of its feelings of "guilt," many journalists at the newspaper indeed felt a strong sense of betrayal by the North. Yoshibumi Wakamiya, interview with the author, 17 December 2009.

97 Editorial, *Asahi Shimbun*, 1 January 2003, 2.

98 *Asahi Shimbun*, 26 January 2003, 2; Wakamiya, *Tatakau Shasetsu*, 49.

99 Noboru Maruyama, "Kenshō Rachi Hōdō – Jiyū de Shinjitsu no Hōdō wa Dekiteiruka [Abduction media coverage – Is free and truthful reporting possible?]," *Sekai* (May 2003), 128.

100 Hasuike, *Rachi*, 88–9.

101 "The spiral of silence" model asserts that "individuals who notice that their personal opinions are spreading will voice these opinions self-confidently in public; those who notice their opinions are 'losing ground' will be inclined to adopt a more reserved attitude and remain silent"; see Glynn et al., *Public Opinion*, 244–7.

102 Masao Okonogi, interview with the author, 11 December 2009; Komori, "Chimmoku no Rasen, Arekara," 13. See also Akio Yamaguchi, interviewed by Katsuyuki Yakushiji, "Liberal Journalism in Japan: An Endangered Species," in "The Rise and Fall of Intellectual Journalism," *Japan Echo* (June 2005), 54.

103 Yamaguchi, interviewed by Yakushiji, "Liberal Journalism in Japan."

104 Yoshibumi Wakamiya, interview with the author, 17 December 2009.

105 "Chimbotsu Nihon ureu Nashonarizumu [Nationalism produced by the concern for 'sinking Japan']," *Weekly AERA* (16 June 2003), 14.

106 McCormack and Wada, "Forever Stepping Back," 87.

107 Maruyama, "Kenshō Rachi Hōdō," 127.

108 Ibid., 128–9.

109 Kazuyoshi Hishiki, "Nicchō Kanren Hōdō – Media ga Baiyō suru Fushin to Zōo no Seron [Media coverage concerning Japan–North Korea relations – Public opinion of distrust and hatred nurtured by the media]," in Kang, Lee, and Mizuno, *Nicchō Kōshō*, 162.

110 Morris-Suzuki, "Politics of Hysteria"; the quote is a translation from p. 231 of the Japanese version. See also Murray Levin, *Political Hysteria in America: The Democratic Capacity for Repression* (New York: Basic Books, 1971).
111 Morris-Suzuki, "Politics of Hysteria," p. 231 of the Japanese version.
112 Ibid.; the quote is from pp. 234–5 of the Japanese version.
113 *Yomiuri Shimbun*, 28 September 2002, 1.
114 Funabashi, *Peninsula Question*, 39.
115 Masahiko Kōmura, "Tokushū Kitachōsen 'Taisei Hatan' no Shinario – Gensoku wo Wasureta Gaikō wa Seikō Shinai [Special edition: The scenario of North Korean regime collapse – Diplomacy without principle cannot succeed]," *Chūōkōron* (December 2002), 47.
116 *Asahi Shimbun*, 10 October 2002, 3.
117 Editorial, *Asahi Shimbun*, 16 October 2002, 2; *Yomiuri Shimbun*, 16 October 2002, 1.
118 Hasuike, *Rachi*, 27.
119 Funabashi, *Peninsula Question*, 40.
120 *Asahi Shimbun*, 24 October 2002, 2; Hasuike, *Rachi*, 55; Hasuike and Ōta, *Rachi Tairon*, 131.
121 Pempel, "Japanese Strategy under Koizumi," 129.
122 Funabashi, *Peninsula Question*.
123 *Yomiuri Shimbun*, 25 October 2002, 2.
124 Funabashi, *Peninsula Question*, 41.
125 Shinoda, *Koizumi Diplomacy*, 107. One abductee, Soga Hitomi, had an American husband, Charles Jenkins, formerly of the United States Army, who had defected to North Korea while stationed in South Korea. The two had met and married in the North, and had two children.
126 Kōmura, "Tokushū Kitachōsen 'Taisei Hatan' no Shinario"; *Asahi Shimbun*, 8 November 2002, 3.
127 Shinoda, *Koizumi Diplomacy*, 108.
128 *Asahi Shimbun*, 24 October 2002, 1.
129 Togo, *Japan's Foreign Policy 1945–2003*, 191.
130 Database of poll conducted by *Asahi Shimbun*, presented to the author by Yoshibumi Wakamiya.
131 *Asahi Shimbun*, 2 November 2002, 3.
132 Japan, Cabinet Office, "Gaikō ni Kansuru Yoron Chōsa."
133 *Yomiuri Shimbun*, 5 October 2002, 2.
134 Editorial, *Yomiuri Shimbun*, 11 December 2002, 3.
135 *Yomiuri Shimbun*, 8 February 2003, 3.

136 Hughes, "Political Economy of Japanese Sanctions towards North Korea," 476.
137 Kitaoka, "Tokushū Kitachōsen," 52.
138 Editorial, *Yomiuri Shimbun*, 26 May 2003, 3.
139 Editorial, *Yomiuri Shimbun*, 3 April 2003, 3; Editorial, *Asahi Shimbun*, 25 June 2003, 2.
140 Isao Kakiya, "Ishihara Tochiji Sensō Hatsugen ni Kinkijyakuyaku Shita Asahi Shimbun [Asahi Shimbun's overreaction to Governor Ishihara's statement on war]," *Seiron* (January 2003), 108–10.
141 Shinichi Kitaoka, former Japanese ambassador to the United Nations, Professor, Graduate Schools for Law and Politics, University of Tokyo, interview with the author, 16 December 2009.
142 Makoto Iokibe, interview with the author, 18 December 2009.
143 *Yomiuri Shimbun*, 7 June 2003, 1; Hughes, *Japan's Re-emergence*, 74–5.
144 Samuels, *Securing Japan*, 100; Editorial, *Yomiuri Shimbun*, 7 June 2003, 3.
145 "Nijyū, Sanjyū Dai Kokkaigiin Chōsa ni Miru – Nihon ga 'Neo-con'-ka Suru [Observations from questionnaire to the Diet members in the twenties and thirties – Japan turning 'neo-con']," *Weekly AERA* (16 June 2003), 12–13.
146 Editorial, *Yomiuri Shimbun*, 17 September 2003, 3.
147 Ibid.; Editorial, *Yomiuri Shimbun*, 24 April 2004, 3.
148 Shinoda, *Koizumi Diplomacy*, 112.
149 Tadokoro, "Change and Continuity in Japan's 'Abnormality,'" 51–2.
150 Masao Okonogi, interview with the author, 11 December 2009.
151 *Yomiuri Shimbun*, 15 October 2003, 3.
152 Masao Okonogi, interview with the author, 11 December 2009.

5. Japanese–North Korean Relations, 2004–06: Debates about Unilateral Sanctions

1 Editorial, *Asahi Shimbun*, 15 May 2004, 2.
2 Ōtake, *Koizumi Junichirō Popyurizumu no Kenkyū*, 224.
3 Asahi Shimbun, 15 May 2004, 3.
4 *Asahi Shimbun*, 23 May 2004, 1–2.
5 Ibid., 4.
6 Ōtake, *Koizumi Junichirō Popyurizumu no Kenkyū*, 229.
7 *Yomiuri Shimbun* Political Section, *Gaikō wo Kenka ni Shita Otoko*, 76–7; Ōtake, *Koizumi Junichirō Popyurizumu no Kenkyū*, 227.
8 Database of poll conducted by *Asahi Shimbun*, presented to the author by Yoshibumi Wakamiya. Only 10 per cent of the respondents answered that they did not regard the abductions to be a significant topic.

9 Ibid.

10 Gilbert Rozman, Kazuhiko Togo, and Joseph P. Ferguson, "Overview," in Rozman, Togo, and Ferguson, *Japanese Strategic Thought toward Asia*, 25.

11 Wada, "Ushinatta Kanōsei no Kaifuku wo," 143.

12 *Yomiuri Shimbun* Political Section, *Gaikō wo Kenka ni shita Otoko*, 48; Ōtake, *Koizumi Junichirō Popyurizumu no Kenkyū*, 225. The membership of the association also largely coincides with that of Rachi-Giren.

13 Ibid.

14 Editorial, *Yomiuri Shimbun*, 30 January 2003, 3.

15 Editorial, *Yomiuri Shimbun*, 2 February 2003, 3; Editorial, *Yomiuri Shimbun*, 28 May 2003, 3; Editorial, *Yomiuri Shimbun*, 26 August 2003, 3.

16 Editorial, *Yomiuri Shimbun*, 10 June 2003, 3.

17 Editorial, *Yomiuri Shimbun*, 14 December 2003, 3.

18 Editorial, *Yomiuri Shimbun*, 23 May 2003, 3; Editorial, *Yomiuri Shimbun*, 19 June 2003, 3.

19 John Swenson-Wright, "The Limits to 'Normalcy': Japanese–Korean Post–Cold War Interactions," in Soeya, Tadokoro, and Welch, *Japan as a "Normal Country"?*, 169; Hitoshi Tanaka, former director general of Asian and Oceanian Affairs, Ministry of Foreign Affairs, Senior Fellow, Japan Center for International Exchange, and Visiting Professor, Graduate School of Public Policy, University of Tokyo, interview with the author, 17 December 2009.

20 Editorial, *Asahi Shimbun*, 3 November 2005, 3.

21 Shinzō Abe, "Tokushū Kitachōsen Mondai no Miezaru Saizensen – Jikan wa Wareware ni Yūri ni Hataraku [Special edition: The invisible frontline of North Korea issues – Time will work to our advantage]," *Chūōkōron* (August 2003), 62.

22 Yoshibumi Wakamiya, interview with the author, 17 December 2009.

23 Hughes, "Political Economy of Japanese Sanctions towards North Korea," 469. Abe's rise in Japanese politics was uncommon, since his popularity solely as a result of the abductions issue eventually would win him his first prime ministership in 2006.

24 Tanaka, *Gaikō no Chikara*, 216–17.

25 Ōtake, *Koizumi Junichirō Popyurizumu no Kenkyū*, 226; *Yomiuri Shimbun* Political Section, *Gaikō wo Kenka ni shita Otoko*, 49–50.

26 Yoshibumi Wakamiya, interview with the author, 17 December 2009.

27 Editorial, *Yomiuri Shimbun*, 14 December 2003, 3.

28 Editorial, *Asahi Shimbun*, 30 January 2004, 2.

29 Editorial, *Yomiuri Shimbun*, 1 February 2004, 3.

30 Editorial, *Yomiuri Shimbun*, 18 February 2004, 3; Editorial, *Yomiuri Shimbun*, 4 March 2004, 3.

31 Editorial, *Yomiuri Shimbun,* 1 February 2004, 3.
32 Editorial, *Asahi Shimbun,* 12 March 2004, 2.
33 Editorial, *Yomiuri Shimbun,* 26 February 2004, 3.
34 Editorial, *Asahi Shimbun,* 12 March 2004, 2; Editorial, *Yomiuri Shimbun,* 23 April 2004, 3.
35 "Sukuu-kai Rachi Ankēto – Zen Shūgiin Giin 480-Nin no Kaitō wo Ikkyo Keisai [Abduction questionnaire by Sukuu-kai: Full disclosure of the replies from all 480 lower house Diet members]," *Seiron* (January 2004), 54–95.
36 *Yomiuri Shimbun,* 17 September 2004, 3; *Asahi Shimbun,* 25 December 2004, 2.
37 *Yomiuri Shimbun,* 17 September 2004, 3. Since neither the Japanese public nor politics in 2004 ever recognized the North Korean claim that the victims and their family members who had already been repatriated to Japan were the only living survivors, the official stance of the Japanese government also had to assume that the other eight abductees who allegedly died in the North were still alive. Even mentioning the possibility that they might already be deceased was taboo in national media. Since North Korea has always claimed that the eight abductees had died, whether Japan believed it or not, and since there is no means for Japan to find out the truth unilaterally, the Japanese assertion that "all remaining victims must be rescued" has been at the core of the stalemate concerning what really constitutes the "full resolution" of the issue.
38 Editorial, *Yomiuri Shimbun,* 11 October 2004, 3; *Yomiuri Shimbun,* 5 November 2004, 3; Database of poll conducted by *Asahi Shimbun,* presented to the author by Yoshibumi Wakamiya.
39 Funabashi, *Peninsula Question,* 61.
40 Sang Jung Kang, "Sanctions against North Korea or East Asian Security Cooperation?" *Asia-Pacific Journal: Japan Focus;* available online at http://www.japanfocus.org/-Kang-Man_Gil_/2014/article.html, accessed 9 June 2009; originally published by *Asahi Shimbun,* 31 December 2004.
41 Hasuike and Ōta, *Rachi Tairon,* 103. When Kazoku-kai's Hasuike asked young LDP politician Ichita Yamamoto to make sure that the party had a specific roadmap predicting the mechanism through which the abduction victims would be retrieved by the imposition of pressure, all Yamamoto could say was that it would be done "strategically."
42 Editorial, *Asahi Shimbun,* 2 July 2004, 3; Editorial, *Yomiuri Shimbun,* 19 July 2004, 3.
43 Watanabe, "Impediments to Relations with Pyongyang," 9; Funabashi, *Peninsula Question,* 60.

44 The most prominent critique of the result was in the international weekly journal of science, *Nature*. Although it did not claim that the DNA was Megumi's, the journal pointed out that, from a purely scientific perspective, the Japanese investigation was inconclusive and insufficient to prove that the remains did not belong to Megumi. When criticism from Japan mounted towards the journal, *Nature*, in an editorial, highly atypical for a science magazine, entitled "Politics versus Reality," countered that "Japan's politicians have to face scientific uncertainty, no matter how uncomfortable it may be," and that "dealing with North Korea is no fun, but it doesn't justify breaking the rules of separation between science and politics." See "Politics versus Reality," *Nature*, 16 March 2005; available online at http://www.nature.com/nature/journal/v434/n7031/full/434257a.html, accessed 15 September 2010. The young chief examiner at Teikyo University who led the DNA test was later promoted to the head of the Forensics Department at the Tokyo Metropolitan Police Department, but he has remained silent on any question concerning the examination. See Hasuike, *Rachi*, 42–4.

45 *Yomiuri Shimbun*, 9 December 2004, 3; *Asahi Shimbun*, 9 December 2004, 2.

46 Editorial, *Yomiuri Shimbun*, 9 December 2004, 3; Editorial, *Asahi Shimbun*, 9 December 2004, 3.

47 Editorial, *Yomiuri Shimbun*, 14 December 2004, 3.

48 *Asahi Shimbun*, 9 December 2004, 2.

49 Ōtake, *Koizumi Junichirō Popyurizumu no Kenkyū*, 233, 237.

50 *Yomiuri Shimbun*, 18 December 2004, 3; Kang, "Sanctions against North Korea or East Asian Security Cooperation?"

51 Editorial, *Yomiuri Shimbun*, 30 January 2005, 3.

52 Funabashi, *Peninsula Question*, 60; Editorial, *Yomiuri Shimbun*, 25 December 2004, 3.

53 Tsuneo Akaha, "Japan and the Recurrent Nuclear Crisis," in Hagström and Söderberg, *North Korea Policy*, 33.

54 The announcement is also a strong indication that even North Korea had concluded by the end of 2004 that diplomatic normalization, which would better enable Koizumi to mediate between the North and the United States, could not be expected. Therefore, from Pyongyang's perspective, making already-hopeless North Korean–Japanese relations worse by its nuclear declaration (and facing the possibility of Japanese sanctions) was not as important as shifting its tactics to force the United States to sit at the negotiating table for a bilateral "big deal" (which it had always preferred over multilateral talks), by using the "atomic card" to which the Americans were most sensitive.

55 For the Japanese government's official version of the linkage between the abductions and all other North Korean issues and the progress of sanctions proposals in that context, see Japan, Ministry of Foreign Affairs, "Abductions of Japanese Citizens by North Korea: Awaiting the Day When We Will Be Reunited" (Tokyo, April 2008); the same pamphlet in Japanese (with more detailed contents) is entitled "Kitachōsen ni yoru Nihonjin Rachi Mondai." See also idem, "Heisei 18 Nendo Rachi Mondai no Kaiketsu Sono-hoka Kitachōsen Tōkyoku ni yoru Jinken Shingai Mondai e no Taisho ni Kansuru Seifu no Torikumi ni tsuite no Hōkoku [2006 report on the government's pursuit of the resolution of the abduction issue and its engagement with other humanitarian violations by the North Korean regime]" (Tokyo, June 2007).

56 Watanabe, "Impediments to Relations with Pyongyang," 7.

57 Morris-Suzuki, "Politics of Hysteria"; the quote is from p. 236 of the Japanese version. Terumasa Nakanishi also concurs, arguing that compared to the abductions issue, the nuclear issue has been regarded by Japanese as "*sanbun-teki* (prosaic and dull)"; see Nakanishi, *Nihon no Kakugo*, 19–20.

58 Weston S. Konishi, "Washington Japanwatch: Japan stuck on abduction issue," *Daily Yomiuri Online*, 30 August 2005.

59 Linus Hagström and Marie Söderberg, "Introduction: Japan, the Great Powers, and the Coordination of North Korea Policy," in Hagström and Söderberg, *North Korea Policy*, 2.

60 Okonogi et al., "Sōgō Tōron," 5.

61 Abe and Sakurai, "Futatabi Tatsu!" 52.

62 Japan, Cabinet Office, "Gaikō ni Kansuru Yoron Chōsa."

63 Editorial, *Asahi Shimbun*, 12 July 2005, 3.

64 For example, Christopher W. Hughes, "Japan and Multilateralism in the North Korean Nuclear Crisis: Road Map or Dead End?" in Hagström and Söderberg, *North Korea Policy*, 166; idem, "Political Economy of Japanese Sanctions towards North Korea," 455–6, 466; Maaike Okano-Heijmans, "Japan as Spoiler in the Six-Party Talks: Single-Issue Politics and Economic Diplomacy toward North Korea," *Japan Focus* (21 October 2008); Hideya Kurata, "The Six Party Talks Still Crucial to Japan's Abduction Issue," AJISS-Commentary 22 (n.p.: Association of Japanese Institutes of Strategic Studies, 25 January 2008).

65 Konishi, "Washington Japanwatch"; Lynn, "Vicarious Traumas," 506.

66 Satō, "Japanese Perspective on North Korea," 58.

67 Hitoshi Tanaka, interview with the author, 17 December 2009.

68 Tahara and Tanaka, *Kokka to Gaikō*, 40, 50, 73.

69 Ibid., 250; Tanaka, *Gaikō no Chikara,* 204.
70 Lynn, "Vicarious Traumas."
71 See, for example, Akaha, "Japan and the Recurrent Nuclear Crisis," 34.
72 Masao Okonogi, interview with the author, 11 December 2009.
73 *Yomiuri Shimbun* Political Section, *Gaikō wo Kenka ni shita Otoko,* 108.
74 Shinoda, *Koizumi Diplomacy,* 151–3.
75 "Public opinion, conservative media alter policy on North Korea," *Japan Times Online,* 19 November 2007; available at http://www.japantimes.co.jp/news/2007/11/19/national/public-opinion-conservative-media-alter-policy-on-north-korea/#.VZrfqmfbLIVQ3.
76 Shinichi Kitaoka, interview with the author, 16 December 2009.
77 *Asahi Shimbun,* 5 July 2006, 1–2; *Asahi Shimbun,* 6 July 2006, 1; *Yomiuri Shimbun,* 6 July 2006, 1.
78 *Asahi Shimbun,* 6 July 2006, 1; *Yomiuri Shimbun,* 6 July 2006, 1.
79 Hisahiko Okazaki, *Kono Kuni wo Mamoru tame no Gaikō Senryaku* [Diplomatic strategies for protecting Japan] (Tokyo: PHP Shinsho, 2007), 199–200.
80 *Asahi Shimbun,* 6 July 2006, 1; *Yomiuri Shimbun,* 6 July 2006, 1.
81 Ibid.
82 *Yomiuri Shimbun,* 6 July 2006, 2.
83 *Yomiuri Shimbun,* 7 July 2006, 3.
84 *Asahi Shimbun,* 17 July 2006, 1; *Yomiuri Shimbun,* 18 July 2006, 3.
85 *Yomiuri Shimbun,* 17 July 2006, 3.
86 *Asahi Shimbun,* 17 July 2006, 1.
87 *Asahi Shimbun,* 19 September 2006, 1; Editorial, *Yomiuri Shimbun,* 20 September 2006, 3.
88 *Asahi Shimbun,* 20 September 2006, 2; Editorial, *Asahi Shimbun,* 20 September 2006, 3.
89 *Yomiuri Shimbun,* 6 July 2006, 2.
90 Abe and Sakurai, "Futatabi Tatsu!" 54; Abe, *Utsukushii Kuni e,* 54.
91 Masao Okonogi, "Sōron [Overview]," in Okonogi, *Kiki no Chōsen Hantō,* 7.
92 Editorial, *Yomiuri Shimbun,* 13 October 2006, 3.
93 Editorial, *Yomiuri Shimbun,* 15 November 2006, 3.
94 *Asahi Shimbun,* 16 October 2006, 1; *Yomiuri Shimbun,* 16 October 2006, 1.

6. Conclusion

1 The Japanese "victim mentality" or "sense of victimhood" towards the West – and especially towards the United States for its use of atomic bombs during the war – has been noticed by many scholars. Steven T.

Benfell, for example, argues that such a mentality resonates powerfully in all Japanese, especially among the older generation, and that the "victimhood" is "a powerful constraint on any political leader seeking to issue a more powerfully worded apology or offer of compensation" to Japan's former enemies and subjugated peoples; see Steven T. Benfell, "Why Can't Japan Apologize? Institutions and War Memory since 1945," *Harvard Asia Quarterly* 6, no. 2 (2002), online.

Although the prevalence of a "victim mentality" towards the West throughout the postwar period cannot be denied, in my view the sense of victimhood towards the West and that towards Japan's neighbours should be separated. Although there is surely a difference in the extent of acceptance among individual Japanese, Japan as a nation has accepted its historic role as the aggressor in its official discourse for most of the postwar period. In this regard, the new surge of "victim mentality" as a result of the North Korea factor in the 2000s was a new strand of societal discourse that needs to be distinguished from our typical understanding of the Japanese sense of victimhood.

Moreover, the main reason Japan has been reluctant to offer powerfully worded apologies or compensation to individuals or states in the West and in Asia also diverges. In the case of the former, it is indeed true that such a mentality played a major role, in addition to the fact that Western countries in general – as victors – have not prioritized the demand for such official compensation on behalf of their citizens. In the case of the latter, however, the chief reason has been economic, not the "victim mentality." In other words, the problem of "where to draw the line" – meaning what constitutes the aggression and atrocities that must be compensated for, and for how much – has prevented the Japanese government from actively stepping into the compensation issue; instead, it has preferred bilateral negotiations for political settlements to ensure that whatever an agreed compensation of a particular state might be, it would be the "final settlement."

2 Masao Okonogi, interview with the author, 11 December 2009; Makoto Iokibe, interview with the author, 18 December 2009.

3 Yoshihide Soeya, "Diplomacy for Japan as a Middle Power," *Japan Echo* (April 2008), 36.

4 Kiichi Fujiwara, "Gaikō wa Seron (Yoron) ni Shitagaubekika – Minshushugi no Seijuku to Taigai Seisaku [Should diplomacy follow public opinion? The democratic maturation and foreign policy]," *Ronza* (March 2008), 78–9.

5 Izumi, "Dealing with North Korea," 36, 38; Haruki Wada, "Tai Kitachōsen Seisaku – Ima Kinkyū ni Hitsuyō to Sareteru Koto [Policies towards North Korea – What is urgently needed]," *Sekai* (May 2008), 157.
6 Hasuike, *Rachi*, 41.
7 "Rachi Chōsa, Nicchō ga Gōi [Japan and North Korea agree on the abduction re-investigation]," *Asahi Shimbun Digital*, 30 May 2014.
8 "Japan, North Korea to hold talks next week on probe into abductions," *Reuters Online*, 25 June 2014.
9 "North Korea delays first report on reinvestigation of abduction issue," *Asahi Shimbun Digital English*, 19 September 2014; "North Korea says abduction probe will take another year," *Japan Times Online*, 19 September 2014.
10 "Japan unwilling to let up on abduction issue," *Japan Times Online*, 4 January 2015.
11 Hasuike, *Rachi*, 38–9.
12 "Number of suspected Japanese abduction victims by North Korea rises to 883," *Japan Times Online*, 2 September 2014.
13 Japan, Cabinet Office, "Gaikō ni Kansuru Yoron Chōsa [Official opinion poll concerning foreign relations of Japan]"; available online at http://survey.gov-online.go.jp/h26/h26-gaiko/index.html, accessed 22 December 2014.
14 "Families fear hundreds left out of abductee debate," *Japan Times Online*, 5 September 2014.
15 "North Korea delays first report on reinvestigation of abduction issue," *Asahi Shimbun Digital English*, 19 September 2014.
16 Okonogi, "Sōron," 9.
17 For example, Masao Okonogi, interview with the author, 11 December 2009; Narushige Michishita, Associate Professor, Security and International Studies Program, National Graduate Institute for Policy Studies, Tokyo, interview with the author, 16 December 2009.
18 Hitoshi Tanaka, interview with the author, 17 December 2009; Kurata, "Six Party Talks."
19 Seung Hyok Lee, "North Korea in South Korea–Japan Relations as a Source of Mutual Security Anxiety among Democratic Societies," *International Relations of the Asia-Pacific* (forthcoming).
20 See, for example, Tsunemi Koyama, "Mattanashi! Ima Koso Nihon-koku Kenpō wo Mukō to Seyo [Now or never! This is the moment to annul the Japanese Constitution]," *Seiron* (September 2004), 71.
21 Hasuike, *Rachi*, 84–5.

22 He once wrote about the Constitution as an example of Japan's "national spirit" being overtaken by "American pragmatism, English utilitarianism, and French-style individualism" that led to a "cultural sickness in [Japan's postwar] politics, economy and society." See Yasuhiro Nakasone, *A State Strategy for the Twenty-First Century* (London: Routledge Curzon, 2002), 108–13.

23 Yasuhiro Nakasone and Shintarō Ishihara, "Tate! Nihon-yo Ima Koso Sengo no Jubaku wo Tachikire [Rise Japan! This is the moment to cut off the spell of the postwar]," *Seiron* (February 2004), 61.

24 Editorial, *Yomiuri Shimbun*, 2 April 2003, 3.

25 Yoshikazu Sakamoto, "The Postwar and the Japanese Constitution: Beyond Constitutional Dilemmas," *Japan Focus* (November 2005); available online at http://japanfocus.org/-Yoshikazu-SAKAMOTO/1847/article.html, accessed 9 June 2009.

26 Yoshihide Soeya, *Nihon no Midoru Pawā Gaikō* [Japan's "middle power" diplomacy] (Tokyo: Chikuma Shinshō, 2005), 16–29, 198–205.

27 Ibid.

28 Editorial, *Asahi Shimbun*, 3 May 2005, 3; Editorial, *Yomiuri Shimbun*, 4 April 2006, 3.

29 John Swenson-Wright, "What Japan's military shift means," *BBC News*, 2 July 2014.

30 "Over half oppose Japan engaging in collective self-defense: Survey," *Japan Times Online*, 26 January 2014.

31 Swenson-Wright, "What Japan's military shift means."

32 "Abe seeks national referendum for amending the Constitution as early as late 2016," *Asahi Shimbun Digital*, 4 February 2015.

33 "Abe is said to have plans to revise pacifist charter," *New York Times*, 5 February 2015; "Beheadings frame a new debate about restraints on Japan's military," *New York Times*, 3 February 2015.

34 Editorial, *Asahi Shimbun*, 3 May 2005, 3; Editorial, *Yomiuri Shimbun*, 4 April 2006, 3.

35 Ibid.

36 Editorial, *Asahi Shimbun*, 3 May 2005, 3.

Bibliography

English-language Sources

"Abe is said to have plans to revise pacifist charter." *New York Times*, 5 February 2015.

"Abe seeks national referendum for amending the Constitution as early as late 2016." *Asahi Shimbun Digital*, 4 February 2015.

Adler, Emanuel. "Constructivism and International Relations." In *Handbook of International Relations*, ed. Walter Carlsnaes, Thomas Risse, and Beth A. Simmons, 95–118. London: Sage, 2005.

Akaha, Tsuneo. "Japan and the Recurrent Nuclear Crisis." In *North Korea Policy: Japan and the Great Powers*, ed. Linus Hagström and Marie Söderberg, 19–37. Oxford, UK: Routledge and European Institute of Japanese Studies, Stockholm School of Economics, 2006.

Asō, Tarō, and Shōichi Watanabe. "A Talk with the Foreign Minister." *Japan Echo*, October 2006, 9–12.

"Beheadings frame a new debate about restraints on Japan's military." *New York Times*, 3 February 2015.

Benfell, Steven T. "Why Can't Japan Apologize? Institutions and War Memory since 1945." *Harvard Asia Quarterly* 6, no. 2 (2002). Online.

Berger, Thomas U. "From Sword to Chrysanthemum: Japan's Culture of Anti-militarism." In *East Asian Security*, ed. Michael E. Brown, Sean M. Lynn-Jones, and Steven E. Miller, 300–31. Cambridge: MIT Press, 1996.

Berger, Thomas U. "Japan's International Relations: The Political and Security Dimensions." In *The International Relations of Northeast Asia*, ed. Samuel S. Kim, 135–69. Lanham, MD: Rowman & Littlefield, 2003.

Berger, Thomas U. "Norms, Identity, and National Security in Germany and Japan." In *The Culture of National Security: Norms and Identity in World*

Politics, ed. Peter J. Katzenstein, 317–56. New York: Columbia University Press, 1996.

Berger, Thomas U. "The Pragmatic Liberalism of an Adaptive State." In *Japan in International Politics: The Foreign Policies of an Adaptive State*, ed. Thomas U. Berger, Mike M. Mochizuki, and Jitsuo Tsuchiyama, 259–99. Boulder, CO: Lynne Rienner, 2007.

Burchill, Scott. "Realism." In *Theories of International Relations*, 2nd ed., ed. Scott Burchill, Andrew Linklater, Matthew Paterson, Christian Reus-Smit, Jacqui True, and Richard Devetak, 70–102. New York: Palgrave Macmillan, 2001.

Campbell, John Creighton. "Media and Policy Change in Japan." In *Media and Politics in Japan*, ed. Susan J. Pharr and Ellis S. Krauss, 187–211. Honolulu: University of Hawai'i Press, 1996.

DiFilippo, Anthony. "Still at Odds: The Japanese Abduction Issue and North Korea's Circumvention." *UNISCI Discussion Papers* 32 (May 2013): 137–70.

Estévez-Abe, Margarita. "Japan's Shift Toward a Westminster System: A Structural Analysis of the 2005 Lower House Election and Its Aftermath." *Asian Survey* 46, no. 4 (2006): 632–51.

"Families fear hundreds left out of abductee debate." *Japan Times Online*, 5 September 2014.

Fouse, David. "Japan's Post–Cold War North Korea Policy: Hedging toward Autonomy?" In *Japan in a Dynamic Asia: Coping with the New Security Challenges*, ed. Yoichiro Sato and Limaye Sato, 135–55. Lanham, MD: Lexington Books, 2006.

Funabashi, Yōichi. *The Peninsula Question: A Chronicle of the Second Korean Nuclear Crisis*. Washington DC: Brookings Institution Press, 2007.

Gilpin, Robert. *War and Change in World Politics*. Cambridge: Cambridge University Press, 1981.

Glynn, Carroll J., Garrett J. O'Keefe, Robert Y. Shapiro, Mark Lindeman, and Susan Herbst. *Public Opinion*, 2nd ed. Boulder, CO: Westview Press, 2004.

Gordon, Andrew. "Society and Politics from Transwar through Postwar Japan." In *Historical Perspectives on Contemporary East Asia*, ed. Merle Goldman and Andrew Gordon, 272–96. Cambridge, MA: Harvard University Press, 2000.

Green, Michael J. *Japan's Reluctant Realism: Foreign Policy Challenges in an Era of Uncertain Power*. New York: Palgrave, 2001.

Grimes, William. "Institutionalized Inertia: Japanese Foreign Policy in the Post–Cold War World." In *International Relations Theory and the Asia-Pacific*, ed. John G. Ikenberry and Michael Mastanduno, 353–85. New York: Columbia University Press, 2003.

Hagström, Linus, and Marie Söderberg. "Introduction: Japan, the Great Powers, and the Coordination of North Korea Policy." In *North Korea Policy: Japan and the Great Powers*, ed. Linus Hagström and Marie Söderberg, 1–18. Oxford, UK: Routledge and European Institute of Japanese Studies, Stockholm School of Economics, 2006.

Hagström, Linus, and Jon Williamsson. "'Remilitarization,' Really? Assessing Change in Japanese Foreign Security Policy." *Asian Security* 5, no. 3 (2009): 242–72.

Hook, Glenn D., Julie Gilson, Christopher W. Hughes, and Hugo Dobson, eds. *Japan's International Relations, Politics, Economics, and Security*, 2nd ed. London; New York: Routledge, 2006.

Hughes, Christopher W. "Japan and Multilateralism in the North Korean Nuclear Crisis: Road Map or Dead End?" In *North Korea Policy: Japan and the Great Powers*, ed. Linus Hagström and Marie Söderberg, 151–70. Oxford, UK: Routledge and European Institute of Japanese Studies, Stockholm School of Economics, 2006.

Hughes, Christopher W. *Japan's Re emergence as a "Normal" Military Power.* New York: Routledge, 2006.

Hughes, Christopher W. "The Political Economy of Japanese Sanctions towards North Korea: Domestic Coalitions and International Systemic Pressures." *Pacific Affairs* 79, no. 3 (2006): 455–81.

Hwang, Balbina. "Seoul's Policy toward Pyongyang: Strategic Culture and the Negligibility of Japan." In *North Korea Policy: Japan and the Great Powers*, ed. Linus Hagström and Marie Söderberg, 53–72. Oxford, UK: Routledge and European Institute of Japanese Studies, Stockholm School of Economics, 2006.

Iokibe, Makoto. "How Japan Has Fulfilled Its Postwar Responsibilities." *Japan Echo*, December 2005, 45–50.

Iokibe, Makoto, Ryōsei Kokubun, Jong-Won Lee, Masao Okonogi, and Masayuki Yamauchi. "Reviewing Japan's Diplomatic Track Record." *Japan Echo*, August 2006, 10–18.

Isozaki, Atsuhito. "Japan–North Korea Relations: The Abe Administration and the Abduction Issue." *Samsung Economic Research Institution (SERI) Quarterly* (July 2013): 67–72.

Izumi, Hajime. "Dealing with North Korea: Time for Japan to Reengage." *Japan Echo*, February 2008, 36–9.

Japan. Ministry of Foreign Affairs. "Abductions of Japanese Citizens by North Korea: Awaiting the Day When We Will Be Reunited." Tokyo, April 2008.

"Japan, North Korea to hold talks next week on probe into abductions." *Reuters Online*, 25 June 2014.

"Japan unwilling to let up on abduction issue." *Japan Times Online*, 4 January 2015.

Kamiya, Matake. "Japanese Foreign Policy toward Northeast Asia." In *Japanese Foreign Policy Today: A Reader*, ed. Takashi Inoguchi and Purnendra Jain, 226–50. New York: Palgrave, 2000.

Kang, Sang Jung. "Sanctions against North Korea or East Asian Security Cooperation?" *Asia-Pacific Journal: Japan Focus*. Available online at http://www.japanfocus.org/-Kang-Man_Gil_/2014/article.html, accessed 9 June 2009; originally published by *Asahi Shimbun*, 31 December 2004.

Katzenstein, Peter J. *Cultural Norms and National Security: Police and Military in Postwar Japan*. Ithaca, NY: Cornell University Press, 1998.

Katzenstein, Peter J. "Japanese Security in Perspective." In *Rethinking Japanese Security: Internal and External Dimensions*, ed. Peter J. Katzenstein, 1–31. New York: Routledge, 2008.

Kawashima, Yutaka. *Japanese Foreign Policy at the Crossroads: Challenges and Options for the Twenty-First Century*. Washington DC: Brookings Institution Press, 2003.

Kim, Hosup, Masayuki Tadokoro, and Brian Bridges. "Managing Another North Korean Crisis: South Korean, Japanese, and U.S. Approaches." *Asian Perspective* 27, no. 3 (2003): 53–83.

Kondō, Motohiro. "The Rise and Fall of Intellectual Journalism." *Japan Echo*, June 2005, 49–50.

Konishi, Weston S. "Washington Japanwatch: Japan stuck on abduction issue." *Daily Yomiuri Online*, 30 August 2005.

Krauss, Ellis S. "The Mass Media and Japanese Politics: Effects and Consequences." In *Media and Politics in Japan*, ed. Susan J. Pharr and Ellis S. Krauss, 355–72. Honolulu: University of Hawai'i Press, 1996.

Kurata, Hideya. "The Six Party Talks Still Crucial to Japan's Abduction Issue." AJISS-Commentary 22. N.p.: Association of Japanese Institutes of Strategic Studies, 25 January 2008.

Lee, Seung Hyok. "North Korea in South Korea–Japan Relations as a Source of Mutual Security Anxiety among Democratic Societies." *International Relations of the Asia-Pacific*. Forthcoming.

Levin, Murray. *Political Hysteria in America: The Democratic Capacity for Repression*. New York: Basic Books, 1971.

Lynn, Hyung Gu. "Vicarious Traumas: Television and Public Opinion in Japan's North Korea Policy." *Pacific Affairs* 79, no. 3 (2006): 483–508.

McCormack, Gavan, and Haruki Wada. "Forever Stepping Back: The Strange Record of 15 Years of Negotiation between Japan and North Korea." In *The Future of US-Korean Relations: The Imbalance of Power*, ed. John Feffer, 81–100. Oxford, UK; New York: Routledge, 2006.

Mearsheimer, John J. *The Tragedy of Great Power Politics.* New York: W.W. Norton, 2003.

Miyashita, Akitoshi. "Where Do Norms Come From? Foundations of Japan's Postwar Pacifism." *International Relations of the Asia-Pacific* 7 (January 2007): 99–120.

Mochizuki, Mike M. "Japan's Changing International Role." In *Japan in International Politics: The Foreign Policies of an Adaptive State,* ed. Thomas U. Berger, Mike M. Mochizuki, and Jitsuo Tsuchiyama, 1–21. Boulder, CO: Lynne Rienner, 2007.

Morgenthau, Hans J. *Politics among Nations: The Struggle for Power and Peace.* New York: McGraw-Hill, 1993.

Morris-Suzuki, Tessa. "The Politics of Hysteria: America's Iraq, Japan's North Korea." *Japan in the World* 710 (13 February 2003). Available online at http://www.iwanami.co.jp/jpworld/top.html, accessed 14 February 2004.

Morris-Suzuki, Tessa. "Refugees, Abductees, 'Returnees': Human Rights in Japan–North Korea Relations." In *North Korea: Toward a Better Understanding,* ed. Sonia Ryang, 129–55. Lanham, MD: Lexington Books, 2009.

Murata, Kōji. "Japanese Domestic Politics and the U.S.–Japan–ROK Security Relationship." In *The Future of U.S.–Korea–Japan Relations: Balancing Values and Interests,* ed. Tae-Hyo Kim and Brad Glosserman, 140–9. Washington, DC: Center for Strategic and International Studies, 2004.

Nakasone, Yasuhiro. *A State Strategy for the Twenty-First Century.* London: Routledge Curzon, 2002.

"North Korea delays first report on reinvestigation of abduction issue." *Asahi Shimbun Digital English,* 19 September 2014.

"North Korea says abduction probe will take another year." *Japan Times Online,* 19 September 2014.

"North Korea's Last Chance for a Diplomatic Solution: An interview with Tanaka Hitoshi." *Japan Echo,* June 2007, 27–30.

"Number of suspected Japanese abduction victims by North Korea rises to 883." *Japan Times Online,* 2 September 2014.

Okano-Heijmans, Maaike. "Japan as Spoiler in the Six-Party Talks: Single-Issue Politics and Economic Diplomacy toward North Korea." *Japan Focus Online,* 21 October 2008.

Open Source Center Media Aid. "Japan – Media Environment Open; State Looms Large." 18 August 2009. Available online at http://fas.org/irp/dni/osc/japan-media.pdf.

Oros, Andrew. "Listening to the People: Japanese Democracy and the New Security Agenda." Commentary C07-3. Washington, DC: Maureen and Mike Mansfield Foundation, 2007. Available online at http://mansfieldfdn.org/

program/research-education-and-communication/asian-opinion-poll-database-commentary/listening-to-the-people-japanese-democracy-and-the-new-security-agenda/.

Oros, Andrew. *Normalizing Japan: Politics, Identity, and the Evolution of Security Practice*. Stanford, CA: Stanford University Press, 2008.

"Over half oppose Japan engaging in collective self-defense: Survey." *Japan Times Online*, 26 January 2014.

Pempel, T.J. "Japanese Strategy under Koizumi." In *Japanese Strategic Thought toward Asia*, ed. Gilbert Rozman, Kazuhiko Togo, and Joseph P. Ferguson, 109–33. New York: Palgrave Macmillan, 2007.

Pharr, Susan J. "Media as Trickster in Japan: A Comparative Perspective." In *Media and Politics in Japan*, ed. Susan J. Pharr and Ellis S. Krauss, 19–41. Honolulu: University of Hawai'i Press, 1996.

"Politics versus Reality." *Nature*, 16 March 2005. Available online at http://www.nature.com/nature/journal/v434/n7031/full/434257a.html, accessed 15 September 2010.

Popkin, Samuel, and Ikuo Kabashima. "Introduction: Changing Media, Changing Politics." *Japanese Journal of Political Science* 8 (April 2007): 1–6.

"Public opinion, conservative media alter policy on North Korea." *Japan Times Online*, 19 November 2007.

Pyle, Kenneth B. *Japan Rising: The Resurgence of Japanese Power and Purpose*. New York: Public Affairs, 2007.

Pyle, Kenneth B. "Profound Forces in the Making of Modern Japan." *Journal of Japanese Studies* 32, no. 2 (2006): 393–418.

Reus-Smit, Christian. "Constructivism." In *Theories of International Relations*, 2nd ed., ed. Scott Burchill, Andrew Linklater, Matthew Paterson, Christian Reus-Smit, Jacqui True, and Richard Devetak, 209–30. New York: Palgrave Macmillan, 2001.

Rozman, Gilbert, Kazuhiko Togo, and Joseph P. Ferguson. "Overview." In *Japanese Strategic Thought toward Asia*, ed. Gilbert Rozman, Kazuhiko Togo, and Joseph P. Ferguson, 1–32. New York: Palgrave Macmillan, 2007.

Sakamoto, Yoshikazu. "The Postwar and the Japanese Constitution: Beyond Constitutional Dilemmas." *Japan Focus*, November 2005. Available online at http://japanfocus.org/-Yoshikazu-SAKAMOTO/1847/article.html, accessed 9 June 2009.

Samuels, Richard J. "Kidnapping Politics in East Asia." *Journal of East Asian Studies* 10, no. 3 (2010): 363–95.

Samuels, Richard J. "New Fighting Power! Japan's Growing Maritime Capabilities and East Asian Security." *International Security* 32 (Winter 2007/08): 84–112.

Samuels, Richard J. *Securing Japan: Tokyo's Grand Strategy and the Future of East Asia.* Ithaca, NY: Cornell University Press, 2007.

Satō, Heigo. "A Japanese Perspective on North Korea: Troubled Bilateral Relations in a Complex Multilateral Framework." *International Journal of Korean Unification Studies* 18, no. 1 (2009): 54–92.

Scalapino, Robert A. "Perspectives on Modern Japanese Foreign Policy." In *The Foreign Policy of Modern Japan,* ed. Robert A. Scalapino, 391–412. Berkeley: University of California Press, 1977.

Schoff, James L. *Political Fences and Bad Neighbors: North Korea Policy Making in Japan and Implications for the United States.* Cambridge, MA: Institute for Foreign Policy Analysis, 2006.

Shinoda, Tomohito. "Becoming More Realistic in the Post–Cold War: Japan's Changing Media and Public Opinion on National Security." *Japanese Journal of Political Science* 8 (2007): 171–90.

Shinoda, Tomohito. *Koizumi Diplomacy: Japan's Kantei Approach to Foreign and Defense Affairs.* Seattle: University of Washington Press, 2007.

Soeya, Yoshihide. "Diplomacy for Japan as a Middle Power." *Japan Echo,* April 2008, 36–41.

Soeya, Yoshihide. "The Minconstrued Shift in Japan's Foreign Policy." *Japan Echo,* June 2006, 16–19.

Steinhoff, Patricia G. "Kidnapped Japanese in North Korea: The New Left Connection." *Journal of Japanese Studies* 30, no. 1 (2004): 123–42.

Swenson-Wright, John. "The Limits to 'Normalcy': Japanese–Korean Post–Cold War Interactions." In *Japan as a "Normal Country"? A Nation in Search of Its Place in the World,* ed. Yoshihide Soeya, Masayuki Tadokoro, and David A. Welch, 146–92. Toronto: University of Toronto Press, 2011.

Swenson-Wright, John. "What Japan's military shift means." *BBC News,* 2 July 2014.

Tadokoro, Masayuki. "Change and Continuity in Japan's 'Abnormality': An Emerging External Attitude of the Japanese Public." In *Japan as a "Normal Country"? A Nation in Search of Its Place in the World,* ed. Yoshihide Soeya, Masayuki Tadokoro, and David A. Welch, 38–71. Toronto: University of Toronto Press, 2011.

Takashima, Nobuyoshi. "The North Korean Abductions … and the Rewriting of Japanese History." Trans. John Junkerman. *Japan Focus.* Available online at http://www.japanfocus.org/-Takashima-Nobuyoshi/1600/article.html.

Tanaka, Akihiko. "Domestic Politics and Foreign Policy." In *Japanese Foreign Policy Today: A Reader,* ed. Takashi Inoguchi and Purnendra Jain, 3–17. New York: Palgrave, 2000.

Togo, Kazuhiko. "Greater Self-Assertion and Nationalism in Japan." *Copenhagen Journal of Asian Studies* 21 (2005): 8–44.

Togo, Kazuhiko. *Japan's Foreign Policy 1945–2003: The Quest for a Proactive Policy.* Leiden, Netherlands: Brill Academic, 2005.

Waltz, Kenneth. *Theory of International Politics.* New York: McGraw-Hill, 1979.

Watanabe, Akio. "Japanese Public Opinion and Foreign Affairs: 1964–1973." In *The Foreign Policy of Modern Japan,* ed. Robert A. Scalapino, 105–45. Berkeley: University of California Press, 1977.

Watanabe, Hirotaka. "Impediments to Relations with Pyongyang." *Japan Echo,* February 2007, 7–15.

Watanuki, Joji. *Politics in Postwar Japanese Society.* Tokyo: University of Tokyo Press, 1977.

Wendt, Alexander. *Social Theory of International Politics.* Cambridge: Cambridge University Press, 1999.

Williams, Brad, and Erik Mobrand. "Explaining Divergent Responses to the North Korean Abductions Issue in Japan and South Korea." *Journal of Asian Studies* 69, no. 2 (2010): 507–36.

Yamaguchi, Akio, interviewed Katsuyuki Yakushiji. "Liberal Journalism in Japan: An Endangered Species." In "The Rise and Fall of Intellectual Journalism. " *Japan Echo,* June 2005, 49–55.

Yamamoto, Takehiko. "Structural and Functional Vulnerabilities in Multilateral Export Control Regimes: A Japanese Perspective." Paper presented at the 2nd International Symposium of the Japan Atomic Industrial Forum, "How to Harmonize Peaceful Uses of Nuclear Energy and Non-Proliferation? Considering the Future of Nuclear Energy Development from Asia," Tokyo, March 2001.

Japanese-language Sources

Abe, Shinzō. "Tokushū Kitachōsen Mondai no Miezaru Saizensen – Jikan wa Wareware ni Yūri ni Hataraku [Special edition: The invisible frontline of North Korea issues – Time will work to our advantage]." *Chūōkōron,* August 2003, 60–3.

Abe, Shinzō. *Utsukushii Kuni e* [Beautiful country Japan]. Tokyo: Bungeishunjū, 2006.

Abe, Shinzō, and Yoshiko Sakurai. "Futatabi Tatsu! Dare ga Kono Kuni wo Mamorunoka [Rising again! Who will protect this country?]." *Seiron,* September 2008, 48–61.

Abe, Shinzō, and Kenzō Yoneda. "Nihon Kakusei no tameni Wareware wa Nani wo Nasubekika [What we must accomplish in order to awaken Japan]." *Seiron*, September 2003, 72–83.

Asahi Shimbunsha Yoron Chōsashitsu. *Nihonjin no Seiji Ishiki: Asahi Shimbun Yoron Chōsa no 30 nen* [Political attitude of the Japanese: Thirty years of *Asahi Shimbun*'s public opinion polling]. Tokyo: Asahi Shimbunsha, 1976.

"Chimbotsu Nihon ureu Nashonarizumu [Nationalism produced by the concern for the 'sinking Japan']." *Weekly AERA*, 16 June 2003, 14–17.

Fujiwara, Kiichi. "Gaikō wa Seron (Yoron) ni Shitagaubekika-Minshushugi no Seijuku to Taigai Seisaku [Should diplomacy follow public opinion? The democratic maturation and foreign policy]." *Ronza*, March 2008, 70–81.

Fukuda, Kazuya. "Tahara Sōichirō-shi no Rekisikan wo Tou [Questioning Mr Tahara's understanding of history]." *Bungeishunjū*, February 2003, 134–41.

Hasuike, Tōru. *Rachi: Sayū no Kakine wo Koeta Tatakai e* [The abduction: Towards a fight beyond the left-right hedge]. Kyoto: Kamogawa Shuppan, 2009.

Hasuike, Tōru, and Masakuni Ōta. *Rachi Tairon* [Abduction debates]. Tokyo: Ohta Shuppan, 2009.

Hayashi, Kaori. "Masumedia Jānarizumu wo Shihai suru 'Saidai Tasū no Saidai Kōfuku' no Saidai Fukō [The absolute tragedy of the 'absolute happiness to absolute majority' principle governing mass media journalism]." *Ronza*, July 2008, 26–31.

Hishiki, Kazuyoshi. "Nicchō Kanren Hōdō – Media ga Baiyō suru Fushin to Zōo no Seron [Media coverage concerning Japan–North Korea relations – Public opinion of distrust and hatred nurtured by the media]." In *Nicchō Kōshō* [Japan–North Korea negotiations], ed. Sang Joong Kang, Jong-Won Lee, and Naoki Mizuno, 159–64. Tokyo: Iwanami Shoten, 2003.

Iokibe, Makoto. "Reisengo no Nihon Gaikō [Japanese diplomacy in the post–Cold War period]." In *Sengo Nihon Gaikōshi* [History of postwar Japanese diplomacy], ed. Makoto Iokibe, 225–66. Tokyo: Yūhikaku ARMA, 1999.

Ishihara, Shintarō, and Shinzō Abe. "Kangan Kokka tono Ketsubetsu no Toki [It is time to say farewell to the country run by eunuch bureaucrats]." *Bungeishunjū*, August 2003, 112–20.

Izumi, Hajime. "Chikakute Tōi Rinjin [Close but far-off neighbour]." In *Sengo Nihon no Taigai Seisaku* [Postwar Japanese foreign policy], ed. Akio Watanabe, 162–81. Tokyo: Yūhikaku Senshō, 1995.

Japan. Cabinet Office. "Gaikō ni Kansuru Yoron Chōsa [Official opinion poll concerning foreign relations of Japan]." Tokyo, October 2002. Available online at http://www8.cao.go.jp/survey/index.htmlQ4, accessed 26 July 2010.

Japan. Cabinet Office. *Gaikō ni Kansuru Yoron Chōsa* [Official opinion poll concerning foreign relations of Japan]. Tokyo, 22 December 2014. Available online at http://survey.gov-online.go.jp/h26/h26-gaiko/index.html.

Japan. Ministry of Foreign Affairs. *Bluebook 1999 online edition, Part 1, Chapter 1, Section 2 (2).* Tokyo 1999. Available online at http://www.mofa.go.jp/mofaj/gaiko/bluebook/99/1st/index.html.

Japan. Ministry of Foreign Affairs. *Bluebook 2007 online edition, Chapter 2 (1).* Tokyo, 2007. Available online at http://www.mofa.go.jp/mofaj/gaiko/bluebook/2007/pdf/pdfs/2_1.pdf.

Japan. Ministry of Foreign Affairs. "Heisei 18 Nendo Rachi Mondai no Kaiketsu Sono-hoka Kitachōsen Tōkyoku ni yoru Jinken Shingai Mondai e no Taisho ni Kansuru Seifu no Torikumi ni tsuite no Hōkoku [2006 report on the government's pursuit of the resolution of the abduction issue and its engagement with other humanitarian violations by the North Korean regime]." Tokyo, June 2007.

Kabashima, Ikuo, Toshio Takeshita, and Yoichi Serikawa. *Media to Seiji* [Media and politics]. Tokyo: Yūhikaku ARMA, 2007.

Kakiya, Isao. "Ishihara Tochiji Sensō Hatsugen ni Kinkijyakuyaku Shita Asahi Shimbun [*Asahi Shimbun*'s overreaction to Governor Ishihara's statement on war]." *Seiron,* January 2003, 108–13.

Kamiya, Matake. "Gunjiryoku e-no Kyohi Hannō wo Kokufuku surunoga Senketsu-da [The first priority must be to overcome the adverse reaction to military power]." *Chūōkōron,* July 2003, 54–7.

Kitaoka, Shinichi. "Tokushū Kitachōsen Narazumono Kokka no Ummei – Sengo Nihon Gaikōshi ni Nokoru Seikō de Aru [Special coverage North Korea: The fate of the 'rogue state' – Historical success in postwar Japanese diplomacy]." *Chūōkōron,* November 2002, 46–52.

Komori, Yōichi. "Chimmoku no Rasen, Arekara [After the spiral of silence]." *Sōgō Jānarizumu Kenkyū,* July 2005, 8–13.

Kōmura, Masahiko. "Tokushū Kitachōsen 'Taisei Hatan' no Shinario – Gensoku wo Wasureta Gaikō wa Seikō Shinai [Special edition: The scenario of North Korean regime collapse – Diplomacy without principle cannot succeed]." *Chūōkōron,* December 2002, 46–9.

Koyama, Tsunemi. "Mattanashi! Ima Koso Nihon-koku Kenpō wo Mukō to Seyo [Now or never! This is the moment to annul the Japanese Constitution]." *Seiron,* September 2004, 64–75.

Kubo, Takuya. *Kokubō-ron: 80 nendai Nihon wo dō Mamoruka* [On national defence: How to defend Japan in the 1980s]. Kyoto: PHP Kenkyūjyo, 1979.

Lee, Jong-Won. 2003. "Datsu-Reisen wo Mezashi, Nessen no Shusenjō wo Fusen Kyōdōtai ni [By overcoming the Cold War, we must pursue a peaceful cooperative body in the main battlefield of the 'hot war']." In *Nicchō Kōshō* [Japan–North Korea negotiations], ed. Sang Joong Kang, Jong-Won Lee, and Naoki Mizuno, 33–44. Tokyo: Iwanami Shoten, 2003.

Maruyama, Noboru. "Kenshō Rachi Hōdō – Jiyū de Shinjitsu no Hōdō wa Dekiteiruka [Abduction media coverage: Is free and truthful reporting possible?]." *Sekai*, May 2003, 127–35.

Matsumoto, Masao. *Yoron (Seron) chosa no Yukue* [The future course of public opinion polling]. Tokyo: Chūōkōron Shinsha, 2003.

Michishita, Narushige. "Kitachōsen no Misairu Gaikō to Kakkoku no Taiō [North Korea's missile diplomacy and each state's responses]." In *Kiki no Chōsen Hantō – Gendai Higashi Ajia to Nihon* [Korean Peninsula in crisis – Contemporary East Asia and Japan], ed. Masao Okonogi, 69–111. Tokyo: Keio University Press, 2006.

Morris-Suzuki, Tessa. "Hisuterī-no Seijigaku – Amerika no Iraku, Nihon no Kitachōsen [The Politics of Hysteria: America's Iraq, Japan's North Korea]." *Sekai*, February 2003, 230–40.

Murata, Kōji. "Kokusai-Kokka no Shimei to Kunō [The mission and trials of the emerging international state: Japanese diplomacy in the 1980s]." In *Sengo Nihon Gaikōshi* [History of postwar Japanese diplomacy], ed. Makoto Iokibe, 188–224. Tokyo: Yūhikaku ARMA, 1999.

Nakanishi, Hiroshi. "Jiritsuteki Kyōchō no Mosaku [Exploring the idea of 'independent cooperation': Japanese diplomacy in the 1970s]." In *Sengo Nihon Gaikōshi* [History of postwar Japanese diplomacy], ed. Makoto Iokibe, 143–86. Tokyo: Yūhikaku ARMA, 1999.

Nakanishi, Hiroshi. "Reisen Shūengo no Nihon no Henyō – Naisei to Chiiki Gaikō [Transformation of post–Cold War Japan – Domestic politics and regional diplomacy]." In *Nihon no Higashi Ajia Kōsō* [Japan's "East Asia" concept], ed. Yoshihide Soeya and Masayuki Tadokoro, 273–99. Tokyo: Keio University Press, 2004.

Nakanishi, Terumasa. "Kitachōsen no Kaku kara Kokka to Kokumin wo Mamorerunoka [Can we protect our nation and our citizens from the North Korean nuclear threat?]." *Seiron*, December 2002, 46–56.

Nakanishi, Terumasa. *Nihon no Kakugo* [Resolution of Japan]. Tokyo: Bungeishunjū, 2005.

Nakasone, Yasuhiro, and Shintarō Ishihara. "Tate! Nihon-yo Ima Koso Sengo no Jubaku wo Tachikire [Rise Japan! This is the moment to cut off the spell of the postwar]." *Seiron*, February 2004, 50–65.

"Nijyū, Sanjyū Dai Kokkaigiin Chōsa ni Miru – Nihon ga 'Neo-con'-ka Suru [Observations from questionnaire to the Diet members in the twenties and thirties – Japan turning 'Neo-con']." *Weekly AERA*, 16 June 2003, 10–13.

Oguma, Eiji, and Yōko Ueno. *Iyashi no Nashonarizumu – Kusanone Hoshu Undō no Jisshō Kenkyū* [A nationalism of "healing": An empirical analysis of the grassroots conservative movement]. Tokyo: Keio University Press, 2003.

Okazaki, Hisahiko. *Kono Kuni wo Mamoru Tame no Gaikō Senryaku* [Diplomatic strategies for protecting Japan]. Tokyo: PHP Shinsho, 2007.

Okonogi, Masao. "Sōron [Overview]." In *Kiki no Chōsen Hantō – Gendai Higashi Ajia to Nihon* [Korean Peninsula in crisis – Contemporary East Asia and Japan], ed. Masao Okonogi, 1–11. Tokyo: Keio University Press, 2006.

Okonogi, Masao, Hajime Izumi, Sang Joong Kang, Naoki Mizuno, and Jong-Won Lee. "Sōgō Tōron: Nicchō Pyongyang Sengen no Rekishiteki/ Kokusaiteki Igi [Historical and international significance of the Pyongyang Declaration]." In *Nicchō Kōshō* [Japan–North Korea negotiations], ed. Sang Joong Kang, Jong-Won Lee, and Naoki Mizuno, 1–30. Tokyo: Iwanami Shoten, 2003.

Ōtake, Hideo. *Koizumi Junichirō Popyurizumu no Kenkyū – Sono Senryaku to Shuhō* [Koizumi's populism: The strategies and techniques]. Tokyo: Toyo Keizai Shimposha, 2006.

Ōtake, Hideo. *Nihon-gata Popyurizumu – Seiji e no Kitai to Genmetsu* [Japan-style populism: Hope and disillusionment towards politics]. Tokyo: Chūōkōron Shinsha, 2003.

Ōtake, Hideo. *Nihon Seiji no Tairitsu-jiku* [The axis of political controversies in Japanese politics]. Tokyo: Chūōkōron Shinsha, 1999.

"Rachi Chōsa, Nicchō ga Gōi [Japan and North Korea agree on the abduction reinvestigation]." *Asahi Shimbun Digital,* 30 May 2014.

Sakamoto, Kazuya. "Dokuritsukoku no Jōken [The conditions of an independent state: Japanese diplomacy in the 1950s]." In *Sengo Nihon Gaikōshi* [History of postwar Japanese diplomacy], ed. Makoto Iokibe, 66–104. Tokyo: Yūhikaku ARMA, 1999.

Satō, Masaru. "Minzoku no Wana – 'Ōkina Monogatari' Shūengo no Nashonarizumu [Trap of 'Nation' – Nationalism after the end of the 'grand narrative']." *Sekai,* July 2005, 86–96.

Sekai Editorial Office. "Chōsen Mondai ni Kansuru Honshi no Hōdō ni tsuite [Concerning our position on Korea-related issues]." *Sekai,* February 2003, 260–6.

Soeya, Yoshihide. *Nihon no Midoru Pawā Gaikō* [Japan's "middle power" diplomacy]. Tokyo: Chikuma Shinshō, 2005.

"Sukuu-kai Rachi Ankēto – Zen Shūgiin Giin 480-Nin no Kaitō wo Ikkyo Keisai [Abduction questionnaire by *Sukuu-kai*: Full disclosure of the replies from all 480 lower house Diet members]." *Seiron,* January 2004, 54–95.

Tahara, Sōichirō. *Koizumi no Nihon wo Yomu* ["Reading" Koizumi's Japan]. Tokyo: Asahi Shimbunsha, 2005.

Tahara, Sōichirō, and Hitoshi Tanaka. *Kokka to Gaikō* [The state and diplomacy]. Tokyo: Kōdansha, 2005.

Tanaka, Hitoshi. *Gaikō no Chikara* [The power of diplomacy]. Tokyo: Nihon Keizai Shimbun Shuppansha, 2009.

Wada, Haruki. "Tai Kitachōsen Seisaku – Ima Kinkyū ni Hitsuyō to Sareteru Koto [Policies towards North Korea – What is urgently needed]." *Sekai*, May 2008, 155–9.

Wada, Haruki. "Ushinatta Kanōsei no Kaifuku wo [Lost opportunity must be restored]." *Sekai*, March 2003, 136–44.

Wada, Haruki, Hideo Yamamuro, Jirō Yamaguchi, Naoki Mizuno, Sōji Takasaki, Hiroshi Tanaka, Sumiko Shimizu, Yōichi Komori, Tadashi Kimiya, Sang Joong Kang, et al. "Kyōdō Teigen: Tai Kitachōsen Seisaku no Tenkan wo [Collective proposal: Shift in North Korea policy is necessary]." *Sekai*, July 2008, 122–35.

Wakamiya, Yoshibumi. *Sengo Hoshu no Ajia-kan* [The postwar conservative view of Asia]. Tokyo: Asahi Senshō, 1995.

Wakamiya, Yoshibumi. *Tatakau Shasetsu* [Fighting newspaper editorials]. Tokyo: Kōdansha, 2008.

Yamakoshi, Shūzō, and Tomohisa Hirai. "Media Hōdō to Seron Chōsa ni miru Nihon no Jiko Imēji [Japan's self-image based on media coverage and public opinion polls]." In *Imēji no Naka no Nihon – Sofuto Pawā Saikō* [Japan as an image – Reconsidering Japan's soft power], ed. Yutaka Ōishi and Nobuto Yamamoto, 39–57. Tokyo: Keio University Press, 2008.

Yamamoto, Shichihei. *Kūki no Kenkyū* [Study of kūki]. Tokyo: Bungeishunjū, 1983.

Yomiuri Shimbun. *Nihon no Yoron* [Japanese public opinion]. Tokyo: Kobundō, 2002.

Yomiuri Shimbun Editorial Committee. *Yomiuri vs. Asahi – Shasetsu Taiketsu Kitachōsen Mondai* [*Yomiuri* versus *Asahi* editorials on North Korean issues]. Tokyo: Chūōkōron Shinsha, 2002.

Yomiuri Shimbun Political Section. *Gaikō wo Kenka ni Shita Otoko – Koizumi Gaikō 2000 Nichi no Shinjitsu* [The man who turned foreign policy into a fight – The truth behind the 2000 days of Koizumi diplomacy]. Tokyo: Shinchōsha, 2006.

Yomiuri Shimbunsha Yoron Chōsashitsu. *Nihonjin no Iken 150* [150 opinions of the Japanese]. Tokyo: Chiseidō, 1982.

Newspaper Editorials and Articles

Yomiuri Shimbun

EDITORIALS

1 September 1998, 3; 3 September 1998, 3; 12 September 1998, 3; 27 December 1998, 3; 1 January 1999, 3; 5 February 1999, 3; 25 March 1999, 3; 1 April 1999, 3; 3 May 1999, 3; 17 June 1999, 3; 1 September 1999, 3; 4 December 1999, 3; 15 December 1999, 3; 8 March 2000, 3; 8 April 2000, 3; 22 May 2000, 3; 18 June 2000, 3; 19 September 2000, 3; 7 October 2000, 3; 24 October 2000, 3; 13 November 2000, 3; 5 May 2001, 3; 23 December 2001, 3; 22 January 2002, 3; 26 January 2002, 3; 26 February 2002, 3; 17 April 2002, 3; 3 May 2002, 3; 9 May 2002, 3; 11 May 2002, 3; 19 June 2002, 3; 4 September 2002, 3; 7 September 2002, 3; 18 September 2002, 3; 19 September 2002, 3; 11 October 2002, 3; 16 October 2002, 3; 5 December 2002, 3; 11 December 2002, 3; 30 January 2003, 3; 2 February 2003, 3; 2 April 2003, 3; 3 April 2003, 3; 24 April 2003, 3; 27 April 2003, 3; 23 May 2003, 3; 26 May 2003, 3; 28 May 2003, 3; 7 June 2003, 3; 10 June 2003, 3; 19 June 2003, 3; 26 August 2003, 3; 17 September 2003, 3; 14 December 2003, 3; 1 February 2004, 3; 18 February 2004, 3; 26 February 2004, 3; 4 March 2004, 3; 23 April 2004, 3; 24 April 2004, 3; 19 July 2004, 3; 11 October 2004, 3; 9 December 2004, 3; 14 December 2004, 3; 25 December 2004, 3; 30 January 2005, 3; 15 February 2005, 3; 24 March 2006, 3; 4 April 2006, 3; 24 July 2006, 3; 20 September 2006, 3; 13 October 2006, 3; 15 November 2006, 3.

ARTICLES

8 April 2000, 3; 5 May 2001, 3; 21 March 2002, 3; 18 September 2002, 1; 18 September 2002, 3; 20 September 2002, 2; 28 September 2002, 1; 5 October 2002, 2; 16 October 2002, 1; 25 October 2002, 2; 13 November 2002, 4; 8 February 2003, 3; 7 June 2003, 1; 15 October 2003, 3; 17 September 2004, 3; 5 November 2004, 3; 9 December 2004, 3; 18 December 2004, 3; 6 July 2006, 1; 6 July 2006, 2; 7 July 2006, 3; 17 July 2006, 3; 18 July 2006, 3; 16 October 2006, 1.

Asahi Shimbun

EDITORIALS

1 September 1998, 5; 5 September 1998, 5; 18 September 1998, 5; 22 September 1998, 5; 21 October 1998, 5; 25 March 1999, 5; 28 August 1999, 5; 4 December 1999, 5; 8 March 2000, 5; 25 March 2000, 5; 3 May 2000, 2; 22 October 2000, 2; 5 May 2001, 2; 2 July 2001, 2; 12 September 2002, 2; 18 September 2002, 2; 22 September 2002, 2; 16 October 2002, 2; 13 November 2002, 2; 9 December 2002,

2; 1 January 2003, 2; 25 June 2003, 2; 17 September 2003, 2; 30 January 2004, 2; 12 March 2004, 2; 15 May 2004, 2; 2 July 2004, 3; 9 December 2004, 3; 3 May 2005, 3; 12 July 2005, 3; 3 November 2005, 3; 20 September 2006, 3.

Articles

1 September 1998, 1; 5 May 2001, 1; 24 December 2001, 1; 24 December 2001, 2; 3 September 2002, 1; 18 September 2002, 1; 18 September 2002, 5; 20 September 2002, 4; 28 September 2002, 3; 10 October 2002, 3; 24 October 2002, 1; 24 October 2002, 2; 2 November 2002, 3; 8 November 2002, 3; 4 December 2002, 4; 27 December 2002, 12–13; 26 January 2003, 2; 1 July 2003, 2; 15 May 2004, 3; 23 May 2004, 1–2; 9 December 2004, 2; 25 December 2004, 2; 5 July 2006, 1; 5 July 2006, 2; 6 July 2006, 1; 17 July 2006, 1; 19 September 2006, 1; 20 September 2006, 2; 16 October 2006, 1.

Interviews (interviewee positions as of December 2009)

Iokibe, Makoto, President of the National Defense Academy of Japan, 18 December 2009.

Kitaoka, Shinichi, former Japanese ambassador to the United Nations, Professor, Graduate Schools for Law and Politics, University of Tokyo, 16 December 2009.

Michishita, Narushige, Associate Professor, Security and International Studies Program, National Graduate Institute for Policy Studies, Tokyo, 16 December 2009.

Okonogi, Masao, Professor, Department of Political Science, Faculty of Law, Keio University, 11 December 2009.

Tanaka, Hitoshi, former director general of Asian and Oceanian Affairs Bureau, Ministry of Foreign Affairs, Senior Fellow, Japan Center for International Exchange, and Visiting Professor, Graduate School of Public Policy, University of Tokyo, 17 December 2009.

Wakamiya, Yoshibumi, former chairman, Editorial Board, *Asahi Shimbun*, columnist, *Asahi Shimbun*, and Guest Professor, University of Tokyo, 17 December 2009.

Index

abductions: background of, 138–9, 143; definition of resolution, 120, 122–3, 154; historical reinterpretations, 70–1, 76, 116–17; humanitarian issue, 67–9, 82, 124, 147; Kim Jong Il's apology, 57, 60; Koizumi and, 59, 100; link to Constitution, 124–5; link to other issues, 65, 70, 82–3, 103–4, 106, 113, 122–3; link to security identity, 3, 70, 116–17; negotiations for, 4, 36–7, 138–9; reinvestigation of, 108, 121; special missing persons, 121–2; societal pressure, 62–3, 65, 75, 109; storyline and narratives, 67–9, 70, 79; temporary return, 80–2; victim mentality, 70, 71, 88, 116, 158; victims, 57, 80–2, 87, 100–1, 108; victims' families, 80, 90–1, 100, 108, 113, 125; Yokota Megumi's DNA, 100–1, 155

Abe, Shinzō: abductions and, 4, 57, 81, 102, 104, 108, 122, 127; Constitution and, 126–7; criticism of leftists/progressives, 73, 77; rise of, 96–7, 109, 113; sanctions and, 93–4, 96–7, 112; views on security identity, 43, 126

airspace, 30

Amami Ōshima, 40

antimilitarism. *See* pacifism

apologies, 25, 57, 71, 74

Armitage, Richard, 58

Asahi Shimbun, 7, 11, 33, 47, 61–2, 65, 74–5, 77, 82

Asō Tarō, 31

atonement. *See* remorse

Ballistic Missile Defense, 35

Bungeishunjū, 12

bureaucrats, 20, 25, 45, 54, 72–3, 109, 118

Bush, George W., 58–9

Cabinet Office, 61, 83, 104, 121

China: criticism of Japan, 48, 71; Exclusive Economic Zone, 40, 53; rise of, 16, 18, 20, 116, 119; Six Party Talks, 13

Chūōkōron, 12

Coast Guard, 30–1, 35, 40, 42–3, 49, 141

COCOM, 6
Cold War, 15–17, 24, 27–8, 38
collective self-defence, 126
comfort women issue, 71
Constitution: Article Nine, 24, 125–7, 133; LDP revision proposal, 127; pacifism of, 24–5, 75, 116, 133; revision debates, 20, 124–8; as security principle, 15, 18, 43, 133

Democratic Party of Japan, 47, 84–6, 97–9
Diet: on emergency legislation, 44, 50, 54, 85–6; Koizumi and, 45, 47–8, 49; lower house, 94, 97; on national security, 33, 35, 50–1, 85–6, 94; and North Korea, 28–9, 36, 49–51; and sanctions, 93–5, 98, 101, 103; upper house, 92
discourse: definition, 6–7; on Japanese security, 3, 6, 17, 27, 32, 38, 41–2, 49–51, 83–8, 109, 116, 125, 128; on North Korea, 61–3, 67–71, 75, 79, 84–8, 93, 95–6, 104, 108, 110, 116–18, 120
Doi Takako, 72, 86

emergency legislation, 44, 49–51, 54, 85–6, 88
European Union, 34

fascism, 26
First Gulf War, 28, 115
foreign policy: of Japan towards Asia, 27; of Japan towards North Korea, 3, 5, 14–15, 27–9, 33, 36, 54, 60, 68, 73, 81–2, 104, 106, 109–10, 113, 120, 122–3; of Japan towards South Korea, 28
Fujiwara, Kiichi, 109
"*fukoku kyōhei*" (rich nation, strong army), 26
Fukuda, Takeo, 50
Fukuda, Yasuo, 50, 81
fushinsen, 30–1, 35–7, 40–3, 49–50, 53–4, 57, 68, 83, 95, 115

Group of Eight, 111

Hangul, 40
Hashimoto, Ryūtarō, 34
Hasuike, Kaoru, 70
Hasuike, Tōru, 70
"*heiwa to yūkō*" principle, 28
Hiranuma, Takeo, 112
Hirazawa, Katsuei, 90

identity: influence on foreign policy, 19–20, 26, 55; of Japan on security, 19–20, 24, 26, 32, 35, 38, 43, 84–6, 109–10, 116, 124
ikan. *See* remorse
iken no kazamuki (discursive trend), 7, 131
International Atomic Energy Agency, 13
International Red Cross, 36
Iokibe, Makoto, 24, 26, 59–60, 85
Ishiba, Shigeru, 83, 93–4
Ishihara, Shintarō, 43, 65
Islamic State, 127
Izumi, Hajime, 104

Japan: "Britannicization" of, 47; communists in, 25, 29, 72, 112; conservatives in, 25, 27; economy of, 16, 26; elections in, 32, 86–7, 92, 97, 127; as "merchant nation," 16; militarism of, 25–6; national consciousness of, 86; as normal

state, 16, 19–20; political parties of, 72, 86, 95; political system of, 20, 25, 43–4; postwar period of, 5, 12, 15–19, 22–7, 31–3, 35–6, 38, 40, 51, 53–4, 56–7, 68–9, 71, 87, 109–10, 116, 125; rightists in, 70–1, 116, 124–6; security principles of, 15–16, 18, 26, 31, 38, 42, 49, 51, 84–5, 109–10, 115, 124, 126, 132–3; socialists in, 25, 29, 36, 72, 86, 112; sovereignty of, 31, 40–1, 67–70, 116; on "use of force," 41–2; "Young Turks," 51, 55
Japan Bank for International Cooperation, 57
Japan Defense Agency, 35
Japanese Communist Party, 72, 112
Japan Socialist Party, 28–9

Kagoshima Prefecture, 40
Kanemaru, Shin, 28, 35
kasha-kurabu. *See* mass media (press club)
Katō, Kōichi, 28
Kazoku-kai, 66, 70, 74, 76–7, 80–1, 91–2, 96, 102, 120, 122, 125, 146–7, 148
Kelly, James, 58
Kim Dae Jung, 103
Kim Il Sung, 28
Kim Jong Il, 53, 56–7, 78, 87, 93–4, 96, 118–19
Kim Jong Nam, 39–41, 52–3, 115
Kim Jong Un, 119
Kitaoka, Shinichi, 84
Koizumi, Junichirō: cabinet of, 44, 47–9, 66, 81, 87, 102, 111; charisma of, 43; China and, 48, 71; "Koizumi's children" and, 51; North Korea and, 39–40, 44–5, 49, 52–5, 58–63, 65, 80, 87, 89–91, 96, 102–3, 108–9, 118, 144; "one phrase politics" and, 46; political legacy of, 43–8, 53–5, 118; populism of, 33, 44–5, 47–8, 52, 54, 87, 97, 102, 109, 118; relations with media, 46, 91–2; on sanctions, 93, 96–7, 99–100, 102–3, 108; South Korea and, 48, 71
Koizumi–Kim Summit, 53, 56–8, 62, 87, 89, 115, 118, 123, 142
Kōmura, Masahiko, 80
Kōno, Tarō, 94
Korean Peninsula, 27, 37; colonial period of, 57–8, 61, 70, 75–6
Korean Peninsula Energy Development Organization, 4, 34, 138
Koreans: in Japan, 91, 95, 111; *Chōsen-Sōren/Jochongryun*, 29, 111, 114
Korean War, 26–7
Korean Worker's Party, 113
kūki (atmosphere), 7, 47, 81, 131
Kyodo News, 126

"liberal adaptive" state, 17, 19
Liberal Democratic Party: Abe's rise in, 97–8; as coalition partner, 33, 117; constitutional revision and, 125, 127; factionalism in, 43, 45, 59, 118; Koizumi's rise in, 45–7; national security strategy of, 26, 49–50; North Korea and, 28–9, 35, 44, 53, 59, 64, 80; pragmatists in, 50; public criticism of, 72; sanctions and, 93, 98–9, 101–2; subcommittees of, 47, 80

Maehara, Seiji, 86
Mainichi Shimbun, 11, 25

Maizuru (Kyoto), 95
Makita, Kunihiko, 74
Mangyongbong-92, 5, 84, 95, 111
mass media: bandwagon of, 10, 78–9, 117–18; "burasagari," 46; importance of editorials, 10–11; influence on politics, 8, 11, 34, 46–7, 81; newspapers, 8, 46; on North Korea, 21, 38, 41, 52, 61–2, 67, 76, 78–9, 81, 117, 119–20; press club, 46; "progressives" in, 74, 77; public criticism of, 74–6, 149; relations with society, 8–10, 11, 38, 77–8, 88, 117; on sanctions, 95–6, 99, 102–3; television, 8, 46, 62, 78
Masumoto, Teruaki, 70
Ministry of Foreign Affairs, 47, 52, 58, 64–5, 73, 90, 113
Modern Korea Institute, 94, 146–7
Mori, Yoshirō, 29, 40
Murayama, Tomiichi, 36
Murayama Statement, 37

Nagata-chō, 46
Nakanishi, Terumasa, 70
Nakasone, Yasuhiro, 125, 160
National Defense Academy of Japan, 60
National Police Agency, 52, 83, 95
Nature, 155
neocolonialism, 27
New Conservative Party, 117
New Komeito Party, 97–9, 117
Nihon Keizai Shimbun (Nikkei), 11, 126
Niigata Prefecture, 84, 95
Nippon Zaidan, 42
Nonaka, Hiromu, 30
norms. *See* identity
North Korea: aid from Japan, 37, 56, 59, 91; bilateral relations with Japan, 4, 16, 18, 20, 28, 36, 60, 86, 95; as dictatorship, 67, 69, 86; diplomatic normalization with Japan, 36–7, 49, 53, 56, 58–63, 68, 73, 82, 89–92, 100–1, 107–8, 119–20, 122–3; missile launched by, 3, 13–14, 20, 57, 83, 111, 122–3; nuclear program and Japanese society, 13–14, 104, 107–8; nuclear program of, 4, 12–14, 20, 56, 58, 83, 103, 105, 113, 122–3, 155; in the West, 20–1
Noto Peninsula, 30

Obuchi, Keizō, 30, 33
Official Development Assistance, 27
Okamoto, Yukio, 65
Okonogi, Masao, 59
Ōtake, Hideo, 10

pachinko money, 29, 95
pacifism: of Japan, 16–17, 19–20, 25–7, 31, 84–5, 116, 125, 128; pacifists, 74; peace naivety, 31; proactive, 126, 128
peaceful use of space, 35
pluralistic repression, 79
postwar consensus, 24–5
prefectural governments, 50–1, 83–4, 95
publicized issues, 8–10, 117
public opinion: influence on Japanese politics, 20, 44, 50, 55, 64–5, 72, 79–82, 85–7, 103–9, 119, 124; meaning in Japan, 6, 7–8; meaning in the West, 130; polls and surveys, 6, 8, 12, 25, 37, 41–2, 47, 51, 61–2, 64, 69, 82–3, 92, 99–100, 102, 105, 121–2, 125–6; towards North Korea, 3, 6, 13–14,

29, 31, 37–8, 41, 43, 49–51, 53–4, 61–2, 64–7, 69, 75, 80, 83, 85–7, 93, 95–6, 101, 103–5, 116, 118–19, 145
Pyongyang Declaration, 56–60, 62–3, 65, 87, 90–1, 93, 96, 99–100, 103–4, 106–7, 109, 118, 120, 123

rachi. *See* abductions
Rachi-Giren, 66, 90, 93, 99, 112
realpolitik, 27
remorse, 24–5, 28, 57, 60, 70–1
resolution (of wartime legacy), 61
Roh Moo Hyun, 102
Ronza, 12
Russia, 5, 13, 110, 112

Sakai (Tottori Prefecture), 95
Sakamoto, Yoshikazu, 125
Sakigake Party, 29
Sanctions: "atsuryoku to taiwa" (pressure and dialogue), 96; Cold War era, 5–6; historical significance of, 3, 109–10, 112, 119; implementation of, 5, 111–14, 120; international community and, 111–12; legislation, 98–9, 109–10, 113; as leverage, 108; origin of, 89, 93–5, 119; public support of, 93, 95–6, 100–3, 108–9, 112, 119, 126
San Francisco Peace Treaty, 68
Sankei Shimbun, 11, 77
Sapio, 77
Satō, Katsumi, 94
Second World War, 15, 30, 40, 56, 59, 71, 128
Seiron, 12, 77, 99
Sekai, 12, 74–5
Self-Defense Forces: collective self-defence and, 126; constitutional revision and, 128; *fushinsen* and, 30–1, 33, 35, 38; international role of, 20, 126–8; legal procedures concerning, 50, 75, 85
sengo shori. *See* resolution
senshu bōei principles, 33, 51, 84
seron. *See* public opinion
Shii, Kazuo, 72
Shinoda, Tomohito, 11, 108
shokuzai-ishiki. *See* remorse
Shūkan Bunshun, 74
Six Party Talks, 13–14, 90, 105–8, 111
Social Democratic Party, 72, 86, 112
societal. *See* public opinion
Soeya, Yoshihide, 125
South Korea, 13–14, 34, 48, 71, 102–3, 124
spiral of silence, 10, 77, 79, 150
spy satellite, 32, 35
Suga, Yoshihide, 121
Sukuu-kai, 66, 74, 76–7, 94–6, 99, 120, 122, 146–7
Sunshine Policy, 103, 124

Taepodong missiles: shock of, 4; Taepodong-1, 4, 13, 30–1, 34, 36–7, 51, 68; Taepodong-2, 5, 110
Tahara, Sōichirō, 76
Takeshita, Noboru, 28
Tanaka, Hitoshi, 58, 74, 81
Tanaka, Makiko, 52
Theater Missile Defense, 32, 35
theories: constructivism, 19–20; international system, 16, 18;

neorealism, 17–18; realism, 17–18; state rationality, 18
Tiananmen Square incident, 6
Tsumi-ishiki. See remorse

United Nations, 4–5, 16, 34, 111–14
United States: alliance with Japan, 16, 20, 35, 75; Koizumi and, 62; National Security Council of, 48; 9/11, 64, 70, 78–9; North Korea and, 13, 14, 34, 58–9, 123; victim mentality of Japan and, 116

Wakamiya, Yoshibumi, 77
Westminster system, 47
World Food Program, 37

Yamamoto, Ichita, 94
Yasukuni Shrine, 48, 71
yokonarabi taishitsu (media bandwagoning), 10
Yokota, Megumi, 100–1, 108–9, 120
Yomiuri Shimbun, 7, 11, 32–3, 41–2, 62, 67, 86, 99, 102, 104
Yoneda, Kenzō, 65
yoron chosa. See public opinion
Yoshida, Shigeru, 25
Yoshida Doctrine, 15–16, 18, 24, 51, 132
yūji-hōsei/kanren-hōan. See emergency legislation

Japan and Global Society

Yoshihide Soeya, Masayuki Tadokoro, and David A. Welch, eds., *Japan as a "Normal Country"? A Nation in Search of Its Place in the World*

Leonard J. Schoppa, ed., *The Evolution of Japan's Party System: Politics and Policy in an Era of Institutional Change*

Masato Kimura and Tosh Minohara, eds., *Tumultuous Decade: Empire, Society, and Diplomacy in 1930s Japan*

Tomoko T. Okagaki, *The Logic of Conformity: Japan's Entry into International Society*

Peter Ennals, *Opening a Window to the West: The Foreign Concession at Kōbe, Japan, 1868–1899*

Seung Hyok Lee, *Japanese Society and the Politics of the North Korean Threat*

www.ingramcontent.com/pod-product-compliance
Lightning Source LLC
LaVergne TN
LVHW090200080826
844660LV00013B/882/J

* 9 7 8 1 4 4 2 6 3 0 3 4 5 *